MANAGEMENT, WORK AND ORGANISATIONS

Series editors: **Gibson Burrell**, Warwick Business School
Mick Marchington, Manchester School of Management, UMIST
Paul Thompson, Department of Business Studies, University of Edinburgh

This series of new textbooks covers the areas of human resource management, employee relations, organisational behaviour and related business and management fields. Each text has been specially commissioned to be written by leading experts in a clear and accessible way. An important feature of the series is the international orientation. The titles will contain serious and challenging material, be analytical rather than prescriptive and be particularly suitable for use by students with no prior specialist knowledge.

The series will be relevant for a number of business and management courses, including MBA and post-experience courses, specialist masters and postgraduate diplomas, professional courses, and final-year undergraduate and related courses. The books will become essential reading at business and management schools worldwide.

Published:

Paul Blyton and Peter Turnbull   **The Dynamics of Employee Relations**
J. Martin Corbett   **Critical Cases in Organisational Behaviour**
Karen Legge   **Human Resource Management**
Harry Scarbrough (ed.)   **The Management of Expertise**

Forthcoming:

Sue Ledwith and Fiona Colgan (eds)   **Women in Organisations**
Helen Newell and John Purcell   **Business Strategy and the Management of Human Resources**
Helen Rainbird   **Training in the Workplace**
Harvie Ramsey   **Involvement at Work**
Michael Rowlinson   **Organisations and Institutions**
Adrian Wilkinson, Mick Marchington, Tom Redman and Ed Snape
   Total Quality Management

THE MANAGEMENT OF EXPERTISE

Edited by

Harry Scarbrough

First published 1996 by
MACMILLAN PRESS LTD
Houndmills, Basingstoke, Hampshire RG21 6XS
and London
Companies and representatives
throughout the world

ISBN 0–333–56869–9 hardcover
ISBN 0–333–56870–2 paperback

A catalogue record for this book is available
from the British Library.

10   9   8   7   6   5   4   3   2   1
05   04   03   02   01   00   99   98   97   96

Copy-edited and typeset by Povey–Edmondson
Okehampton and Rochdale, England

Printed and bound in Great Britain by
Antony Rowe Ltd
Chippenham, Wiltshire,
England

Published in the United States of America 1996 by
ST. MARTIN'S PRESS, INC.,
Scholarly and Reference Division
175 Fifth Avenue, New York, N.Y. 10010

Contents

Part 3: Institutional change and the management of expertise

Preface

'There's no grand design. People are just reaching out in the dark, touching hands' (A computer designer on the process of developing software – Kidder, 1981).

This book is 'reaching out in the dark' too. It addresses the nexus between wider patterns of industrial change and the deployment of expertise inside and outside organisations. Despite its escalating importance, the management of expertise is only now beginning to emerge as a topic in its own right out of the fragmented studies that currently typify the field. The latter are scatttered across a range of literatures including, variously, the management of professionals, the diffusion of innovations, the design of new technologies, and the development of corporate competences. Reframing these issues in terms of the management of expertise is not to deny the validity of these approaches, but rather to draw their cognate concerns into a sharper, unifying focus on expertise itself and the dynamics of its formation and deployment.

Doing this involves drawing on the work of a number of contributors, and it is worth saying a little about this book's composition of authors and chapters. Contrary to the usual sequence where teaching follows the text, this book actually developed out of a teaching programme – an eponymous option on the full time MBA programme at Warwick Business School. The programme afforded an opportunity to draw on the interests (and expertise) of a number of the faculty members at Warwick – Gibson Burrell, Martin Corbett, Louise Fitzgerald and Jacky Swan – to provide a sustained and integrated exploration of this topic. Moreover, the book, like the teaching programme, draws not only on the considerable research of the Warwick faculty, but also – through our wider networks of teaching and research contacts – on the valuable experience of Lynn Ashburner and Brian Baxter.

If the institutional logic behind this book is reasonably flexible and syncretic, so too is the intellectual logic that is outlined in its Introductory chapter and underpins its shape and structure. Partly this logic is counter-positional: to critique received wisdom on the management of experts or knowledge workers, and, more broadly, to question whether this focus is appropriate to the new mode of knowledge production that characterises the late twentieth century. Partly too, the logic is integrative: to make sense of the concurrent experience of a range of knowledge-based occupations whose management is being radically reshaped by institutional and technological change. The standard professional model of knowledge-based work is of limited value here. The fact, say, that these groups vary widely in their embodiment of the classical professional traits explains little of the commonality of experience posed by exposure to market forces, deregulation and organisational restructuring. In contrast, the focus on expertise developed here posits more fluid, contingent and less institutionally bounded social formations. This offers both an inclusive framework encompassing diverse localised applications of expert knowledge, and an account of the tendential conditions confronting knowledge-based occupations at large.

The dynamics of expertise increasingly transcend particular technological and structural circumstances to present broadly similar dilemmas to managers and organisations across a wide swathe of industrial settings. Sometimes these dilemmas take the form of innovation, sometimes resistance to change; sometimes they are merely functional trade-offs, at other times intensely political challenges to the status quo. Of course, this book can only provide a modest contribution to empirical studies of these differential effects. However its distinctive focus, coupled with the geometry of its constituent parts, helps to project a new and emergent horizon in understanding what it means to manage expertise.

Reference

Kidder, Tracy (1981) *The Soul of a New Machine* (New York: Avon).

Notes on the contributors

Lynn Ashburner, formerly of the Centre for Corporate Strategy and Change, Warwick Business School, is a Lecturer in the Department of Management and Finance at the University of Nottingham. Her practical experience includes organisation development roles at Pilkington Brothers. Latterly her research interests have focused on large-scale change processes in UK hospitals, and the broader issues of professionalism and work organisation.

Brian Baxter is a Director of Kiddy & Partners, a UK-based firm of management consultants and organisational psychologists. He received his first degree in psychology at Edinburgh University, and his PhD from the Department of Behaviour in Organisations, Lancaster University. Since the late 1970s he has worked as management consultant and manager, initially with Arthur Andersen and the W.S. Atkins Group. His assignments have covered strategic reorganisation, business reviews and reorientation activities, organisation development and managing change. His current interests are in the area of helping organisations to develop a post-modern outlook on their approaches to business life. He is also a Visiting Fellow at Lancaster University.

Gibson Burrell was formerly in the Department of Behaviour in Organizations at the University of Lancaster and is now Associate Chair (Academic Development) at Warwick Business School. He is currently interested in *fin de siècle* thinking in the area of management.

J. Martin Corbett is Senior Lecturer in Industrial Relations and Organisational Behaviour at Warwick Business School. His current research interests include the psychology of working with smart machines and the design of human-centred manufacturing systems. He has written a number of books, the most recent of which – *Critical Cases in Organisational Behaviour* – also features in the 'Management, Work and Organisations' series.

Louise Fitzgerald is Senior Lecturer in Organizational Development, Warwick Business School. Her research and consultancy interests are focused on the management of change and restructuring in the UK National Health Service. Work with colleagues at Warwick's Centre for Corporate Strategy and Change has produced a number of papers and books on these topics, the most recent being *The New Public Management in Action* (in press).

Harry Scarbrough is a Lecturer in Industrial Relations and Organizational Behaviour, Warwick Business School. He has written and researched extensively on the organisational implications of IT, including *Technology and Organization: Power, Meaning and Design* (with J. Martin Corbett). His current interests are focused on the management of so-called 'knowledge assets' in organisational contexts.

Jacky Swan is a chartered psychologist, formerly of Aston University and currently Lecturer in Industrial Relations and Organisational Behaviour, Warwick Business School. Her research interests and publications focus on cross-national differences in the roles of professional associations in technology design and diffusion, and on the managerial cognitions in decisions about new technology. She is currently principal researcher on an ESRC project investigating the impact of European professional associations for production control on the diffusion of technology.

Introduction

Historians remember periods of industrial change for their spectacular breakthroughs, but managers of the time more likely curse them for their distinctive constraints. For however broad and far-reaching the frontal advance of new technologies or organisational forms, managerial tasks invariably cluster round the troubling 'reverse salients' (Hughes, 1987) where advance has slowed or stalled. Such salients sometimes surface as bottlenecks in the wider pattern of change. The people and practices that are least amenable to change define the rate of progress for everything else. It is equally possible, though, to see them as strategic sites for directing and extending the scope of industrial change. It is here that many innovations are generated and 'critical success factors' cluster. In other words, such salients can operate equally as a focus for managerial concern, a site of innovation and a locus for the leveraged exercise of power and resistance. This combination of sticky progress and political uncertainty may well be the bane of many managers' lives, but it is also the crucible in which enduring competitive advantages can be forged.

This book argues that current patterns of industrial change are gradually smoothing away technological and structural constraints to disclose expertise as one of the most critical reverse salients confronting management (see Figure 1.1). On the one hand the spread of information technonlogy (IT) is 'hollowing out' organisations. Jobs and tasks are gradually being polarised into two groups; those that involve routine information-processing and those addressing the knowledgeable interpretation of such information (Zuboff, 1988). On

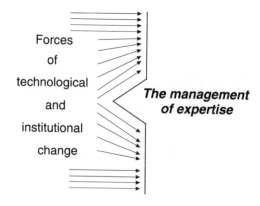

FIGURE I.1   Expertise as a 'reverse salient'

the other hand, the exoskeleton of organisational forms is being reshaped by deregulation and the globalization of market-forces. As corpulent bureaucracies are progressively downsized, concentrations of expertise become key nodes in the newly emerging network organisations.

These trends help to explain the buzz of interest around 'knowledge work', 'core competences' and the like as managers search for a new management paradigm for knowledge-based work. This book aims to address that interest, firstly by presenting some new ways of thinking about the expertise issue, and secondly by exploring the latter through empirical studies of the formation and regulation of specialist expertise. The phrase 'management of expertise' itself needs a little introduction because it is a way of analysing managerial practices that cuts across the usual functional divisions between research and development, human resource management and so on. However, suffice to say that it involves a focus on expertise itself, not on professionals, knowledge workers or expert groups as such, and that it encompasses the formation and regulation of expertise in a range of organisational settings. This is not to say that expert groups do not figure in the studies collected here, but rather that the more plastic and dynamic qualities of expertise are our principal concern. Focusing solely on the day-to-day problems of managing 'knowledge workers' and 'professionals' would mean overlooking the impact of far-reaching changes on the production and distribution of knowledge. The latter have had an enormous effect in freeing expertise from its traditional habitats of professional and functional structures. Compared to this, a survey of the attributes of particular expert groups is relatively small beer.

Again some post-modern studies have challenged the validity of talking about expertise and knowledge workers at all. They claim that these terms are simply ways of legitimising elitist control. Equating knowledge with objective truth is privileging one set of voices over others. In response to this critique, it is worth saying that this book consciously avoids adding to an already over-populated and often uncritical literature by focusing on expertise and not on knowledge workers and their pastimes. In fact, we would go further and argue that this current questioning of knowledge claims can only be understood through an appreciation of expertise. For such questioning actually seems to reflect the 'Tower of Babel' effect produced by a vast increase in the outpouring of specialised knowledges and technologies (Jones, 1982). The latter, and the associated growth in specialist forms of expertise, seems to be much more important than any widespread philosophical retreat from knowledge itself.

Admittedly the traditional knowledge-producing institutions of science and the professions have found it impossible to assimilate and integrate all of these fragmentary knowledges, and this has tended to undermine their claims to exclusive authority. However this has not occurred through the sudden onset of lay scepticism, but through the emergence of competing and alternative bodies of expertise. One obvious example from the legal arena is the frequency with which the claims of forensic scientists in a number of criminal cases have been overturned either by rival expert witnesses or by new techniques that have cast doubt on previous findings. Moreover, as competition grows between the claims and scope of different bodies of expertise, it actually creates new areas of uncertainty upon which other, newer sources of expertise can feed. Thus the market for expertise expands, even as our store of scientific certainties dwindles (Giddens, 1994).

Significance and paradox in expertise

This perspective obviously implies a distinctive view of expertise. Put simply, expertise is broadly defined here as 'knowledge in the world' not 'knowledge of the world'. Expertise is understood as encompassing a wide range of sociocognitive formations, including diffuse occupational networks, the expertise of specialist groups and even the established liberal professions. Although these formations are being addressed in a distinctive way here, it is their practical significance that makes them interesting. In the first instance this involves a recognition of the increasing importance not just of knowledge workers as an occupational grouping but of expertise itself as an engine of competitive performance. Technological and socioeconomic changes have eroded long-standing constraints such as industrial relations problems and the technical limitations of production systems, and in so doing have cleared the way for knowledge and expertise finally to surface as the most critical sources of competitiveness. With capital and technological solutions readily available, and the managerial prerogative unassailed by ideological rivals, the management of expertise has emerged as a crucial modality of organisational life; that is, both the driver of change, but equally the biggest barrier to it.

Testifying to this point are the huge number of change processes and innovations that are either driven by expertise or are predicated on important changes in its distribution and deployment. To mention just an illustrative sample of such instances, this book includes material on; the importance of expert knowledge and networks in the adoption of new technologies in manufacturing industry, the role of IT experts in the development of strategic IT systems in financial services, and the emergence of clinician managers as part of the organisational changes in the UK National Health Service. In each case, despite important differences of history and context, specialist expertise has emerged as the crucial instrument of change. Technologies, management techniques and even the clash of political and ideological forces revolve around the way in which expertise is formed and deployed.

Of course to say that expertise is central to change is not to say that it will always support it. Expertise may become the crucial locale for resistance to change – witness the struggles of doctors and other professional groups against unwelcome organisational change. So the management of expertise is not just about exploiting its competitive benefits, but must also address its role as a barrier to change. In the latter context, therefore, the management of expertise often centres on radical attempts to overturn time-hallowed institutions and methods for organising and deploying expert groups. Professionalism and in-house technical functions, disciplinary knowledge and basic research all give way to *ad hoc* project teams, subcontracting and applied research.

These complex patterns of resistance and change help to explain the paradoxical impressions created by current trends around expertise. Contrast, for example, the explosion in the numbers of self-styled 'experts' within society – ranging from the exotic, such as canine psychologists, to mundane specialists on life-style and diet – with the declining influence of the professional associations that have been the traditional guardians of expert knowledge. A similar paradox is apparent in business firms whose senior managers agonise about their corporate competences while happily bulldozing the in-house technical functions that used to be the repositories for such competences.

At a societal level, such paradoxes seem to be linked to the emergence of what has been termed late-modern or post-modern society. This kind of society represents a break with the modern era, when expertise was primarily embodied in professional groups and as such played a crucial role in both social control and technological advance. The knowledge of the modern expert rooted itself in scientific claims to absolute truth, and brooked no interrogation by users, clients or, in some cases, victims (Bauman, 1989). Now, expertise is increasingly bought and sold outside the professional arena and claims to truth are being tested in the same way as any other product – by customers in the marketplace.

This shift in the epistemological status of expertise has led some post-modern theorists to proclaim the 'death of the expert'. For example White and Taket define the expert as 'a modern figure, emerging in the 19th Century, a creation of liberal discourses, who plays an integral part in governing and controlling individuals and populations at a distance' (White and Taket, 1994, p. 735). From their post-modern standpoint they describe the corpse of this modern expert, with 'its stench of rationality, reason and privilege' (ibid., p.747). But before we subject expertise to a detailed autopsy we might care to consider, paraphrasing Mark Twain, that reports of the death of the expert have been greatly exaggerated. It is not simply the rapid growth in the number of knowledge worker occupations that should give us pause here, but also the dangers of equating the impact of expertise with the fate of one occupational group or another. Although expertise is always applied and transmitted through such groups, its societal role is shaped by factors that lie outside the control of expert groups themselves.

Thus one of the important effects of the industrial change noted earlier is that expertise no longer ranks as merely the intellectual property of professional or functional specialisms. Nor, similarly, can the societal role of expertise be reduced to the epistemological status of experts' knowledge claims. Even if it is true, as White and Taket claim, that expert knowledge can no longer be viewed as possessing scientific objectivity, it does not follow that the real social and material effects of expertise are correspondingly effaced. The uncertain and tentative nature of knowledge in our late-modern period is less the result of philosophical scepticism about scientific objectivity than of a huge explosion in the growth of specialised knowledges in every walk of life. Insofar as the classical scientific model of knowledge production has been overthrown, it is because scientific and professional institutions have proved to be unable to contain this explosion. Indeed, with the market becoming the dominant means of transmitting knowledge, the idea of an objective scientific framework integrating these fragmentary knowledges is simply rendered obsolete. In this context, the only epistemological caveat that really counts is *caveat emptor*.

These points help to explain why expertise is the distinctive focus of this book, and not its social coordinates of occupational and professional group-ings. New technologies, new ways of transmitting and marketing knowledge and new distributions of knowledge within organisations all demand a conceptual framework that is able to address expertise directly and not merely the institutional forms through which it is deployed. The interface between managers and professionals, and indeed the place of experts within organisations, need to be part of that framework, but so too does the wider prospectus of technological and sectoral change, which is so important in shaping these visible expressions of the management of expertise.

Expertise and change

This book not only presents a new analytical framework for understanding the role of expertise, it also develops this framework through an empirical survey of the management of expertise across a range of sectoral and occupational settings. These include both public and private sector organisations, managers and professionals, hierarchies and networks. What all these settings have in common is deep and extensive organisational change that depends critically upon the management of expertise. So crucial is the deployment of expertise to these patterns of change, in fact, that it asserts itself above the specific features of each locale. This saliency is well illustrated by the following examples, which also help to convey a flavour of the sectors and issues addressed in later chapters.

- In less than ten years from its establishment in 1985, the Direct Line insurance company succeeded in capturing a major share of the market for motor insurance in the UK (in the process its founder and chief executive, Peter Wood, became the highest paid executive in Britain). It did so by selling its insurance products directly over the phone at a much lower cost than traditional companies that still employed their own branch networks and intermediaries. Competitive success was partly dependent on an ensemble of technological systems; the phone network, laserprinters and, most importantly, database systems that allowed Direct Line to give immediate quotes for any make of car, adjust their rates frequently and respond to customers without them needing to remember long-winded policy numbers. However none of these systems were at all innovative in their own right; the computer at the heart of the business was a second-hand IBM mainframe. The competitive advantage actually came from top management's unique blend of insurance and computing expertise that put technology, product and distribution together in an innovative configuration. Where established companies had rigid organisational and professional boundaries between their insurance actuaries and their IT experts, Direct Line was established by a group of four senior managers, each of whom combined a detailed knowledge of insurance with hands-on computing and programming skills.

This case highlights the role of expertise in competitive innovation, supplying the novel combination of knowledges upon which new products and services are based. However, since expertise also involves the control and system-atisation of knowledge, it may also become a major barrier to such innovations (Starbuck, 1992). We only have to turn to the well-ordered professional expertise of Direct Line's competitors to see the sometimes sclerotic effect of established expert groups. Thus the Direct Line case also indirectly demonstrates a more widely experienced feature of expertise: the tension between *openness*, meaning the unceasing and extensive search for new knowledge, and *closure* which denotes social control and the development of professional standards. The latter is exemplified by the exclusivity and task controls associated with professional groupings, whereas the former is usefully illustrated by the following example of interorganisational networks.

- In manufacturing industry, technological change is heavily conditioned by the distribution of expertise across sectors. Knowledge networks, in the form of occupational communities, consultancies or professional associations, play an important part not only in transmitting new techniques and systems but also in shaping the knowledge that is applied at company level. The impact of such networks on patterns of technological change is therefore profound, but not necessarily beneficial. Some of the 'innovations' promoted by such networks may prove highly counterproductive for the firms involved.

To say that innovation is not inherently positive or progressive is to point to the important relationship between knowledge and social values. We do not need to relativize all forms of knowledge or see them as dependent on particular cultural contexts to see the effects of their selective application in social value terms. Although the dominance of competitive forces often obscures or neutralises this issue in the private sector, it immediately surfaces when the focus switches to institutions that are regulated by more explicit value criteria. Put simply, innovation and change promote certain values at the expense of others. It follows that the role of expert groups in advancing or retarding such change is to some extent part of a political and ideological clash. And by the same token, the ultimate outcomes of such a clash, as highlighted by the example below, may well hinge on the success or failure of attempts to revise or rework established knowledge bases and assumptions.

- In the UK National Health Service, medical professionals are confronted by organisational changes that create quasi-markets for health care. These changes obviously involve structural and even cultural changes. Deeper than that, though, they demand changes in the skills and knowledge of these professional groups. Be it energetically or reluctantly, doctors are taking on managerial tasks that put decision making and organising skills at the core of what they do.

In each of these examples the immediate motivating (and constraining) force is supplied not by formal strategy, technology or the marketplace, but by the knowledge base, status and internal cohesion of the different expert groups involved. As innovation and change increasingly revolve around these issues, there are corresponding shifts in the way in which expertise is organised and deployed. These shifts often mean difficult and painful reorientations of structure and culture. They may be confined to individual organisations, or may occur across whole sectors – as we see for instance in the insurance industry sparked by Direct Line's competitive innovations. But these local differences should not blind us to their common and generic inheritance from the social and technological movements mentioned earlier.

Challenges to the management of expertise

Despite their sectoral and occupational differences, a common denominator of each of the above examples is their challenge to traditional ways of organising and managing expertise. This common challenge seems to reflect the working through of longer-term trends in society and their powerful alliance with the specific impacts of technological and institutional change. Such trends are also implicated in a widespread shift in power and resources towards knowledge production and knowledge workers. This has been popularly debated in terms of a transition from industrial to post-industrial (Bell, 1973) or 'knowledge society'. Champions of this view argue that advanced societies are experiencing an historical transformation in which social structures dating back to the Industrial Revolution are giving way to distinct new societal forms. This is a society based on an explosion of scientific and technical knowledge, where the knowledge worker reigns supreme.

The post-industrial prophecies seem to be validated by long-term secular trends in late-modern society. Organisations *are* becoming more knowledge intensive, and this is matched by the impressive occupational growth of knowledge worker groups. Yet the more our social institutions outwardly display the predicted appearance of post-industrial forms, the more banally optimistic appear the conclusions of post-industrial theorising. For example writers point to the uneven and socially divisive effects of these changes; that for every IT expert or business analyst we see dozens of deskilled information workers and word-processor typists swelling the ranks of low-level white collar workers (Lyon, 1988).

However, such sociological critiques of the impact of the post-industrial economy are only part of a broader reappraisal. Post-industrialism rightly points to the increasing importance of knowledge in industrial society, but this central argument is also its weakest point. Its view of knowledge production privileges scientific and abstract forms of knowledge over tacit or context-dependent forms. It then plots a linear extrapolation of the societal effects of such knowledge production in a way that is both mechanistic and politically naive. Emphasizing the causation of formal scientific knowledge is hard to square not only with the way in which knowledge is actually used – to create profits, to buttress power inequalities and so on – but also with the reciprocal effect of social and economic changes on knowledge production.

An important revision of these post-industrial accounts is provided by a study of 'The new production of knowledge' (Gibbons *et al.*, 1994). This argues persuasively that advanced societies are witnessing a profound shift from so-called 'Mode 1' to 'Mode 2' forms of knowledge production. Mode 1 they describe as 'a form of knowledge production – a complex of ideas, values, norms – that has grown up to control the diffusion of the Newtonian model to more and more fields of enquiry and ensure its compliance with what is considered sound scientific practice' (ibid., p. 2). However Mode 1 is no longer the dominant mode of knowledge production. Rather it provides a platform for Mode 2, as outlined in Table I.1.

The implications of this shift for the management of expertise are profound: 'in mode 1 knowledge was accumulated through the professionalisation of specialisation largely institutionalised in the universities . . . Mode 2 knowledge is accumulated through the repeated configuration of human resources in flexible, essentially transient forms of organisation' (ibid., p.9). The new mode of knowledge production is associated with radical change in the social and institutional locales. No longer bounded by professional structures and academic disciplines, knowledge production moves away from traditional sites such as universities, government research establishments and corporate laboratories into the context of use and application.

What are the causes of this shift from Mode 1 to Mode 2 dominance ? The study highlights a number of factors, including the massification of education and research creating many sites of Mode 1 knowledge production. However, by emphasising two specific trends – the impact of IT and the expansion in the market for knowledge – they go beyond the unspecified supply-side account advanced by post-industrial theory to locate knowledge production in a wider social context of demand and distribution. Equally importantly, the analysis of

TABLE I.1 **Changing modes of knowledge production**

Mode 1	Mode 2
Problems defined by academic community	Knowledge produced in context of application
Disciplinary knowledge	Transdisciplinary knowledge
Homogeneity	Heterogeneity
Hierarchical and stable organisations	Heterarchical and transient organisations
Quality control by the 'invisible college'	Socially accountable and reflexive

these trends helps to relocate the debate from the *global* ramifications of shifting modes of knowledge production towards the *local* formation and distribution of expertise. This pinpoints the crucial role played by micro-level processes around, first, the adoption of IT and, second increasing market competition in shaping and defining expertise in late-modern society. It is in this predominantly organisational arena of innovation and change that many of the problems (and solutions) associated with long-term societal trends are first addressed.

Technological change

The impact of new information and communication technology has certainly been an important contributor to the new mode of knowledge production. It has facilitated the emergence of new networks of researchers and knowledge workers who are not grounded in traditional disciplinary communities. However the effect of IT as a 'technoeconomic paradigm' is more than its instrumental value for the exchange of research findings. Nowhere is this more evident than in the *informational* effects of IT. It is information flows not the technology itself that have such pervasive effects on the management of expertise. Previous forms of technological change merely replaced one expert group with another. Although IT has this localised effect too, its impact extends to the distribution of knowledge within the organisation as a whole. The ability of IT systems both to 'automate' and to 'informate' work (Zuboff, 1988) means that they not only enhance *control* over physical operations but also produce *representations* of such operations that enhance the possibility of remote control and decision making.

This double-edged effect of IT produces an organisational transparency that has awesome implications for managerial structures. As information about organisational activities becomes more generally available and ceases to be the localised property of particular groups, organisational hierarchies are restructured, reengineered and delayered. Paradoxically, many decision-making processes are decentralised not out of any democratic impulse but because central monitoring and control is now more pervasive than ever before. The effect of such transparency is to identify and ultimately eliminate managerial roles that only act as linkages in the chain of command.

The radical impact of such changes is fully apparent in our initial example of the Direct Line company. While traditional insurance firms had developed multilevel hierarchies, Direct Line was able to provide the same generic product by effectively collapsing their cumbersome bureaucracy into a flatter and leaner organisational form. The Direct Line case thus clearly exemplifies the competitive potential of IT. At the same time though, the company's information systems provide an equally outstanding example of another, more ominous, consequence of IT use: the ruthless separation of the *processing* of information from its *interpretation*. Where the first only requires the exercise of routine clerical data-handling skills, the second demands the exercise of judgement based on specialist knowledge (Newman and Newman, 1985). This separation threatens white-collar workers in much the same way that Taylorism's divorce of mental and manual work threatened blue-collar workers. Thus Direct Line's astounding business growth produced far more jobs for telesales people than for managers. And although these information workers made use of the sophisticated computer database systems, their data-inputting and information-handling work was simultaneously monitored by the very systems they were using.

But if the future facing the mass of information workers seems bleak, some groups will benefit. Interpretive tasks may be concentrated in small, highly knowledgeable groups whose decisions and judgements are amplified a hundred-fold by the information systems that implement them. For an illustration we only have to turn to the money markets of the City. Here the concentration of knowledge and judgement in the hands of so-called 'masters of the universe' – small but highly rewarded teams of deal makers – expresses the near-perfect match between the codified commodity of money values and the processing power of IT systems. Although the deal makers are often portrayed as poker players, the gambling metaphor conceals the hidden apparatus of information flows that allows these players to deploy massive resources with such fine precision of timing and intent. Although this is an extreme example, the same leveraging effect applies even in workaday contexts. In a sea of information, the islands of expertise become the defining geography of organisations.

The effects of IT are normally portrayed as a technological success story, but its polarising effects on work are as much a consequence of failure as of success. IT is certainly capable of commodifying many forms of knowledge into software packages and systems, yet expert systems that have specifically targeted human cognitive capacities have still failed to penetrate important knowledge domains. This failure is usually explained in terms of rules dependency. Expert systems can only apply a given set of rules unthinkingly, whereas humans are able to select which rules to apply to changing situations (Dreyfus, 1979). It is precisely this failure of IT application that has preserved the role of human expertise, while its success in rationalizing other tasks has actually helped to enhance its global significance.

Institutional change

The effects of IT on expertise also extend to the institutional forms through which it is organised. Expertise may be organised within the institutional forms of markets, bureaucracies, professional firms or networks. IT influences the choice of institutional forms in two major ways. First, the codification of expertise may allow hierarchical controls and employment relationships to be replaced by a market transaction (Child, 1987). To take a simple example, when the craft knowledge of the IT worker is turned into a software package, the organisation of knowledge shifts from hierarchical control to a transaction in the marketplace. IT also enhances the use of remote control and monitoring devices. This has paved the way for market or quasi-market mechanisms to take the place of customary forms such as functional structures and the centralised allocation of expert resources.

As well as the technical options advanced by IT, the use of market mechanisms to regulate expertise has also been boosted by more blatantly political factors. In the UK and many other Western countries, governments have sought to reduce the power and resources available to classical professions such as medicine and the law, and to state sponsored groups such as social workers and teachers. Such moves have often been justified in terms of free-market ideologies, but the desire to control ballooning welfare budgets has been an equally pressing factor. One of the practical consequences of such moves, however, has been the polarisation of professional groups into those who have had to endure an increasingly meagre diet of state support and those who have been able to find sustenance elsewhere, principally the private sector (Crompton, 1992). More generally, government policies such as privatisation and deregulation have served to extend greatly the scope of market mechanisms into a wide variety of professional and expert occupational niches. One effect has been a sometimes subtle, sometimes dramatic change in the nature of professional expertise. This has lost some of its ethical and rhetorical baggage and has increasingly been marketed as a commodity.

But the shift towards market-based means of regulating expertise does not always involve the outright 'marketisation' of activities. The number of experts who have found their work unceremoniously 'out-sourced' is probably far fewer than the number subject to tight financial and personnel controls that effectively emulate market disciplines. Central technical functions and R&D labs are converted from corporate overhead into cost centres, profit centres or strategic business units (Whittington, 1991). Though not full-blooded 'exposure' to the market, this marketised bureaucracy has important effects nonetheless. Whilst expertise was previously *allocated* according to the experts' own criteria, it is now increasingly commodified and *marketed* according to customer needs. And whilst the interaction of expert groups with user groups was controlled by an overarching hierarchy, control now operates through the contracts regulating transactions. Users, patients and clients alike all become 'customers'. The overall effect is to install the vocabulary and incentives of the market as the principal means of regulating expertise.

This is not to say that market forces and management hierarchies are mutually exclusive or simply substitute for one another. Institutional change often means markets and management hierarchies evolving in lock-step fashion. Greater market exposure for organisational subunits will have effects on the internal management structure. As 'ivory-tower' technical functions, for instance, are transformed into hard-nosed profit-centres or strategic business units, the power and scope of business management will tend to increase and the autonomy of expert groups reduce (Figure I.2).

This effect is neatly illustrated by a recent study of 'market-driven change' in R&D labs and NHS hospitals (Whittington *et al.*, 1994) which found that increased external market pressures led in both sectors to decentralisation and debureaucratisation. This was accompanied by the introduction and increasing domination of business management practices and the erosion of professional control. Administrators were replaced by managers and 'support' functions mutated into functional specialisms within the evolving management structure. The once all-pervading influence of the wider professional community shrank to a localised 'subculture' within the wider managerial regime. Moreover the shrinking of professional control was accompanied by subtle revisions in the ethos and practices of the professionals themselves. Managerial perceptions and practices diffused widely throughout the organisation. R&D experts and doctors alike increasingly found themselves attending to commercial issues of market share and organisational performance.

FIGURE I.2   Expertise and modes of control

These changes in the management process had important impacts on the production and application of specialist knowledge. In the R&D labs this meant a shift from a long-term to a short-term time horizon and from basic to applied research. One research manager described the shift thus: 'The bottom-line is a strong influence upon people. One is always worried that decentralization will cut people's time horizons. . . Which guy focussed on next December is going to do long-term research – or even medium-term development' (Whittington, 1990, p. 200). More broadly, in both R&D labs and hospitals it meant giving priority to the commodification of knowledge. This 'blackboxing', in the words of one of the R&D experts, involved objectifying knowledge into discrete, marketable packages.

Although much of the recent debate about organisational change has been dominated by this shift from hierarchical to market control, this is only one strand of the broader pattern of industrial 'disorganisation' (Lash and Urry, 1987) and the dispersal of economic activity into widely scattered coalitions of smaller units. In many ways this pattern defies the neat polarity of market versus hierarchy. In particular it has given rise to a focus on 'networks' as crucial means of organising economic and technological activity.

Over time the concept of a 'network' has come to mean a number of different, sometimes contradictory things. Some studies take an institutional focus, defining networks as the middle ground between market and hierarchy where activities are lubricated by shared norms and mutual trust. Other studies, however, focus simply on the performative qualities of networks. Empirical studies, for instance, have demonstrated the importance of networks in fostering innovation.

> Information passed through networks is 'thicker' than information obtained in the market and 'freer' than that communicated in a hierarchy . . . The open-ended, relational features of networks, with their relative absence of explicit 'quid pro quo' behaviour, greatly enhance their ability to transmit and learn new knowledge and skills (Powell, 1991, p. 272).

Given the distribution of technological knowledge across a number of user and supplier groups, the formation of a network may be critical to successful innovation. In the process, as De Bresson and Clark note, the activities of the network may succeed in transforming markets and hierarchies alike: 'The conditions of competition and the shape of the market has been transformed by the strategic act of innovation and the mobilization of a network' (De Bresson and Clark, 1992, p. 156). The critical role of networks powerfully underlines our general theme because it highlights the distribution of the specialist knowledges employed in innovation across many firms in a sector. In that context, it also draws attention to the existence of capillary-like 'knowledge communities' in particular sectors or occupational groups (Borum and Kristensen, 1991). The amorphous social affiliations of such communities provide ample scope for the sharing and transmission of both formal and tacit forms of knowledge, the latter often through stories and parables. As Spender puts it, 'the processes of knowledge generation are emergent and depend on the existence of communities-in-practice' (1992, p. 412).

Finally, at the microlevel of work organisation these sweeping institutional trends have their corollary in radical changes to the internal structuring of expertise. The organisation of product development, to cite a paradigm case, has seen the gradual eclipse of the classic linear model of science-push and market-pull with its functional separation of expertise into R&D, product engineering and marketing departments. Under the pressures of shortening product cycles, sequential and functionally segmented processes have given way to multifunctional project teams and overlapping problem solving (Clark and Fujimoto, 1989). Bertodo (1988), for example, describes the break-up of the functional regime at Rover Cars in the UK and the compression of product development through multi functional teams, parallel working and early prototyping. The wider implications of such changes, however, are outlined in a significant aside that brings to mind some of the comments of the R&D experts in Whittington's study: 'The attainment of a reliable and dependable product over a short development cycle is critically linked with the side-tracking of all innovation and "new" technology into a separate evolutionary stream, separate from the product renewal programme' (Bertodo, 1988, p. 708).

For some organisations, of course, 'sidetracking' innovation out of the mainstream can ultimately mean shunting it into the sidings. Organisational changes affect the quality as well as the distribution of expertise. Thus they can have strategic ramifications for the organisation's ability to innovate – its 'innovation capacity' (Whipp and Clark, 1986) – that extend well beyond their immediate impact on the expert groups involved.

Structure of this book

The management of expertise is too broad and complex a topic to be amenable to a regimented division of intellectual labour or uniform cross-sectional comparisons. Instead each of the following chapters explores in depth some of the themes and levels of analysis that have emerged from this discussion. The aim of this interweaving and layering of different sectoral and occupational experiences can be summed up as 'bootstrapping'. This – the origin of the computer term 'booting up' – meaning to pull ourselves up by our bootstraps, involves using our existing fragmentary knowledge base to create new understandings and insights (Hofstadter, 1980). This aim is partly one of exploration: using a range of studies to map out different patterns of expertise and to examine its critical role in a variety of settings. However we aim to do more than survey the generality of the management of expertise. Having developed a framework that identifies critical issues in the management of expertise, the following chapters offer a chance to explore those issues across an ensemble of sectors and occupational groupings that offer both striking contrasts and surprising similarities.

The emphasis throughout is on an empirically grounded account of the management of expertise. Studies of different industrial and occupational settings not only allow us to test our prospectus against the backdrop of sectoral and technological differences, but also give a flavour of the extensive social networks through which expertise is transmitted. The latter range from the minutely task-specific skills of the individual expert to the diffuse occupational groupings that define that expert's working assumptions.

Each chapter begins with a brief editorial introduction that relates it to the themes outlined here and locates it substantively in the wider debates around the management of expertise. The chapters are organised into three parts that map onto the cardinal forms of change confronting the deployment of expertise. Part 1 – 'Expertise in a Societal Perspective' – deals with the experience of expert groups under the shifting regimes of knowledge production and societal validation that characterise the current epoch. Thus in the first chapter Harry Scarbrough develops a new perspective on the management of expertise that is capable of addressing the radical change in recipes and practices. Is the professional model still a valid framework for analysing and managing expert groups, or do intimations of post-professional forms of work organisation demand new thinking and new approaches?

In the following chapter Gibson Burrell takes a critical view of some of the post-industrial theorising that has coloured our perceptions of the societal role of knowledge workers and expert groups. By locating such groups within the evolution of Britain's service class, self-comforting assumptions about their manifest destiny are replaced by nagging doubts as to their role and ultimate fate in a post-modern society and global capitalist economy.

Brian Baxter further develops the critical social theory perspective by outlining, in Chapter 3, the changing conceptions and practices of management consultancy. As the consultancy model becomes an increasingly important reference point for both the organisation and the intellectual analysis of expertise, this chapter has a relevance that extends beyond the consultancy industry itself. The competing meanings provided by modern and post-modern analyses give us a useful framework for examining the shifting patterns of consultancy work.

Part 2, 'Expertise and Technological Innovation' deals with the technological implications of the management of expertise. In Chapter 4 Martin Corbett takes us into the complex flows of knowledge and information that are involved in technological design. By examining key features of the designers' expertise – assumptions, tacit knowledge and values – we are able to understand design as an outcome of a particular negotiated distribution of expertise between designer and user.

Chapter 5 by Jacky Swan puts expert–user relationships into a wider perspective by examining the networks of expertise that promote the diffusion of technologies. Defining technological innovations as complex, multifaceted bundles of knowledge allows us to see their dependence on existing intrasectoral and professional distributions of expertise. This study of the role of a professional association in promoting production and inventory control systems shows how far innovation processes at the organisational level are actually dependent upon wider social networks and professional projects.

In the following chapter Harry Scarbrough explores the interaction of expertise, innovation and management in the financial services sector. Here the focus shifts from experts' location within extensive sectoral networks to their position within managerial hierarchies. A more central role in such hierarchies seemed to be a corollary of the emergence of 'strategic IT' applications in the 1980s. The analysis of IS expertise, however, highlights important constraints on its ability to make IT strategic. A paired comparison of half a dozen IT projects demonstrates the processes involved in the social construction of strategic knowledge around IT.

Part 3 'Expertise and Institutional Change', examines the impact of the break-up of professional functional structures and the extension of market mechanisms through studies of the UK National Health Service (NHS), manufacturing industry and the financial services sector.

Chapter 7 by Harry Scarbrough investigates one of the important consequences of changes in traditional, functional regimes for managing technical expertise. This is the extension of managerial responsibility for the formation and deployment of expertise. Companies are faced with pressures to make effective use of scarce technical expertise, yet much managerial knowledge about the capabilities and knowledges of different expert groups is swept away by organisational change. This at a time when organisations are concerned to identify their 'core competences' for competitive advantage. The overlapping knowledges and experience provided by functional career ladders at least ensured managers a degree of tacit knowledge about the experts under their control. Now, without functional structures to provide a collective memory of expert capabilities it becomes difficult to apply them effectively to the ever-changing roster of projects and technologies that market forces generate. One symptom, and putative solution, to this loss of intimate managerial knowledge is the development of elaborate frameworks and systems to identify and record competences and skills. This chapter reports case-study findings on the relative success of such initiatives in a sample of large UK firms.

Lynn Ashburner and Louise Fitzgerald's Chapter 8 deals with the interplay between the advance of market pressures and the development of management structures and practices in the NHS. Here we see market mechanisms sparking the diffusion of managerial practices in the context of long-established professional demarcations and controls. Importantly, though, the spread of managerial concepts and discourse is not confined to the establishment of formal managerial structures. Equally important is the development of managerial disciplines within the professional groups providing medical care; education and socialisation helping to bring about a hybridisation of professional and managerial practices and commitments.

While NHS changes reflect a key policy assumption that medical expertise can be regulated through the market, in the final chapter Harry Scarbrough explores some of the limitations of the market as an institutional means of organising expertise. It examines the so-called 'make–buy' problem as it surfaces in a sample of IT projects drawn from the financial services sector. Detailed analysis of each case not only shows the constraints on the use of the market mechanism, especially in strategic applications and innovation, but also the extent to which the transfer and construction of knowledge depends on social processes and structures. The *ad hoc* 'strategies of social closure' adopted by in-house functions and external suppliers play an important role in generating different forms of technological innovation.

References

Bauman, Z. (1989) *Modernity and the Holocaust* (Oxford: Polity Press).

Bell, D. (1973) *The Coming of Post-industrial Society* (New York: Basic Books).

Bertodo, R. G. (1988) 'Evolution of an engineering organisation', *International Journal of Technology Management*, vol. 3, no. 6, pp. 693–710.

Borum, F. and Kristensen, P. H. (1991) *Technological Innovation and Organisational Change: Danish patterns of knowledge, networks and culture* (Copenhagen: New Social Science Monographs).

Child, J. (1987) 'Information technology, organisation and the response to strategic challenges', *California Management Review*, vol. 30, pp. 33–49.

Clark, K. B. and Fujimoto, T. (1989), 'Overlapping problem-solving in product development' in K. Ferdows (ed.), *Managing International Manufacturing* (Amsterdam: North-Holland), pp. 127–52.

Crompton, R. (1992) 'Professions in the current context', *Work, Employment and Society*, special issue, 'A decade of change', pp. 147–66.

De Bresson, C. and Clark, P. (1992) 'Strategic Acts, Networks and Sector transformation', in T. M. Khalil and B. A. Bayraktar (eds), *Management of Technology III* (Norcross, Georgia: Institute of Industrial Engineers), pp. 155–64.

Dreyfus, H. (1979) *What Computers Can't Do* (New York: Harper & Row).

Gibbons, M., Limoges, C., Nowotny, H., Schwartzman, S., Scott, P. and Trow, M. (1994) *The New Production of Knowledge: The dynamics of science and research in contemporary societies* (London: Sage).

Giddens, A. (1994) 'Living in a post-traditional society', in U. Beck, A. Giddens and S. Lash, *Reflexive Modernization: Politics, tradition and aesthetics in the modern social order* (Oxford: Blackwell).

Hofstadter, D. R. (1980) *Godel, Escher, Bach: An eternal golden braid* (Harmondsworth: Penguin).

Hughes, T. P. (1987) 'The evolution of large technological systems', in W. E. Bijker, T. Hughes and T. J. Pinch (eds), *The Social Construction of Technological Systems* (London: MIT Press).

Jones, B. (1982) *Sleepers Wake! Technology and the future of work* (Melbourne: Oxford University Press).

Lash, S. and Urry, J. (1987) *The End of Organised Capitalism* (Cambridge: Polity Press).

Lyon, D. (1988) *The Information Society: Issues and illusions* (Cambridge: Polity Press).

Newman, J. and Newman, R. (1985) 'Information work: The new divorce?', *British Journal of Sociology*, vol. 24, pp. 497–515.

Powell, W. W. (1991) 'Neither market nor hierarchy: network forms of organisation', in G. Thompson, J. Frances, R. Levacic and J. Mitchell, *Markets, Hierarchies and Networks: The coordination of social life* (London: Sage), pp. 265–77.

Starbuck, W. (1992) 'Learning by knowledge intensive firms', *Journal of Management Studies*, vol. 29, no. 6, pp. 713–40.

Whipp, R. and Clark, P. (1986) *Innovation in the Auto Industry* (London: Frances Pinter).

Spender, J. C. (1992) 'Knowledge management: Putting your technology strategy on track', *Management of Technology III* (New York: Institute of Industrial Engineers).

White, L. and Taket, A. (1994), 'The death of the expert', *Journal of the Operational Research Society*, vol. 45, no. 7, pp. 733–748.

Whittington, R. (1990) 'The changing structures of R&D', in R. Loveridge and M. Pitt (eds), *The Strategic Management of Technological Innovation* (London: Wiley).

Whittington, R. (1991) 'Changing control strategies in industrial R&D', *R&D Management*, vol. 21, pp. 43–53.

Whittington, R., McNulty, T. and Whipp, R. (1994) 'Market-driven change in professional services: Problems and Processes', *Journal of Management Studies*, vol. 31, no. 6, pp. 829–46.

Zuboff, S. (1988) *In the Age of the Smart Machine* (London: Heinemann).

PART 1

SOCIETAL PERSPECTIVES ON EXPERTISE

CHAPTER 1

Understanding and managing expertise

Harry Scarbrough

Expertise has traditionally been viewed as the near exclusive property of professional groups. The sweeping technological and institutional changes outlined in the Introduction, however, have begun to unravel the nexus that connects the social appropriation of knowledge to professional jurisdictions. Yet the gradual unlocking of expertise from professional control does not mean that it has taken on the ambient, free-floating form of pure knowledge. Although expertise is now more widely distributed and more contingently deployed than before, the same kind of questions that were addressed by the professional model – what counts as expertise, and how do groups acquire it? – remain valid. What is different is that answering these questions means casting our conceptual net even wider to take in not only professionalism but also more diffuse and coincidental formations of knowledge and social relations.

Reframing expertise in this way provides new insights into the management process around expert groups. The structural conflict of professional and managerial norms seems less important than the interpenetration of managerial and expert practices. And antagonistic cultural relations increasingly defer to the economics of commodifying expertise, and their sometime contradictory implications for management and organisations.

Perspectives on expertise

Global changes in organisation and technology are making expertise a more critical resource, and its management more central to organisational performance. These changes are disrupting standard managerial recipes, but are an equally ominous threat to the existing ways of thinking about expertise that underpin them. This threat is greatest for conventional models of professionalism, which have tended to dominate debates on the managerial aspects of expertise. The latter have bred an interest in the 'management of professionals' that presents the expertise issue primarily in terms of the clash of norms and values between two differentially socialised groups. With commitments to knowledge and some ethical baggage to boot, professionals and their practices are seen as either directly or obliquely clashing with hard-nosed business managers. Of course this approach has thrown up its own controversies. There are nagging definitional problems, for instance, that centre on the ontological, and therefore unanswerable, question: what is a profession? Until now, though, most of the stresses and strains on the professional model could be accommodated simply by shifting stance from the definitional problem to a focus on the process of 'professionalising'. This meant that emergent occupational groups could always be accommodated because they were by definition engaged in the professionalising project.

At the heart of this professional version of expertise, setting aside the trappings of State sponsorship and regulation, is a particular conception of the relationship between work and social relations. Put very simply – for the professions literature is rich and extensive – the professional model highlights the central importance of task uncertainty to the organisation of knowledge-based work (Jamous and Pelloile, 1970). The argument runs that tasks with a high degree of uncertainty involve a degree of autonomy and non-trivial discretion, thereby frustrating the usual managerial imperatives of efficiency and control. In turn, such task uncertainty is related to the development of cohesive professional groupings, either functionally – discretion requiring a professional ethos of self-regulation (Merton, 1949) – or politically, discretion conferring power (Johnson, 1972). However both functional and political explanations tend to take as their central focus the development of boundaries or 'jurisdictions' in knowledge-based work (Abbott, 1988). The evolution of such boundaries is seen as an index of the advance or retreat of professionalism. The extension of management control or user influence, for instance, is seen as a process of 'deprofessionalisation' (Haug, 1973).

There are some important drawbacks to applying the professional model to current trends in organisations and expertise. It focuses on task uncertainty as a given feature of a particular production system, yet neglects the extent to which the system itself is a product of discrete bodies of expert knowledge. Task uncertainty arguably needs to be seen not as an *a priori* fact of organisational life, but as something that is actively constructed through expertise. This involves disentangling the existential uncertainty of organisational life from uncertainties constructed and controlled by expert groups. This is, to use a medical metaphor, the distinction between the life-threatening uncertainty of cancer, and the uncertainty of the wound made by the surgeon's healing scalpel. In this example professional knowledge first absorbs the existential uncertainty of a particular condition, and then reintroduces it as an operational uncertainty to be controlled by a suitably qualified and competent professional (Baer, 1986).

Moreover this focus on tasks rather than knowledges helps to blind the professional model to the more dynamic qualities of expertise. The new flows of knowledge produced by IT systems, the effect of market forces on professional jurisdictions and the role of expertise in innovation all constitute a challenge to professional orthodoxy. In addition, making professionalism an ideal-typical benchmark may mean neglecting subtle evolutionary changes in the context, knowledge base and power relationships of such groups. The very fact, for instance, that we need to discriminate in such precise semantic fashion between terms such as 'clients', 'customers' and 'users' to denote the receivers of expert services suggests some of the complexity of the underlying relations of power and knowledge. Concepts of professionalism that view such relations as a zero-sum game only expose their own self-referential tendencies. An outstanding example of this is the argument that the institutional changes of the 1980s and 1990s involve a shift in occupational paradigm from classic professionalism to so-called 'organisational profession-alism' (Friedson 1986). Whereas the liberal professions exercise power *over* organisations and control their task domain through professional and regulatory regimes, organisational professionals, it is said, exercise power *within* organisations and control tasks only by dint of their access to specialised knowledge and skills. The irony of this account is that it is tries to explain powerful trends in occupational development in terms of the very model that is threatened by them.

This is not to say that professionalism necessarily ceases to be an important consideration in the management of expert groups. Its declining significance as an organising principle for expert work does not preclude it from continuing to evoke powerful meanings and identities for groups and individuals. The *idea* of professionalism then, if not its practice, is likely to endure as an ideological resource to be selectively invoked by managers or expert groups according to circumstances – indeed it may be even more fervently invoked as its practice wanes.

Rather, the point of this critique is to suggest that a focus on expertise is both more inclusive and more dynamic than the professional model's rather static focus on defining and controlling boundaries. We can explain many of the features of professionalism in terms of the management of expertise, but not vice versa. Moreover a focus on expertise highlights the uneven but graduated distribution of expertise between specialist groups, suppliers and users. Expertise is diffusely constituted by the interplay of social, economic and technological forces. In that sense it not only highlights the implications of the control of certain kinds of work, but the way that control is influenced by wider patterns of social legitimation, economic value and technological change.

These dynamic and distributed qualities suggest a point-by-point reappraisal of perspectives on expertise. The first item in this roll-call is the importance of seeing expertise as a contingent, socially distributed phenomenon. Expertise is not only the preserve of tightly knit groups of experts and professionals, but is produced, transmitted, bought and sold in many different social settings. The codifying effects of technology mean that expertise can no longer be equated with hermetic expert practices since expert knowledge may be readily transformed into more accessible forms. Software packages turn what were once jealously guarded 'tricks of the trade' into market commodities.

Second, it needs to address the shift in knowledge production from invention to use and from disciplinary to transdisciplinary knowledge. As the advance of market mechanisms involves a faster turnover of knowledge into commercial value, the distance between the locus of invention and the locus of use is correspondingly reduced. While disciplinary knowledge and ivory tower institutions decline, the formation and propagation of expertise increasingly occurs across disciplinary and institutional boundaries, and knowledge-producing groups are subject to increasing pressure to externalize their knowledge into the context of marketing and use.

Third, it needs to provide a framework for understanding expertise in the context of the economic performance of organisations. Expertise is not a thing to be possessed but a form of work that creates value through knowledge and which therefore commands a price in the marketplace. As standardised technologies diffuse so readily across the global marketplace, the secret of competitive advantage increasingly derives from the non-standard insights and interpretations produced by expertise within and across organisational boundaries.

In sum, these points seem to demand a transdisciplinary account of expertise that at least acknowledges some of its multifaceted implications. The scope of such an account has already been hinted at in some previous case examples. The Direct Line case mentioned in the Introduction, for instance, shows a firm reaping the economic and competitive rewards of new combinations of expertise. In the NHS example, new combinations of expertise are a crucial part of a power-struggle, the outcomes of which will shape the NHS for many years to come. And the adoption of new technology in industry shows the importance of the way in which knowledge is distributed both between groups, and between formal and tacit forms. Figure 1.1 provides a simple graphic representation of these interdependent elements of expertise.[1] It describes forms of work that act as a medium for the creation and transmission of interrelated power, knowledge and economic effects – which are characterised by instability and fluidity, and whose meaning and implications are largely contingent on the context of their deployment. This contingent analysis perhaps strikes a discordant note against the classical orchestration of professionalism and occupational control, yet it also seems more suited to the current ecology of expertise. Uprooted from its professional and disciplinary fastnesses, expertise has to fend for itself in a mixed economy of material and symbolic forces where occupational controls are weak and state regulation in retreat.

Developing a molar interpretation of expertise to match this mixed economy involves suspending strict disciplinary categories and recognising the localised and sometimes contradictory coexistence of multiple networks of causation. More specifically it maps a conceptual space, across the disciplines as it were, in which to locate the shaping contingencies and effects of expertise. As such it addresses work processes whose unfolding simultaneously enfolds and normalises social and political relations, knowledge bases and economic values. For example, although I have noted the politicality of organisational change in the NHS, the politics of expertise here are not simply a clash of different vested interests. They are being driven by an explicit economic agenda to do with market disciplines and are being worked through by subtle changes in the knowledge base of doctors.

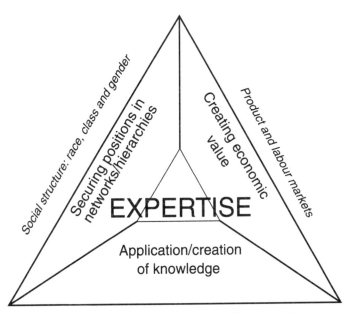

Knowledge communities and occupational groupings

FIGURE 1.1   **A perspective on expertise**

A further advantage of this broad and inclusive view of expertise is that it produces a relativistic treatment of its distribution. Relativistic not only in the sense of bracketing the truth-value claims of different groups, but also in terms of locating expertise in the shifting relationships between different social groups. This is important because many areas of expertise are confronted by the gradual leeching of knowledge into user or customer groups. In the IT field, for example, IT experts have had to adjust their knowledge base and even their self-image to accommodate increases in user knowledge, particularly the rise of assertively knowledgeable 'power users'. Instead of viewing expertise as an emblematic property of professional domains, this approach allows us to relate it to processes of industrial change and their fuzzier conjunctions of specialist knowledges with socially strategic locations. It highlights the sinuous contours of expertise, twisting and shifting to reflect the changing landscapes of knowledge production and industrial change.

As for the conceptual mapping of these landscapes, it would be trite simply to suggest that expertise can be viewed from a number of different perspectives. Certainly the different aspects of expertise need unpacking, and this is addressed under various headings below. However expertise is primarily and distinctively important as a site for the joint production of knowledge, economic value and social relations. As it evolves in particular localised settings, it reflects but also begins to shape its wider institutional context. Thus Figure 1.1 is not merely a reminder that expertise is amenable to a variety of differentiated perspectives but also an invitation to explore these integrating dynamics.

The politics of expertise

Expertise can be understood as the medium through which knowledge grasps power, while power shapes knowledge. This is not a one-to-one correspondence, however, but a complex working out of many possible configurations within a particular work context. The inequality of knowledge between expert and user or client may be implicated with power relations in a number of different ways. Thus in some contexts expertise can be understood as a kind of modern alchemy, turning the baser forms of power into the lustrous forms of technology and knowledge. In other contexts expertise represents the rate of political return to groups that have invested in specialist forms of knowledge. In neither case, though, can we apply any general formula or rate of exchange to the power–knowledge translation. Indeed one of the things to be learned from post-industrial predictions of societal change – and one of the reasons for studying expertise in preference – is the dismal failure of generalisations about the relationship between knowledge and power in society. There may be a certain logic to the notion that the knowledge-generating occupations or the 'technocracy' would inevitably assume dominant positions in a society based on knowledge. Galbraith, for instance, claims that power 'goes to the factor which is hardest to obtain or hardest to replace . . . it adheres to the one that has greatest inelasticity of supply at the margin' (Galbraith, 1969, p. 67). However this logic is based on the heroic assumption that power is awarded broadly according to productive contribution to organisations and to society in general.

Organisational and occupational studies show how naive that assumption is. Power is taken, not given, and expertise is about mobilising knowledge and economic scarcity to seize it (Fischer, 1990). As Stehr notes, 'Knowledge . . . constitutes a capacity for action' (Stehr, 1994, p. 120) Thus within organisations expert power certainly reflects control of knowledge and labour-market scarcity, but it is also a more immediate consequence of enlisting these variables as political tools. When this strategy is successful, as Figure 1.2 indicates, expertise may be sustained by recursive relationships between a group's control of techniques and its strategic position in decision-making processes.

The medical profession provides some excellent examples of such recursive relationships. Medical practitioners have generally been able to assert firm control over expert diagnostic systems and other technologies to ensure that their expertise remains central to key decisions in treatment process – and, by

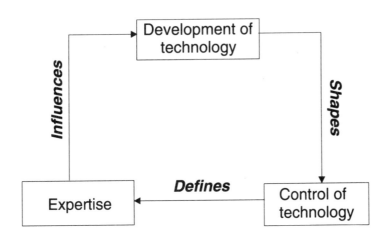

FIGURE 1.2   **Recursive relations in the reproduction of expertise**

the by, that other groups such as nurses, pharmacists and radiologists are largely excluded from such decisions. To complete the circuit, their arguments for control often draw on self-validating claims to vital forms of knowledge. Thus in one UK study (Child *et al.*, 1984), doctors successfully argued for control over a diagnostic system on the grounds that expert medical judgement was still needed to gauge the truthfulness of patients' responses to the system.

In this context it is hardly surprising that the professions are often seen as institutionalised forms of power holding by particular social groups (Johnson, 1972), even though, as Armstrong's work (1984, 1985) demonstrates, such power is to a degree dependent on acquiescence in wider structures of ownership and control. Such acquiescence is secured in part by processes of interprofessional competition, as different occupational groups seek to cannibalise the valuable knowledge and techniques of others while retaining a monopoly of their own. Armstrong's account of such processes also serves to highlight the fluid and contingent features of expertise, as occupational knowledge-bases are eroded or political exclusions fail. He contrasts the fate of the engineering profession in the UK – which he argues, failed to retain control of its most valuable techniques – with the accounting profession. The latter has insinuated itself as the dominant form of expertise mediating between business organisations and the owners of capital. As a result its particular world-view has effectively become one of the structural realities that such businesses face.

Knowledge and cognition in expertise

The production and communication of knowledge effectively distinguishes expertise from other forms of work, and is a crucial influence on its formation and deployment. In fact it is the far-reaching changes in these very areas that threaten the validity and viability of the professional model of expertise. On the other hand, knowledge and expertise are not synonymous. One of the biggest flaws of post-industrial theory, as Abercrombie and Urry note, was to equate knowledge with power: 'Knowledge is power is a misleading slogan. Knowledge may well be important to the maintenance of power, but that does not mean the knowledgeable are powerful' (Abercrombie and Urry, 1983, p. 62). This is one of the reasons for defining knowledge as only one facet of expertise. Also, relating the possession of knowledge to the exercise of power would be neglecting the important, if often tacit and contingent, forms of knowledge possessed by less powerful social groups. This would not only be colluding with attempts to justify power inequalities in knowledge terms (Knights *et al.*, 1993), but also glossing over the tendency for social institutions to naturalise and take for granted the knowledge deployed by lower-status groups in society.

The usefulness of this distinction between expertise and knowledge is further underlined when we turn from the knowledge of individuals and groups to knowledge in organisations. Depending on their aims, organisations draw on a variety of different sources of knowledge, but not all of it is embodied in individuals or groups. In fact certain kinds of knowledge can truly be said to be organisational in that they are impersonally distributed and sedimented in the rules and relationships of an organisation's structure and systems (Kogut and Zander, 1992).

These points still leave a number of unanswered questions about the nature of knowledge itself. Specifically, there is the epistemological issue of the relationship between knowledge and truth. In a late-modern or post-modern age it is no longer assumed that knowledge equates with truth in anything but a relativistic or localised sense (Law, 1991). Social studies of science have even challenged the commonly held view that scientific knowledge is actually a reflection of an *objective* reality. They suggest instead that the sciences are socially constructed ways of understanding reality. Some post-modern writers take this view even further, and argue that all forms of knowledge, including much vaunted forms of expertise, are merely 'stories' of no greater validity than any others (Lawson, 1989).

Fortunately one of the advantages of a modest sociological approach to these questions is the ability to set aside consideration of ultimate truth or reality for another day (Berger and Luckmann, 1967). Accepting simply that all knowledge production is a social activity – a view accepted on all sides since the work of Thomas Kuhn (1962) – the preferred approach here is to bracket the claims of objectivists and post-modernists alike in favour of a sociological analysis of the means by which knowledge is distributed, validated and accepted in different social contexts. Whether or not all forms of knowledge are merely plausible 'stories', the crucial question for a sociological study of expertise is how expert groups manage to distance their knowledge from such story-telling and present it as something more objective and portentous. In other words, the emphasis slips from truth to value and from epistemology to production and distribution. The crucial question becomes this: how is knowledge produced, distributed and valued across different social contexts?

In the literature, answers to this question can be roughly arrayed to form a continuum. At one extreme knowledge is viewed in terms of its discrete content and its functional value (for example Sveiby and Lloyd, 1987; Machlup, 1990; Ericsson and Smith, 1991). In what can be termed this 'content theory', knowledge is seen as an objective entity that is acquired by individuals through learning and specialization and embodied, owned and controlled in a variety of forms. At the other extreme, knowledge is defined as a diffuse, collective phenonemon, shaped by patterns of social relations and with predominantly political effects (cf. McNeil, 1987; Latour, 1987; Lyotard, 1984). The emphasis of such 'relational' theory on the social institutions that shape and validate knowledge often leads to a highly relativistic account. In this view, professional knowledge is a rhetorical complex that functions as a handy means of achieving control over important tasks and status (Alvesson, 1993).

Both theoretical approaches have their advantages and disadvantages. Content theories usefully highlight the development of coherent bodies of thought and the effect of their transmission and application on different social settings. Studies of the diffusion of innovations remind us of the powerful effects of such discrete packages of knowledge, and their ability to generalise themselves across enormous cultural and geographical distances. On the other hand, a focus on the cognitive content of knowledge abstracts it from its social setting, making it difficult to handle questions of value and status. It can provide exemplary data on, say, the number of chess games that grand masters hold in their heads, but it cannot explain the differential value attached to different sets of cognitive skills. For example combat pilots typically have around 350 flying hours when they join their squadrons, yet after 600 hours of supervised practice college-trained typists are viewed as barely competent (Gentner, 1988). Clearly the enormous difference in status (and salary) attaching to these respective roles has little to do with individual skills and much more with societal attributions, particularly with regard to gender.

But if the content view is too focused on individual skills, relational theory threatens to throw everything back into the soup of generalised social relations. Either that or the arguments for the rhetorical nature of knowledge collapse sociological questions back into epistemological ones. Issues of diffusion and innovation are neglected, as too are the socially grounded determinants of the success and failure of different knowledge claims.

One way of handling these competing accounts is to turn them into dimensions of a typology. Blackler (1994), for instance, elaborates on these dimensions with a typology that encompasses five categories of knowledge: embodied, embedded, embrained, encultured and encoded. The problem with this, as with any typology, is that it imposes a static framework upon what are often dynamic processes; a particular failing given the shifts and elisions between one form of knowledge and another. An alternative approach, and the one preferred here, is to focus on the social construction of knowledge. This means reframing the content and relational aspects of knowledge in terms of the social processes and structures through which knowledge is constructed.

To speak of the social construction of knowledge does not imply that particular social groups arbitrarily construct their own truths and beliefs. Knowledge is seen not as a choice but as a provisional accomplishment of social groups and social processes. It also involves attending to the wider social structures that shape these processes; the latter being a necessary corrective to the depiction of knowledge as free-floating facts or narratives. By highlighting the structural aspects of knowledge and expertise, it makes a kind of figure-ground sense of, respectively, the relations between tacit and formal knowledges, between knowledges applied in the immediate work process and the wider context of knowledge production, and between discrete, specialised bodies of knowledge and widely diffused understandings or world-views.

Over time, the relationships between process and social structure are broadly dialectical. Preexisting and sedimented knowledge bases, for instance, constrain the production of new forms of knowledge and validate or qualify their claims. But equally, processes of innovation and diffusion transform the knowledges of a particular work process (taking the form of technologies or rules of action, say) into widely held, structural forms that in turn provide the backcloth for other work processes. Thus Whipp and Clark (1986) describe how 'strategic innovations' within the Rover car firm radically changed the operating rules and relations within the company and thereby laid down 'structural repertoires' that heavily influenced future performance. Similarly the widespread adoption of IBM's PC operating system had the effect of defining an 'industry standard' that subsequently defined the parameters for further innovations in that sector.

The social construction approach thus gives us a sense of the 'duality' of knowledge; that discrete bodies of knowledge are not defined simply in terms of their innate cause–effect propositions but are also related to, and validated by, a wider socially embedded structure of knowledge, be it occupational norms, technological infrastructure, disciplinary knowledge or structural repertoires. This is an important point because management often view knowledge as a purely cognitive phenomenon, thus forgetting that its social construction not only draws on knowledge work at the point of production, but on a wider occupational and technological infrastructure that extends well beyond the environs of the firm itself.

As an illustration of this important link between the immediate application and creation of knowledge and its structural distribution, we can usefully compare the knowledge of the IT expert with the knowledge of the human resource management (HRM) practitioner. In the former case, since IT produces predictable material effects that are independent of the immediate social context, the attendant specialist expertise is much more readily standardised and diffused through product and labour-markets. Against this mediating backdrop of market values, the organisational application of IT expertise (practical) is effectively distanced from the societal validation of the occupation's knowledge-claims (rhetorical and ideological). In contrast the HRM expert's knowledge base is localised and tacit and he or she finds it is difficult to demonstrate predictable and tangible effects from its application. The result is that HRM expertise struggles to validate itself at firm level and is more likely to face fundamental criticism of 'the emperor's new clothes' kind. Thus, even accepting that HRM and IT expertise are epistemological equals, the latter does not have to achieve the same degree of rhetorical closure at the level of the organisation. Rather, the claims of IT expertise are continuously tested at the institutional level of product and labour markets through, for instance technology prototyping, user–supplier relations and the labour marketability of technical competences.

Economics and expertise

The economic issues around expertise can be briefly discussed in terms of two main questions: one is to do with the way knowledge creates economic value, the other with the relationship between economic forces and the construction and distribution of knowledge. As for the first, some studies highlight the embodied knowledge of individual experts and specialists, taking 'professional service' or 'knowledge-intensive firms' as their paradigm of firm behaviour. The implication is that organisations are basically vehicles for the application of individually applied expertise, with human resource policies and labour-market issues consequently taking centre stage (Maister, 1985). In contrast a growing number of studies embrace a full-blown knowledge-based analysis of corporate performance. That is, organisational actions are related not to internal structures or external market forces but to the nature and distribution of knowledge within the firm. Competitiveness and innovation comes not from individual experts but from the configuration and acquisition of knowledge within the firm as a whole. Corporate competences and organisational learning define the stocks and flows of knowledge. Thus Quinn asserts, 'The organisation of enterprises and effective strategies will depend more on the development and deployment of intellectual resources than on the management of physical assets' (Quinn, 1992, p. 48).

Secondly, and echoing comments on the power and knowledge dimensions noted above, seeing expertise as a medium for the appropriation of economic value helps to qualify any assumptions of economic determinism. Market forces do not operate directly or unambiguously on organisations. Specialised bodies of expertise are employed to read the economic runes, and their interpretations effectively construct the realities that organisations face (Morgan, 1990). In the UK, for example, we need look no further than the collusive alliance of accounting expertise with City institutions for an explanation of the distinctively short-term, financially oriented interpretations of market forces that have come to predominate in the boardrooms of large firms. Moreover expertise not only interprets market forces but also directly shapes them through the medium of strategic innovations that restructure the competitive rules in a sector. As Starbuck puts it in his study of knowledge intensive firms: 'Successful firms cause their environments to have uncorrectable problems. Firms and their environments change symbiotically' (Starbuck, 1992, p. 721) In other words, in the economic arena as much as in the arenas of power and knowledge, expertise stands out as a region of indeterminacy that defies narrow disciplinary accounts.

Pausing here to summarise the discussion so far, this indeterminacy and resistance to reductive analysis reflects the distinctive role of expertise in late-modern society:

- The formation of expertise is seen as a *contingent* phenomenon, dependent on the coincidence of particular social groups with valued knowledges. Although there are wider structural predispositions favouring the emergence of particular forms of expertise, the fluidity of knowledge coupled with the active opportunism of social groups effectively translates such predispositions into the contingent resources from which expertise is constructed.
- As a soluble matrix of knowledge and social relations, expertise in the current context is characterised by its *fragmentation and transience*. It therefore bears little relationship to the teleologically assured evolution of the classical professions, or the systemic effects of disciplinary bodies of knowledge (Foucault, 1979).
- The *interdependency* of knowledge and socioeconomic relations is reflected in the diverse effects of expertise, where cognitive competences are advanced alongside the political interests of particular groups and their claims on resources. Conversely, shifts in the management and organisation of expertise are likely to produce consequential changes in its integral formation. Thus a change in power relations or a more intensive regime for the marketing and commodification of expertise would not only generate important political and economic issues around expert groups, but would simultaneously advance shifts in their knowledg base.

Managing expertise

So far we have established that societal trends have established expertise as a critical moment in industrial change: the principal 'reverse salient' to the application of technology and the pursuit of competitive advantage. At the same time orthodox approaches to the management of expertise are being undermined by the global shift in the societal mode of knowledge production. The growing emphasis on networked forms of knowledge production and the impact of IT are transforming the means by which expertise is constituted, marketed and deployed.

What these global trends mean for organisational processes of managing expertise, however, is less clear. Expertise is certainly a problem for management; the one point of agreement in an otherwise disparate literature. But the nature of that problem and the wider relationship between expertise and management is much more contentious. A popular view amongst managers seems to equate managing expertise with the frustrations of controlling 'prima donnas', a task that has been likened to 'herding cats'. This popular motif has potential therapeutic value for distressed managers, but it ignores the reasons why expertise is both vital and intractable in equal measure, focusing instead on short-term strategies of control.

More thoughtful managerial approaches tend to see expertise in terms of professionalism. Specifically, they define a problematic of structural conflict between the 'professional' goals and norms of expert groups and the narrowly defined organisational goals pursued by management (Katz, 1988). On the one hand, gaining access to the professionals' knowledge base involves tolerating their commitment to professional standards within work processes. On the other hand, managers are constantly seeking greater control of such processes to achieve efficiency goals. Many different solutions are proffered for this supposedly inherent conflict, but all tend to converge on the same general principle; namely, that of constructing boundaries between managers and experts that preserve the essential integrity of professional forms of work while locating them within the wider fabric of organisational goals. So pervasive is this approach that we can see it operating at several different levels. At the organisational level, for instance, it is apparent in Mintzberg's (1983) notion of 'professional bureaucracies'. The latter are contrasted with the direct managerial control of work that is typical of 'machine bureaucracy' inasmuch as professional groups are given considerable control over their own work. Coordination is achieved not through hierarchy but through the standardisation of skills, with the standards themselves being defined by external, self-governing professional associations. Instead of a singular managerial hierarchy, therefore, professional bureaucracies are characterised by 'parallel administrative hierarchies, one democratic and bottom-up for the professionals, and a second machine bureaucratic and top-down for the support staff' (Mintzberg, 1983, p. 198).

Bailyn, by way of contrast, focuses on processes of decision making, and in particular on a claimed distinction between 'strategic' and 'operational' autonomy – the first being 'the freedom to set one's own research agenda' and the second 'the freedom once a problem has been set to attack it by means determined by oneself, within given organisational resource constraints' (Bailyn, 1988, p. 227). Happily, and conveniently, her study concludes that operational autonomy is most important to scientists and technicians while strategic autonomy has greater relevance to managers.

The distinction between different kinds of autonomy finds parallels in many other organisational studies; in Weick's (1979) distinction between premise control and behavioural or output controls, for instance. More recently it has resurfaced in a cultural guise. Thus Raelin defines the management of expertise as bridging the gap between the culture of the organisation and the culture of the professional: 'The inherent conflict between managers and professionals results basically from a clash of cultures: the corporate culture, which captures the commitment of managers, and the professional culture which socialises professionals' (Raelin, 1991, p. 1).

Be they concerned with structure, culture or decision making, these studies all differentiate carefully between managerial and professional functions in organisations. Given the argument already developed here though, this boundary setting and differentiation seems anchored to a narrowly defined view of expertise and its management. Cultural accounts of expertise, for example, imply an overly socialised view of the formation and management of expert groups. Likewise, locating expert–manager tensions at the point of production involves neglecting the effect of the wider dynamics of expertise, including economic pressures and the political and cognitive legacies of the evolution of professions and knowledge communities.

We obtain a very different view, however, if we focus not on the professional groups that instantiate expertise, but rather on the changeability and contingency of expertise itself; the latter reflecting, for instance, the impact of technological change and such market-related factors as outsourcing and commodification. Studies that highlight such contingencies effectively sweep aside the expert–manager conflict and its presumed universality in favour of a detailed examination of the operation of labour markets, technological trends and organisational strategies. They suggest that expertise is ceasing to be the calling card of cohesive social elites and becoming instead a corporate currency of variable status and value.

Whalley's research into the management of 'technical workers' in two UK firms, one 'high tech' and the other 'low tech', provides an important example of this approach. First, it dismisses 'managers versus professionals' accounts by exposing the malleability of expert motivation and orientation:

> The assumption that technical and managerial orientations are somehow incompatible involves the same kind of error incurred in treating knowledge as an autonomous source of labour market power ... Engineers have to respond to a market dominated by the interests of employers. Technical orientations are not so fixed as to be impervious to employers' distributions of rewards and advantages (Whalley, 1986, p. 109).

Whalley notes that technical workers rationally invest in the 'equity' of particular skills and, further, that their investments are influenced by the returns arising from corporate policy and the wider labour market. Thus, in his high-tech firm, technical expertise was valued for its own sake and many of the staff exhibited a technical orientation to their work. On the other hand staff in the low-tech engineering firm had little interest in technology *per se*, and saw their career development primarily in terms of managerial progression. As a result the much-touted clash of values between managers and experts simply did not arise. So dominant were managerial values, and so negligible the technical ones, that career progression within the organisation was simply a function of managerial perceptions of individuals' trustworthiness: 'The various grades of technical work were more accurately characterized as being levels of organisational trustworthiness than of technical skill' (ibid., p. 226).

The corollary of these points, of course, is that management emerge not as the hapless victims of temperamental expert groups but as their creators. Thus, in Whalley's study only the high-tech organisation experienced the classic problems of expertise management. It therefore seems reasonable to argue that such problems are a product of managerial strategy rather than of intrinsic orientations or cultures.

However, defining the management of expertise as, in effect, a consequence of capital accumulation rather than managerial rationalisation does not discount the real problems that it generates. Rather it helps to reframe them. Instead of a conflict *between* organisational and professional goals, the focus shifts to tensions – principally between efficiency and innovation – *within* organisational goals. Nor are such tensions merely frictional in their effects. If professional control is no longer the bugbear it used to be, the underlying indeterminacy of expertise persists in providing a locus of resistance and contradiction. Expertise resists management control in the same way that it resists codification into expert systems: because crucial forms of knowledge are embedded in social relations. As Collins puts it: 'The locus of knowledge appears to be not the individual but the group; what we are as individuals is but a symptom of the groups in which the irreducible quantum of knowledge is located' (Collins, 1990, p. 6).

To say that knowledge is socially constructed is also a statement about the indivisibility of particular sets of social relations and particular kinds of knowledge. This in turn suggests an important parallel with the old Marxist distinction between labour and labour power. Labour can be bought and sold as a commodity, but 'labour power' can only be extracted within socialised systems of production. In the same way, knowledge can be acquired as a commodity, in the form of artefacts or techniques, but the active construction and application of knowledge – 'knowledge power' as it were, or expertise as I have termed it here – depends upon socialised processes and relationships. This parallel thus gives us a sense of the way in which expertise, or 'living' knowledge to apply the Marxist term, may have contradictory implications for management, even when it is embodied in 'organisational professionals' whose recruitment and deployment are a direct consequence of organisational goals.

However, there the parallel ends, for the managerial implications of extracting knowledge power are inversely related to the techniques applied to labour power. Thus, roughly speaking, the quality of labour is enhanced by simple repetition whereas knowledge is impoverished. In the same vein, specialisation enhances management control of manual labour but inhibits control of knowledge by deepening it and making it more opaque. Also, while the objects of labour are literally to hand and the labour process is bounded by the physical workplace, knowledge is reflexive and distributed across internal and external knowledge networks. Expertise involves importing, reinterpreting and applying these extensively distributed knowledges to a localised work process.

It follows that managerial strategies based on the intensification of labour, typically involving increasing cycle times and repetition, may prove highly counterproductive for the management of expertise. To be sure, to the extent that expertise is embodied through the physical actions of keying in a computer programme, calculating figures, writing a book and so on, it can be interpreted as a labour process. Friedman's (1989) study of computer systems development, for example, highlights the role of managerial strategies such as 'direct control' and 'responsible autonomy' in controlling such processes. However management's pursuit of the intensification of expertise has to be set alongside their equally ardent pursuit of, to coin a phrase, 'extensification' – this term simply denoting the managerial incentives to exploit knowledge networks through, for instance, the formation of transdisciplinary knowledges, involvement in professional communities, contacts with users and suppliers, and the hiring of consultants.

Thus expertise poses a distinctive challenge to management. For while labour power may frustrate management control, knowledge power poses a direct and radical challenge to organisational forms. Hitherto the nature of that challenge has typically been seen in purely structural terms. Since Burns and Stalker (1961), organisation theorists have focused on the tension between 'mechanistic' and 'organic' forms of organisation, with the latter seen as encouraging flexibility and the sharing of knowledge and information. Latterly, however, under the impact of market and IT-related change, the nature of the challenge has increasingly shifted from the terrain of internal structure to that of external networks and relationships. Now the organic form is increasingly found in transdisciplinary teams and market-driven settings rather than in market-insulated specialist functions. Moreover the explosion of specialist knowledges and their reconfiguration as an array of consultants and suppliers means that there are even greater incentives to expose in-house expertise to a networked environment.

From a managerial standpoint the results may be uncomfortable, threatening, as they do, the cosy, unitary assumptions that managers typically seek to foster. Tapping different forms of expertise may involve internalising some of the cultural baggage, social networks and status trappings through which it is constructed. This inevitably makes it difficult to normalise such expertise within the organisation, not least because the experts themselves are likely to be mobile, with an incentive to sustain their marketability through interorganisational moves and continued involvement in the wider occupational culture and networks. As Spender notes: 'In due course the management of the technologically-intensive firm is forced towards a pluralistic form of organisation in which the organisation itself becomes a community of communities' (Spender, 1992, p. 412).

Symptomatic of organisations facing this problem are the adoption of some features of the scientific or academic community. These adaptations are sometimes cosmetic – the campus-style layout and architecture of 'science park' businesses (Massey *et al.*, 1992) for instance. But others seem to be more serious attempts at finding organisational means of tapping into narrow but distended chains of expertise.

The cultivation of informal knowledge networks, for instance, is a good example of the dilemmas that expertise may create for management. One recent study encompassing R&D scientists and academic specialists (Kreiner and Schultz, 1993) found that the usual strictures of good management practice had to be set aside if such networks were to operate effectively. In particular the study suggests that management practices around expertise may eagerly exploit the space offered by the 'informal organisation', and even defend such informality against the extension of managerial rationality and control. Thus, in order to encourage these anarchic knowledge networks while delimiting their impact on control and efficiency, management may engage in what can be termed 'indulgency' strategies (Gouldner, 1954) – that is, holding formal rules in abeyance as long as important operational objectives are achieved. Such strategies involve, amongst other things: formal communications whose subtext is 'ignore this communication'; consciously limiting the amount of control and direction exercised by management; and avoiding too much formal awareness of these practices so as to sustain 'deniability' for senior management. In other words the extensification of expertise involves creating or tolerating interstitial space and time in which limited rule autonomy can be exploited to innovative effect.

These interstitial practices are most likely to be found in the immediate vicinity of innovation processes, since it is here that the tensions between organisational planning and control and the unpredictable nature of knowledge networking and production are most keenly felt. In this context, Peters (1988) describes the effectiveness of 'skunkworks' as a means of organising innovation. In his account, these loosely organised small groups combine high levels of motivation with the 'organic' relationships needed to tap and apply extensive networks of knowledge and information. There is an emphasis on internal competition, teamwork, and contacts with users and customers.

However, as even Peters would accept, freewheeling informality is not a complete solution to the demands of innovation. Deeply ingrained experience and expertise is also an important element in the success of skunkworks, but it may be difficult to sustain in organisational contexts where personal success is calibrated by position in the managerial hierarchy. In order to avoid career structures that turn the best technical experts into mediocre managers, some organisations have developed 'dual career' ladders. This involves developing an alternative career path that is based on scientific or technical prowess and offers equivalent rewards and status to the managerial route. At ICL in

Britain, for instance, 3000 development staff are eligible for a career structure that ultimately leads to the job titles 'distinguished engineer', or 'fellow'.

The structural implications of managing expertise are not simply a question, though, of formal relationships and career patterns. There is also the problem of developing management structures that are capable of addressing the intensity, extensibility and opacity of expert work. Management technologies that control the work process through proxy indicators of input and output are highly limited. They rely upon a degree of self-policing and self-managing to be effective. In addition the measures they offer are rarely self-explanatory enough to allow remote control of the work process. Rather they need to be interpreted by managers with an informed understanding of that process: 'it seems it takes professionals to manage professionals' (Whittington, 1991, p. 52).

This need for overlapping knowledge bases between managers and experts has effectively preempted a simple hierarchical division between managerial control and productive work in favour of a tapering blend of managerial authority and expertise. That is, the nearer to the expert work process the more that coordination and control depends on expertise rather than managerial authority. Thus the managerial positions closest to expertise will often be filled by so-called 'player-managers' (Whalley, 1986) who have been promoted from the ranks of those they now direct. This graduated pattern has several advantages from the organisational point of view. Apart from the control issues noted earlier, a further important factor is the motivation of the experts themselves. Even if organisations do not develop elaborate dual career ladders of the ICL kind, player–manager roles effectively constitute a specialist career path that, however truncated it may be, has some positive effects on motivation and retention.

This graduated overlap between expertise and management is most closely associated with bureaucratic structures that insulate expert groups from the wider business environment. Decentralization and the blurring of structural demarcations, however, tend to force managerial tasks and knowledges through to the heart of expertise itself. Increasingly, therefore, management and expertise interpenetrate and intertwine. It has always been possible to argue that the professional ethos implicitly involved a degree of self-management. Now the discrete knowledge bases of expert groups are being reworked to include explicit managerial components.

This development effectively scotches the notion that management and experts are monolithic groups or that their relationship can be reduced to a simple functional or political division. Rather it serves to reinforce the patchwork picture of control and interpenetration, which more usefully characterises the interplay of management and expertise. Even though managers and experts may be formally bracketed as separate groupings, the fluid interaction of their knowledges and world views extends far beyond their immediate organisational interface. Nor does this merely imply a one-way importation of managerial discourse into professional work. Studies of top management have shown, for instance, that strategy making is heavily coloured by occupational background and training. Thus, according to sectoral and national context, some forms of expertise are able to achieve a central role within management while others are marginalised. To cite an obvious example: management in German manufacturing industry is dominated by engineering expertise and a culture of technik; a word that has no direct equivalent in English (Lee and Smith, 1992). Conversely, in Britain engineering expertise is generally excluded from strategic decisions in favour of the financial calculability promoted by the accounting professions. This is, of course, 'a peculiarly British view of management, which regards it as something quite distinct from technical expertise: which, indeed, in its more virulent versions, actually regards technical expertise as a disqualification for managerial positions' (Armstrong, 1992, p. 43).

The effect of these dominant professional knowledges and world-views is, however, primarily ambient rather than direct. Management practice, even at senior levels, is more pragmatic than professional (Reed and Anthony, 1992) and formal knowledges exercise a limited influence on highly organisation-specific decision-making processes. Moreover the internationalisation of business tends to normalise the cultural peculiarities of different management groups. It follows that in many cases the strategic implications of expertise only surface fully when they feature in hard-headed economic calculations around forming and managing different forms of specialist knowledge.

Paradoxically this is most likely to happen when the cultural and political saliency of expertise has been either downgraded or assimilated within the management structure. This assimilation produces a subtle but important shift in the dynamics of managing expertise. The traditional managerial hostility to the status trappings and power of the professionals undergoes a quiet transformation. With near unstoppable organisational pressures towards rationalisation and cost reduction threatening the professional virtues of self-discipline, peer control and innovation, management may find themselves in the ironic position of becoming 'defenders of the faith'; seeking to revive the vestiges of professionalism through 'indulgency patterns' and informal support for pseudo-professional norms.

These dangers are greatest when management have ruthlessly decentralised their organisation such that specialist expertise has been fragmented and devolved to market-facing business units. As the management of such units are driven by short-term financial targets, they are less likely to reinvest in the seedcorn knowledges and skills upon which future products and services will be based. It is in this context that arguments for the strategic management of knowledge assets are most compelling, with the latter being variously labelled as 'capabilities', 'routines', 'core competences' or 'core skills' (Stalk *et al.*, 1992; Nelson and Winter, 1982; Pralahad and Hamel, 1990; Klein *et al.*, 1991).

Pralahad and Hamel describe core competencies such as Sony's prowess in miniaturisation or Philip's optical-media expertise in the following terms:

Core competence is communication, involvement and a deep commitment to working across organisational boundaries. It involves many levels of people and all functions . . . Core competence does not diminish with use . . . But competencies still need to be nurtured and protected, knowledge fades if it is not used. Competencies are the glue that binds existing businesses. They are also the engine for new business development (Pralahad and Hmael, 1990, p. 82).

Of course, concerns about knowledge assets are only relevant when companies pursue long-term competitive strategies based on innovation. In that sense, the managerial constraints posed by expertise no longer take on an explicit, political form but are built into serial trade-offs between competing strategic objectives. Nonetheless, to return to the earlier analysis of 'knowledge power', the economic value to be gained from expertise depends upon fostering the social processes and structures through which knowledge is constructed. Breaking down professional demarcations and functional boundaries does not solve the expertise problem, but rather changes and relocates it. Instead of wrestling with the boundary conditions defined by their relationship with professional groups, management now confront expertise as a powerful but fragile resource.

Clearly, the extension of managerial control brings with it an extension of managerial responsibilities. This, along with the limitations of market mechanisms, is one of the subtexts of the knowledge-assets debate. Managers are realising that structural changes that weaken professional career structures and controls – the fragmentation of large specialist functions into market-facing business units or project teams, for example – mean substituting remote forms of managerial control for the more intimate relationships and tacit knowledges that characterised the earlier regime. Reflexive forms of knowledge management have to be contrived, ranging from information systems and skills databases through to new frameworks for strategic management.

Conclusion

To summarise the key points, this chapter began by outlining the challenges in both theory and practice to the professional model of expertise. The professional model has traditionally focused on the evolution of different occupational groups as the principal means through which knowledge is appropriated in society. It assumes an elective affinity between the application of knowledge and the development of professional forms of social relations.

This affinity is increasingly challenged, however, both by the incursion of managerial and market controls into professional domains, and by the wider proliferation of sites of knowledge production and innovation.

Choosing to perceive such changes solely in terms of their impact on professionalism would be neglecting the broader, socially distributed terrain of knowledge production. In particular it would be glossing over the need for a more inclusive account of the joint evolution of social relations, knowledge and economic value in complex matrices of work and control. In addressing this need, this chapter has developed a picture of expertise as forms of work that mediate the translation of wider social institutions and knowledge networks into material and symbolic production processes. At the same time, expertise has been presented as an active agent in constructing its own environment. The contingencies out of which expertise is crystallised are in turn enlisted by expert groups in their strategies of resistance and control, and reworked symbolically and materially through processes of interpretation and innovation. Thus while management and expertise are alike in being highly contingent practices, their structural affiliations provide cross-cutting bases of action. Experts act as the plenipotentiaries of shifting technological innovations and occupational networks, while management are more securely ensconced in established structures of power and control. The management of expertise, then, is not just about functional or political conflicts but ultimately about the active blending of these competing bases of action in a particular social context.

Note

1. The analysis of expertise in terms of power, knowledge and tradeability was originally developed by James Fleck of the University of Edinburgh. See the paper 'Expertise: Knowledge, Tradeability and Power' presented to the workshop on Exploring Expertise, University of Edinburgh, 1992.

References

Abbott, A. (1988) *The System of Professions* (London: University of Chicago Press).

Abercrombie, N. and Urry, J. (1983) *Capital, Labour and the Middle Classes* (London: Allen & Unwin).

Alvesson, M. (1993) 'Organisation as rhetoric: knowledge-intensive firms and the struggle with ambiguity', *Journal of Management Studies*, vol. 30, pp. 997–1016.

Armstrong, P. (1984) 'Competition between the organisational professions and the evolution of management control strategies', in K. Thompson (ed.) *Work, Employment and Unemployment* (Milton Keynes: Open University Press), pp. 97–120.

Armstrong, P. (1985) 'Changing management control strategies: The role of competition between accountancy and other organisational professions', *Accounting, Organisations and Society*, vol. 10, pp. 129–48.

Armstrong, P. (1992) 'The engineering dimension and the management education movement' in G.L. Lee and C. Smith, *Engineers and Management: International comparisons* (London: Routledge), pp. 41–53.

Baer, W.C. (1986) 'Expertise and Professional Standards', *Work and Occupations*, vol. 13, no. 4, pp. 532–52.

Bailyn, L. (1988) 'Autonomy in the Industrial R&D Lab', in R. Katz, (ed.) *Managing Professionals in Innovative Organisations* (New York: Ballinger), pp. 223-36.

Berger, P. and Luckmann, T. (1967) *The social construction of reality: A treatise in the sociology of knowledge* (New York: Doubleday Anchor Books).

Blackler, F. (1994) 'Late capitalism, Knowledge and Theories of Practice', *British Academy of Management*, Annual Conference, Lancaster University, September 1994.

Burns T. and Stalker G.M. (1961) *The Management of Innovation* (London: Tavistock).

Child, J., Loveridge, R., Harvey, J. and Spencer, A. (1984) 'Microelectronics and the Quality of Employment in Services', in P. Marstrand (ed.), *New Technology and the Future of Work and Skills* (London: Frances Pinter).

Collins, H.M. (1990) *Artificial Experts: Social knowledge and intelligent machines* (London: MIT Press).

Ericsson, K.A. and Smith, J. (eds) (1991) *Towards a General Theory of Expertise: Prospects and limits* (Cambridge: Cambridge University Press).

Fischer, F. (1990) *Technocracy and the Politics of Expertise* (London: Sage).

Foucault, M. (1979) *Discipline and Punish* (Harmondsworth: Penguin).

Friedman, A. with Cornford, D. (1989) *Computer Systems Development: History, organisation and implementation* (Chichester: John Wiley & Sons).

Friedson, E. (1986) *Professional Powers* (Chicago: University of Chicago Press).

Galbraith, J.K. (1969) *The New Industrial State* (Harmondsworth: Penguin).

Gentner, D.R. (1988) 'Expertise in typewriting', in M.T. Chi, R. Glaser and M.J. Farr (eds) *The nature of expertise* (Hillsdale, NJ: Lawrence Erlbaum Associates).

Gouldner, A.W. (1954) *Wildcat Strike* (London: Routledge & Kegan Paul).

Haug, M.R. (1973) 'Deprofessionalization: an alternative hypothesis for the future', *Sociological Review Monographs*, vol. 20, pp. 195–211.

Hofstadter, D.R. (1980) *Godel, Escher, Bach: An eternal golden braid* (Harmondsworth: Penguin).

Jamous, H. and Peloille, B. (1970) 'Professions or self-perpetuating systems?' in J.A. Jackson (ed.), *Professions and Professionalization* (London: Cambridge University Press).

Johnson, T. (1972) *Professions and Power* (London: Macmillan).

Katz, R. (ed.) (1988) *Managing Professionals in Innovative Organisations* (New York: Ballinger).

Klein, J. A., Edge, G. M. and Kass, T. (1991) 'Skill-based competition', *Journal of General Management*, vol. 16, no. 4 (Summer), pp. 1–15.

Knights, D., Murray, F. and Willmott, H. (1993) 'Networking as knowledge work: A study of interorganisational development in the financial services sector', *Journal of Management Studies*, vol. 30, pp. 975–96.

Kogut, B. and Zander, U. (1992) 'Knowledge of the firm, combinative capabilities and the replication of technology', *Organisation Science*, vol. 3, no. 3, pp. 383–97.

Kreiner, K. and Schultz, M. (1993) 'Informal collaboration in R&D. The formation of networks across organisations', *Organisation Studies*, vol. 14, no. 2, pp. 189–209.

Kuhn, T. S. (1962) *The Structure of Scientific Revolutions* (Chicago: University of Chicago Press).

Latour, B. (1987) *Science in Action* (Milton Keynes: Open University Press).

Law, J. (ed.) (1991) *A Sociology of Monsters: Essays on power, technology and domination* (London: Routledge).

Lawson, H. (1989) 'Stories about stories', in H. Lawson and L. Appignanesi, *Dismantling truth: Reality in the Postmodern World* (London: Weidenfeld & Nicolson).

Lee, G. L. and Smith, C. (eds) (1992) *Engineers and Management: International comparisons* (London: Routledge).

Lyotard, J-F. (1984) *The Postmodern Condition: A report on knowledge* (Manchester: Manchester University Press).

Machlup, F. (1990) *Knowledge: Its creation, distribution and economic significance*, Vol. 1; (Princeton, NJ: Princeton University Press).

Maister, D. H. (1985) 'The one-firm firm: what makes it successful', *Sloan Management Review*, vol. 27, no. 1, pp. 3–13.

Massey, D., Quintas, P. and Wield, D. (1992) *High-tech Fantasies: Science parks in society, science and space* (London: Routledge).

McNeil, M. (ed.) (1987) *Gender and Expertise* (London: Free Association Books).

Merton, R. K. (1949) *Social Theory and Social Structure* (Chicago: Free Press).

Mintzberg, H. (1983) *Structure in Fives: Designing effective organizations* (Englewood Cliffs, NJ: Prentice-Hall).

Morgan, G. (1990) *Organisations in Society* (London: Macmillan).

Nelson, R. and Winter, S. (1982) *An Evolutionary Theory of Organizational Change* (Cambridge, Mass.: Harvard University Press).

Peters, T. J. (1988) 'A skunkworks tale', in R. Katz, (ed.) *Managing Professionals in Innovative Organizations* (New York: Ballinger).

Pralahad, C. K. and Hamel, G. (1990) 'The core competence of the corporation', *Harvard Business Review*, May–June, pp. 79–91.

Quinn, J. B. (1992) 'The intelligent enterprise: a new paradigm', *Academy of Management Executive*, vol. 6, no. 4, pp. 48–63.

Raelin, J. A. (1991) *The Clash of Cultures: Managers managing professionals* (Boston, Mass.: Harvard Business School Press).

Reed, M. and Anthony, P. (1992) 'Professionalizing management and managing professionalization: British management in the 1980's', *Journal of Management Studies*, vol. 29, no. 5, pp. 591–613.

Stalk, G, Evans, P. and Shulman, L. E. (1992) ' Competing on capabilities: The new rules of corporate strategy', *Harvard Business Review*, vol. 92, pp. 57–69.

Starbuck, W. H. (1992) 'Learning by knowledge intensive firms', *Journal of Management Studies*, vol. 29, no. 6 (November), pp. 713–40.

Stehr, N. (1994) *Knowledge Societies* (London: Sage).

Sveiby K. and Lloyd, T. (1987) *Managing Knowhow: Add value by valuing creativity* (London: Bloomsbury).

Weick, K. E. (1979) *The Social Psychology of Organizing* (Reading, Mass.: Addison-Wesley).

Whalley, P. (1986) *The Social Production of Technical Work* (London: Macmillan).

Whipp, R. and Clark, P. (1986) *Innovation and the Auto Industry: Production, process and work organization* (London: Frances Pinter).

Whittington, R. (1991) 'Changing control strategies in industrial R&D', *R&D Management*, vol. 21, pp. 43–53.

CHAPTER 2

Hard times for the salariat?

Gibson Burrell

Viewing the management of expertise through the lens of social theory produces interesting refractions of cause and effect. The post-modern fragmentation of expert authority creates a space for the recognition of many voices and knowledges. But does this acceptance of diversity reflect a liberating and democratic shift in social sensibilities or the final subordination of knowledge production to global markets and capitals? This chapter addresses the fate of expert groups as an important component of the service class in Britain. While experts are often portrayed as powerful and Machiavellian actors on society's stage, the growth of consumer knowledge and the organisational changes wrought by capitalists suggest that the roles of scapegoat and victim may have to be added to their repertoire.

Introduction

The knowledge-worker 'debate' has received some impetus from the likes of Robert Reich (1991) who said shortly before taking up the office of US secretary of state for labour that America's future no longer lay with its business organisations, but with the abilities and skills of its most highly trained individuals. These 'symbolic analytical' workers had a role, in Reich's view, that was reminiscent of Daniel Bell's and Peter Drucker's writings, which saw 'knowledge' workers as the new key resource of the 'post-capitalist' society.

Reich's arguments have influenced Britain's Gordon Brown (*Guardian*, 6 September 1994), but we must treat these political speeches carefully for there is much to confuse us in the definitional landscape with which 'knowledge' is highly camouflaged. Blackler (1994) has done as much as anyone to seek clarification of the term and to situate the debate in wider organisational frameworks. At the societal level, however, the opaqueness one finds associated with all forms of 'consultancy-speak' has all too often clouded our understanding of what, if anything, is going on.

The 'knowledge society' is usually associated with the emergence of problems of uncertainty. Where are we going and where have we been creates concerns about the uncertain nature of the past, present and future. Few have as much certainty as Fukuyama (1992, p. 4) evinces when he says we have reached 'the end point of mankind's ideological evolution and universalisation of Western democracy as the final form of human government'.

Certainly we have to recognise that changes are underway at three different levels – individual, organisational and societal. There are increased demands for esoteric individual skills. Changing demands are being faced by those charged with managing organisational routines. And finally there are changes in institutional and societal factors that forms a context for the other two types of change. Given the usual privileging of factors that takes place, which forms a context for the other two types of change, we are much more likely to neglect the latter and focus on the former sets of circumstances. This chapter is an attempt to redress that balance by concentrating upon societal and global-level forces.

Pace White and Taket (1994), even today the concept of 'expertise' is often individualised into the notion of the lone, tormented expert whose brilliant work is carried out in splendid isolation. 'Doc' Emmett Brown in 'Back to the Future', Frankenstein himself and Inspector Morse in the eponymous TV detective series, are just a few examples of the individual expression of 'expertise' in its popularised form. In the Anglophone world, as is clear to see, the concept of the individual has become highly developed. Whereas the understated French *'je'* and the German *'ich'* denote the singular, in English it is a huge, self-aggrandising 'I' in all its capitalised fullness that governs our concept of the individual. Whereas collectivism predominates in many cultures, in the English-speaking world it is the individualistic imperative that influences our views of almost everything – including the concept of 'expertise'. For us, but not everyone, expertise means *the* expert.

Within the West, the middle-class baby-boomer generation has assumed that life-long employment within caring organisational forms will be the reward of those who remain loyal to the organisation, These 'core' knowledge-workers put their expertise at the service of 'local' senior management and would reap the benefits of evincing such commitment. The so-called 'Generation X' of recent analysis, on the other hand, finds the large organisation untrustworthy and thus commits itself only to itself, to its own self-belief. The skills and expertise of Generation X are meant to be portable, temporary and constantly renewed. Above all they are individually based. Not for this generation commitment to any one learning organisation but solely to learning itself. Learning is thus part of a new 'Enlightenment' where the portability of knowledge, its lightness and transferability are emphasised as supportive of the individual's peripatetic 'career' rather than as giving the static local expert heavy but stabilising gravitas. Knowledge is no longer career ballast for the organisation man or woman. It is career mobility for the enlightened individual who now flits like a butterfly.

Following on from our finely honed individualism, there is a sense of the role of self in the grand sweep of history and of our having a place in major, transformatory events. In many cultures influenced by Confucianism, for example, the self is but part of a continuous stream of historical movement in which the existential theme is continuity with the ancestors and the enduring conservatism of any social change. In cultures where English is the dominant language, there is often a sense of transitoriness and of the unexceptional individual as a witness to major events that will change the shape of the global situation. All is flux and the new. So insecure are we in our world that we believe this world is undergoing major epochal changes all the time. And thus it is with expertise.

The idea that one is living through such major transformations fulfils the function of giving the individual a role, a narrative or story line, an ending and a sense of direction upon which to build one's life. If one is to be a spear carrier, it is better to be one in an *important* play. 'Post-industrialism' is such a dramatic narrative. It rose to prominence in the 1970s and has persisted in one form or another until the present day. Whilst 'post-industrialism' is a term that does give individuals a role for themselves, it certainly does not rely on the individual level of analysis for its intellectual underpinnings. Since it is often termed the theory of post-industrial society, it should be clear that it operates primarily at a collective or supra-individual level. It forms a guide for individuals, however, showing them how they might think, behave and develop within this modern epoch. It is unhappily playful.

Post-industrial society

This term was originally developed by Daniel Bell (1973) in the USA and Alain Touraine (1970) in France. The sense of being 'post-anything', of course, fits in with the epochal change perspective that Lakatos (1970) called *rupturism*. This notion refers to breaks or caesurist splits with the past and the belief that what comes next is of a revolutionarily different kind. Rupturism relies upon a belief that one understands the past and can recognise in the present many signs of a break, out of which will develop, or have already developed, very different forms of social organisation. Rupturism puts the theorist where the action is and involves the reader in a sense of being in a place and time where the old is being transmuted into the new. It is narcissistic and self-congratulatory.

There is a tremendous diversity of 'post-something' labels because many leading theorists show a deep-seated commitment to narcissistic rupturism. They know that their readers in the English-speaking world would much prefer to be bit players in historical dramas than mere passive observers. The 'post-something' label engenders this participative rather than analytical stance from its first signallings. It is a consumer-oriented symbolic device. For we are not merely observing the rupture; we are involved in the sound and fury of tearing.

For Bell and Touraine, industrialism was the name of the colossus that bestrode humankind for a century or more. But it can no longer claim total dominance, for what is now happening is beyond the 'industrial' altogether. 'It is bigger, deeper and more important than the Industrial Revolution . . . . The present moment represents nothing less than the second great divide in "human history"' (Toffler, 1970, p. 21).

Of note here is the emphasis Bell places upon the collectivity of individuals who now work within post-industrial societies. The lone researcher, if she or he ever existed within the confines of early industrialism, has now disappeared. Research is collectivised, organised and transformed so that it now takes place within research institutes backed up by the most modern forms of organising collective human action. Lone researchers cannot be tolerated; and in the same way as industrialism insistently pushes out the lone entrepreneur in the face of the multinational corporation, post-industrialism displaces the lone seeker after knowledge in the face of 'big science' (Ravetz, 1973). Big science requires big research grants and big facilities. Doc's garage or Frankenstein's cellars can no longer compete with the multimillion dollar facilities in the huge research laboratories of the late twentieth century. The computing power of a Cray or set of Crays, the skilled labour of doctoral students or post-doctoral fellows, the access to external resources and networks of other scholars and so on are just not available to the isolated, unfunded expert. The organisation of expertise in the post-industrial society is thus an organisational form built upon size, access to resources and considerable expenditure of time in networking. What drives it, however, is not money but 'brains'.

We can see clearly from Table 2.1 that Bell highlights the significance of information or knowledge or expertise in the society of the future. Our way of life, based upon the powered machine, the factories in which to place them and a market for manufactured goods, is being replaced by one in which the control of, access to, and dissemination of knowledge is becoming crucial. The post-industrial order is characterised by growth in service occupations at the expense of manufacturing goods, thus creating a huge growth in the number of professionals. These professional groupings specialise in the production and control of codified knowledge – systematic, organised, coordinated information that forms a major resource upon which the nation-state's economic future depends. This shift in the locus of economic strength becomes matched with a shift in political power so that industrialists give way to professionals as key actors in the political system of the post-industrial society. Work itself loses the connotations of drudgery that developed during the era of industrialism, and leisure activity rises to centrality in the lives of the population.

TABLE 2.1   A comparison between industrial and post-industrial societies

	Industrialism	*Post-industrialism*
Major relationship	Against nature	Between organisations
Dominant sector of the economy	Secondary	Tertiary, quaternary, quinary
Key resource	Energy	Information
Key goal	Economic growth	Codification of theoretical knowledge
Numerically 'dominant' group	Semi-skilled worker	Professional/technical Scientists
Response to the future	*Ad hoc* adaptiveness	Forecasting
Key mechanisms	Machinery	Knowledge
Key institutional form	Business firm	Research institute
Key agent	Business men	Scientists
Key base of agent	Property	Technical institute
Transmission of base	Inheritance	Education

Source: Bell, 1973.

Expertise then enters the historical stage and displaces capital as the basis of the socioeconomic order. What the expert possesses is a new form of power that transcends that based upon money – it is knowledge that is not available elsewhere at any price.

In Touraine's perspective this shift in power is crucial. The events in France, particularly Paris, in 1968 convinced many French writers of major shifts in socio-political forces. It was not the Communist Party that led *les evenements* of May 1968, but the highly skilled technical workers in new high-technology industries. This 'new working class' was seen, albeit briefly, as an expert group who would quickly lose touch with the 'old' working class, whose politics were based upon Marxist-inspired theory, and who would come to represent a new militant and *very* powerful grouping in French society. This new working class was to post-industrial society what the old working class had been to industrial society. It was the dynamic force that would inevitably drive socioeconomic events in the future. Thus, for Touraine's class-based analysis, post-industrialism heralded an expert group who, for first time, could wrest the reins of the economy from the state and return them to the workforce. Members of the new working class were to be found in hugely expensive, state-funded enterprises such as the nuclear energy industry, they were to be found at the forefront of the technological innovation and the investment schemes that private industry was interested in, they were to be found anywhere where there was a need for technical expertise and highly skilled labour. The new working class was only one stride away from the commanding heights of the post-industrial economy (Gallie, 1979). More than that, its level of 'alienation' (Blauner, 1963) from the industries of the post-industrial era was much higher than had been imagined. Rather than being less alienated than, say, that stereotyped drone of industrialism, the automobile worker – the members of the French new working class seemed to be *more* alienated than their predecessors. So, not only did they have relatively enormous power at their disposal, they were also possessed of reasons for using it.

We can see then, that for Bell, based around Route 128 in the Boston area of the USA in the early 1970s, the key actor was likely to be the laboratory scientist. For Touraine, in post-*les evenements* France, the key actor was likely to be the highly skilled technician. Both sets of actors were seen as crucial within post-industrialism theory, but on different sides of the Atlantic they were attributed with differential significance.

Basic criticisms of the theory of post-industrialism

First, some have argued that the rupture with the past is much less in evidence than the major theorists maintain. Indeed there may be no rupture at all. The trend towards the service occupations is not a recent phenomenon. From the early 1800s manufacturing and services both expanded at the expense of agriculture and often the service sector outstripped the secondary sector in growth rate. The blue-collar 'horny handed son of toil' (*sic*) has never been the predominant member of the economy, for a higher proportion of paid employees have always worked in agriculture and services combined than in the manufacturing sector. As agriculture declined, its numbers were taken up by the service sector. The most significant change, then, has been from agriculture to elsewhere in the economy and not from manufacturing to services.

Second, the service sector is a very heterogeneous body, and as we have seen, the Touraine–Bell difference in focus reveals a failure to distinguish analytically between quite different groups within the sector. Braverman's thesis of deskilling points to the 'removal of knowledge' from many groups within the category whilst the hyperskilling of a few other internal groupings may well have taken place. Post-industrial society predicts power for a new group of employees, but the prediction itself makes the identified group immediately vulnerable to countervailing forces.

Third, as other chapters in this book will demonstrate, how far the codification of knowledge has taken place remains very unclear. The service-sector concept remains far too broad to encapsulate changes of a precise nature in different sectors in different places at different times. Knowledge codification is a contested terrain and the outcomes of this contest cannot be easily prejudged for they are not predetermined. Human action, political organisation and skill, and historical accident can all affect the outcome.

Finally, both Bell and Touraine, and their followers, have been critical of Marxian analyses: the former almost entirely; the latter seeing Marxism as a dated, if valuable, orientation. Yet economic determinism is quite strongly represented in their writings. The shift from primary to secondary to tertiary sectors of the economy (even where it is seen incorrectly) is an economic imperative that post-industrialists use to bolster and structure their models. What is happening in the cultural, political and consumption spheres passes them by as being of secondary importance.

Before we leave post-industrialism, however, we should not assume that simply because it is theoretically flawed it had no impact on practice. There is clear evidence of post-industrial thought in the Thatcher government's economic and employment policy of the early 1980s. Just as the theory of industrialism (Kerr *et al.*, 1963) influenced UNICEF, UNESCO and the various aid agencies when dealing with developing countries, the theory of post-industrialism, somewhat simplified, lay behind Conservative restructuring. The shift in emphasis from manufacturing to the service sector, the reforms in the financial sector, the encouragement of city technology colleges and the obvious rejection of the CBI in favour of the Institute of Directors, all point to a restructuring of the British economic base that was based upon a crude understanding of the *predictive* nature of post-industrial theory. It was said that if this is what *will* happen, let us get there faster than anyone else. Britain was the first industrial society; under the Tories in the 1980s it was claimed that this particular social entity would become the first post-industrial society without, should it need to be said, capital losing its preeminence (Abercombie and Urry, 1983, p. 62).

The end of organised capitalism

Lash and Urry (1987) discuss the importance of capital in the coming epoch but note that it is changing in composition. Table 2.2 shows in point form how they conceptualise their particular rupturist scenario – a world of disorganised capitalism.

TABLE 2.2   Disorganised capitalism

The central features of disorganised capitalism

- Decline of the City; growth of small towns
- Deconcentration of industrial capital nationally
- Rise of the flexible firm
- Growth in significance of service class
- The end of Fordism and mass production – mass market notions
- The rise of flexible specialisation
- The rise of post-modernism as a cultural form
- The questioning of science and technology

Like Bell, Touraine and others, Lash and Urry focus on the service sector, although they give a broad hint of their conceptual proclivities by terming the key figures 'the service class'. The rise of the service class features very highly in their conceptual structure, and its preeminence within 'disorganised capitalism' fits in well with a text, like theirs, written in the late 1980s.

Since then, of course, capitalism's development has yet again been stunted. The attempt to ingest East Germany into a world capitalist system and the break-up of the Soviet Union, the signs of slowing down, if not the collapse of the Japanese economic miracle, and the deflationary effects of the 'peace dividend' all point to an economic system in trouble. The growth throughout the 1980s of the economic system and its concomitant development of the service class have ended. What we now face is an attack upon the service class in a variety of forms. Throughout the 1980s its power was contested. Without much exaggeration we can now say its very existence is contested.

The service class is described by Lash and Urry (1987) as having the following features:

- Professional/managerial groups, for example engineers, planners, managers, social workers.
- Their own organisational resources, for example universities, associations.
- Their own cultural resources, for example justification of position through superior qualification.
- Are not owners but 'service' capital.
- Enjoy superior working conditions, exercise authority, have 'careers'.
- Possess credentials (either organisation specific or general).
- Depend heavily on knowledge, education and science.

With the decline in Fordism and the rise of technocracies and *ad hocracies* (Mintzberg, 1985) it became possible to imagine that one could see power shifts towards 'knowledge workers' in the service class – including, of course, the growth of management buyouts such as the one orchestrated by P. Judge of Cadbury, which resulted in a 'windfall' of £45 million to him personally. But more than this had been going on in the late 1980s. Lash and Urry have been part of the movement that has focused not so much on post-industrialism as on post-modernity (Figure 2.1). The writers on post-modernity tend to claim that industrialism is at an end, but the changes we are now undergoing affect much more than the economic base of society. What is happening is a critique of and a description of the downfall of 'modernity' – the bedrock upon which many of our views on science's place, rationality, large bureaucratic structures, the state, the city and so on rests. As Hall states:

> our world is being remade. Mass production, the mass consumer, the big city, big brother state, the sprawling housing estate, and the nation-state are in decline: flexibility, diversity, differentiation and mobility, communication, decentralisation and internationalisation are in the ascendant. In the process, our own identities, our sense of self, our own subjectivities are being transformed. We are in transition to a new era (Hall, 1988, p. 12).

Knowledge's role in post-modernity is very unclear, for a plurality of expertise is now widely recognised. Consider for example how the quizzes of the modern period relied upon high culture as *the* valued source of information. The BBC's 'University Challenge', for example, once fitted very closely with the classical subjects of philosophy, music, art and theatre. Today, general knowledge means a 'trivial pursuit' of 'top twenty hits', football scores from past cup finals and information derived from non-upper-middle-class courses. Knowledge has come to be democratised in class terms, although much respect is still held for those who possess it. With this widening or pluralisation of the general knowledge base has also come a broadening of what passes for knowledge. As we shall see in a moment, knowledge has begun a move away from a totally phallocentric view (but has by no means completed that move). Post-modernism has to some extent allowed for 'female' interests and concerns, for 'female' knowledge and history to be voiced. But we should not assume that this is merely another word for the pluralism so deeply entrenched in liberal democratic ideology. For liberal pluralism assumes some politics are superior to others (say parliamentary politics to local politics) and some economic forms are superior to others (say hierarchical forms to anarchistic ones), despite tolerating their non-bureaucratic forms. Post-modernism is not about tolerance of difference; it is about the celebration of difference. It is not about *primus inter pares* (first among equals), which is the motto of liberal democracy. It is about complete diversity without hierarchy – 'anything goes'. Post-modernism stands against hierarchy. Forms of expertise may be used for power plays but they are part of a plurality of competing perspectives. For example consumption patterns are subject to tremendous expert influences; drug-taking requires quite sophisticated forms of knowledge and training; car buying necessitates expertise about price, performance, extras, resale value, service intervals and so on. Even training shoes are bought only after a careful exchange of knowledge with the supplier. Under post-modernism the consumer becomes the expert. Everyone might be famous for 15 minutes and everyone might be the most sophisticated consumer of some product for another 15 minutes. Knowledge in production has been overshadowed by knowledge in consumption. And yet it is the service class which tends to have both forms of knowledge to hand. But what of the service class? Compared with its high-water mark of the late 1980s it is now in retreat – everywhere. In the 1980s changes in patterns of consumption and expertise were very important and interesting in terms of the shifts in power they represented (Friedson, 1986).

Changes in patterns of consumption of expertise

Figure 2.1 relates political issues to the changing nature of the consumer. It shows that a considerable divergence exists in the relationship between the expert and his/her customer/consumer. This relationship is fundamentally one of power and sections of the service sector can be classified by the political nature of the relationship. Beginning on the right-hand side:

- *The professional/patient relationship.* This has existed since the professions of law and medicine developed. The customer has little influence whilst the practitioner has huge amounts of power. The literature on the professions is vast and needs little discussion here, except to say that in the 1980s, as we shall see, this relationship came under attack.
- *The semi-professional/client relationship.* Under the Conservative government the client has been given much more control and the semi-professions have come

under intensive pressure. The client has more influence to shape the need than was ever the case previously (pace Bell).

- *The new working class/customer relationship.* This is the weakest power relationship for the expert who is only responsive to customer need but does not shape it. Expertise here is bought and sold in ways that do not invest service-sector members with anything like the power Bell envisaged for them.

Specifically in the UK, the Conservative Government has consciously sought to move these powerful knowledge-workers on the right-hand side of the continuum to positions closer to the left. This it has done in medicine, university teaching, school teaching, the law, in government and many other areas of expert knowledge.

Some cases of attempted relocation have been more successful than others. None have been easily achieved. Nevertheless the most powerful of the professionals in the UK have been targeted for attack and the basic aim has been to shift the basis of the expert's relationship to the way she or he defines

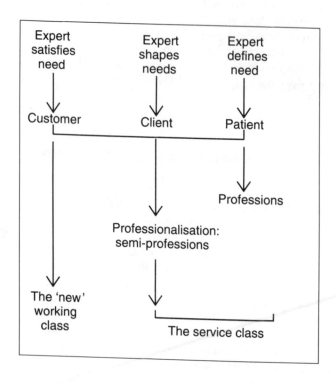

FIGURE 2.1   Power, expertise and 'needs'

the *needs* of the patient or student. It is now much more common for the patient or student to have 'a charter' and a reconstituted view of what is possible within the relationship. Whilst the Conservative government has not removed all knowledge-workers from the fortress of 'patient–expert' relations, it has certainly reduced the numbers thus protected.

However in the 1990s new pressures have been brought to bear to be added to government policy. The service class now faces the following forces:

- In the West it faces delayering, downsizing, automation and besmirching.
- In Japan it faces the breakdown of the 'jobs-for-life' period in Keiretsu growth as mobility of an *inter*-company kind becomes conceivable for the service class member.
- In Eastern Europe and Russia kleptocracy has replaced the service classes' major support system, which lay in bureaucracy.

For global capital, the managerial knowledge-worker, seen just five years ago as the *support* of the world system of economic activity, is now under threat as the *problem* of the global system. In the high-level discussions of the super-information highway the concern is increasingly about multinational companies (and networks thereof) and how these will be managed on a day-to-day basis. But once the networks are established, the emphasis will not lie upon empowered managers playing a role in a decentralised system; it will be upon a centralised schematisation in which one or two global players do as much as possible to circumvent the power of their own lower-order staff. The lessons of May 1968 still live on.

As Calas and Smircich (1993) have shown, the globalisation process, insofar as it affects management, has moved the locus of power from previously decentralised and now newly delayered companies to very small corporate headquarters located in some 'transnational' space. At the Seville Expo of 1991, for example, Coca-Cola refused to base itself in the USA building and set up instead in the World Trade Building. The gap left in these multinationals by successive waves of delayering has been filled by a high proportion of women who are stereotypically skilled in 'healing the wound' left by delayering. Thus the decline in the service class is further evidenced, in some eyes, by its feminisation (Calas and Smircich, 1993).

However the concept of expertise has made its appearance here yet again. Is this feminisation of the service class not another reminder that the expertise senior management defines as being necessary to the organisation is being lost then relocated? Does recognising expertise take the form of luring it in yet again? Despite Calas and Smircich's justifiably suspicious approach to the new 'expertise' that is being sought and encouraged, might we not wish to argue that expertise of unusual kinds will always empower its possessor? If so, the wave of relayering now going on defines *new* expertise as crucial to the organisation for its survival. Of course the organisational superordinates are defining, ordering and monitoring this expertise, which places it well down in the scenario laid out in Figure 2.1. Nevertheless it demonstrates the point that new expertise will always be identified and sought after. The organisation can never control all the forms of expertise that it will come to define as essential. Indeed there is a sense in which knowledge already possessed by the organisation will be defined not so much as expertise but more as knowledge it does not possess. Prophets are not recognised in their homeland.

Well, not always, perhaps. Ricardo Semler is quite famous in his native Brazil and has attempted to impact upon the Anglophone world through his book *Maverick* (1993). The story supposedly is that 'Mr Semler is turning the world of work upside down' (*Guardian*, 28 September 1993, pp. 2–3). Expertise is recognised to exist throughout the organisation in Sao Paulo. Employees reorganise their factories, central computers have been dispensed with; so too have filing cabinets. Memos are confined to one page. Semler does not have a desk and there is no receptionist. He 'empowers' his employees. Semler argues that 'modern times' are over and what is problematically happening to the giant corporations of the present century, such as IBM, has no solution. Because, it is said, this is an historical process coming to an end. To democratise the organisation, Semler has shed seven layers of management. This has created, he claims, an end to autocracy; for each manager is assessed by the workforce anonymously on a scale of 0 to 100. Scores around 50 are not good enough. The election of managers is to come next, as are self-set salaries. The pyramidic structure has gone, to be replaced by three concentric circles, and 'the books' are open to everyone. Clearly, then, knowledge and skills are seen as residing throughout the 200-person organisation and not just in senior management. Managers, hired for their abilities to command, organise and lead, will find themselves facing a workforce who are now asked to command, organise and lead themselves. As Keegan (1993, p. 3) says: 'the trouble is that the corporate world is run by people not exactly busting keen to lose their parking lots, let alone to subject themselves to monthly scrutiny by people whom currently, they can hire and fire. Even corporate turkeys don't vote for Christmas'. And this is the issue. Middle management are now perceived to be corporate turkeys: anti-democratic, anti-change and ripe for culling.

Speaking of prophets, Tom Peters has also put a gloss on this issue. He claims that a radical restructuring of corporate staff will be necessary whether the firm is British or German or Swiss or Swedish or American. 'It is that bad'.

When I was here in May, I came across a short newspaper article that reported on a speech by the Chief Executive Officer of Asea Brown Boveri. With no headline on the article, with no major story involved, he commented that during that first year of Asea's owning Brown Boveri they had managed to modestly trim the corporate staff of Brown Boveri back from its prior 4000 people down to 100. Now some of you snicker when I say that, some of you weep. Some of you become ill at your stomach. All three responses are appropriate. My simple comment, whether you are a middle manager, whether you are chief executive officer, is if you look at that number and think it is amusing, you do not understand what is going on around you (Peters, 1990, p. 1).

A great believer in the notion of us living in an age of information technology, Peters also claims that the new advances will bring about shifts in what we regard as expert fields and in what we regard as expertise. One example of each is to be found in this extract of his paper.

> In a catalogue that comes from the Toilet Bowl Division of American Standard there is a picture of American Standard's top of the line, $36,000, 'Smart' bathtub. In Japan, 10 percent of the toilets are now 'Smart' toilets, and they are now heading for 'Smart Smart' toilets. The new toilets in Japan take all of a person's vital signs, blood pressure and so on, and electronically transmit them directly to one's doctor. A toilet is not a toilet (Peters, 1990, p. 18).

Maybe, he opines, the best description of where we are heading from a products standpoint was in a speech given by a professor from the University of Miami in 1989 to the International Airline Pilots Association describing the aircraft of the year 2005. He said the crew would consist of one pilot and one dog, the pilot's role being to feed and nurture the dog. The dog's role would be to bite the pilot if he tried to touch anything.

Is this what we have come to then – the surveillance of intelligent, skilled human beings by electronic toilets and vicious dogs? But the information some human beings use is much more valuable than many existing collections of humanity grouped in large firms. The Official Airline Guide, which contains data on airline schedules, is valued more highly than many of the airlines represented within it. The *TV Guide* in the US was worth $3 billion which made it more valuable than the companies who made the programmes it contained. (Peters, 1990, p. 5).

So, is delayering and IT displacing whole firms, and all middle managers in all firms? Dopson and Stewart (1990) think not. For them, the management of expertise does not revolve around mass sackings, enhanced surveillance, greater control and worsening job conditions. The service class, for them, has to be seen as a complex body in which countervailing trends may well be at work. They do not accept that there is a concerted attack upon middle management through restructuring and IT (Scarbrough and Burrell, 1994).

Cycles of dissatisfaction

It would be as well for us to recognise that if there were to be such an offensive on these particular members of the service class it would not be for the first time (Fletcher, 1973). Townsend's book *Up the Organisation* (1970) certainly owed its popularity to the chord it struck with many senior management from whose ranks Townsend was drawn. If one compares Semler's *Maverick* (1993) with *Up the Organisation*, there are some remarkable similarities: 'hot desking', no central computers, a reduction in filing cabinets, single-page memos, employee empowerment and a recognition of widespread managerial ability are all to be found, even though the works were published 20 years apart. But Berle and Means (1932) had also raised, along with Burnham (1945), the spectre of a 'managerial revolution' where bureaucrats would displace plutocrats at the cost of the world we then knew and loved. Do you notice any similarity in the phasing of these anti-middle-management attacks? Might it not be that, in times of economic recession, the blame for poor performance might be laid at the doors of expert functionaries rather than their superiors? Thus, is there a connection between the dominant views of the management of expertise and the state of the economy? Perhaps it is wrong to utilise 'post-this' 'post-that' labels when these suggest a linearity in human societies and how they develop. Might it not be that there is a circularity in approaches to the management of expertise? Certainly Friedman (1977) and Ramsay (1977) have demonstrated the likelihood of managerial control systems of industrial staff being tied into the economic cycle. Could it not be that managerial control systems for skilled technical and expert groups are equally analysable in this light? Whatever the periodicity of this cycle, or even if its existence is in question, it is clearly possible to argue that a wholescale delayering of expert groups from middle-management ranks has taken place globally. This is predicted neither in theories of post-industrialism nor in the post-modernising approaches to 'the end of organised capitalism' thesis.

Conclusions

Expertise has become a vogue issue. Why? Is it not because senior management want solutions to their dependence on this perceived bottleneck in corporate affairs? Expertise *can* be dispensed with if economic and/or political circumstances dictate. Whether one speaks of the new working class, professionals, experts or knowledge-workers, theories that place them as a category at ever-increasing levels of power within organisations are manifestly inaccurate. Even accountants, once powerful (Amstrong, 1984), are being delayered very rapidly (Ezzamel, 1993) from large firms. Theories that are unilinear and predictive of the rise to influence of knowledge-intensive firms because of social and institutional pressures do not contain the realisation that socioeconomic pressures may well change. It is much wiser to recognise that there were some aspects of the theory of post-industrialism that had a real impact on British government thinking in the early 1980s. Some aspects they sought to bring into being; others they sought to supress. It is much wiser to recognise that some aspects of post-modernism, particularly its emphasis upon the consumer, would shift the emphasis in analysis from production to consumption. In so doing, the move would also shift some forms of power towards the consumer and away from the producer. When this was married to governmental pressures to reduce the power of expert groups it could not directly control, we witnessed a real pull away from the concept of professions and their patients in the direction of the concept of salaried wage earners and their customers. In reducing the power of the salariat, of course, the power of senior management was correspondingly enhanced.

Added to this, the very mobility of Generation X and its rejection of the Protestant work ethic accelerate the concerned search of senior management for 'open' forms of knowledge that exist outside the control of company experts. The Protestant work ethic and its links to professionalism are indeed crucial here, for they play directly into the hands of those who seek to 'lock' knowledge-workers into extant reward systems within single institutional forms. The paradox is, of course, that by locking knowledge-workers into one organisation one cannot have an openness of expertise. Their prisons may be gilded but incarceration of the expert implies that, for other organisations, her or his expertise will be denied them. This starts to look suspiciously like a Marxian contradiction in which the interest of the individual (firm) operates in direct opposition to the good of capital generally.

But by opening up the organisation to a constant ebb and flow of new expertise, and by circumventing the old expertise as best it might, capital forces the old professional, cosmopolitan worker to play into the hands of capital generally. Whilst individual organisations might lose commitment, loyalty and control from within their knowledge-workers, 'their' workers are now part of a liberated, deregulated system. Knowledge is no longer as parochial as it was. It is globalised, not balkanised.

However it is also much wiser to recognise that the threats to middle management and expert ranks are *by no means* new. There appear to have been waves of this anti-managerialism. These occur about the time (as it happens), when the debate focuses in on the issue of 'managerialism' itself. To raise the spectre of 'managerialism' is to seek an antagonistic reaction from within corporate ownership. If that well-paid bellweather, Tom Peters, is saying that management should be reduced in scope, size and number, then one must assume that many senior executives had got there first in their thinking (if not their pronouncements). Yet as we have seen, previous authors and well-respected consultants have said almost identical things to this in the past – regularly.

Thus the salariat is a group of expert, highly skilled managers and technicians. The role they have fulfilled, are fulfilling and will fulfil in contemporary society is open to much debate. How we label them and how we label the society in which we seek to find them will differ according to the theoretical framework we seek to use. They are important actors on an important stage, but their real worth is clouded in views about our *own* worth. For almost all those who read this are likely to be members of the salariat who are both Anglophone and individualistically inclined. The service class is *their* class and they have a vested interest in seeing its role enhanced. The sociology of knowledge unfortunately explains this chapter away as a self-centred *cri de coeur* of 'giz a job' from a salaried official.

References

Abercombie, N. E. and Urry, J. (1983) *Capital, Labour and the Middle Classes* (London: Allen & Unwin).

Armstrong, P. (1984) 'Competition between the organisational professions and the evolution of management control strategies', in K. Thompson (ed.) *Work, Employment and Unemployment* (Milton Keynes: Open University Press), pp. 97–120.

Berle, A. and Means, G. (1932) *The Modern Corporation and Private Property* (New York: Macmillan).

Bell, D. (1973) *The Coming of Post-industrial Society* (New York: Basic Books).

Blackler, F. (1994) 'Late capitalism, knowledge and theories of practice', *British Academy of Management, Annual Conference*, Lancaster.

Blauner, R. (1963) *Alienation and Freedom* (Chicago, Ill: University of Chicago Press).

Burnham, J. (1945) *Managerial Revolution* (New York: Day)

Calas, M. and Smircich, L. (1993) 'Dangerous liaison: the feminine in management meets globalization', *Business Horizons*, April, pp. 73–83.

Dopson S. and Stewart, R. (1990) 'Whatever's happening to middle management?', *British Journal of Management*, vol. 1, pp. 3–16.

Ezzamel M. (1993) unpublished paper presented at Warwick Business School, January 1994.

Fletcher, R. (1973) 'The End of Management', in J. Child (ed.), *Man and Organisation* (London: Allen & Unwin).

Friedman, A. (1977) *Industry and Labour* (London: Macmillan).

Friedson, E. (1986) *Professional Powers* (Chicago: University of Chicago Press).

Fukuyama, F. (1992) *The End of History* (Harmondsworth: Penguin).

Gallie, D. (1979) *In Search of the New Working Class* (Cambridge: Cambridge University Press).

Guardian (1988) 'A New Way Forward?', 28 September.

Hall, S. (1988) 'Modern Times, New Times', *Marxism Today*, October.

Keegan, V. (1993) 'Has work reached the end of the line?', *Guardian*, 28 September 1993, pp. 2–3.

Kerr, C., Harbison, D., Dunlop, J. and Myers, C. (1963) *Industrialism and Industrial Man* (Harmondsworth: Penguin).

Lakatos, I. (1974) 'Time and Theory in Sociology', in J. Rex (ed.), *Sociology* (London: Routledge).

Lash, S. and Urry, J. (1987) *The End of Organised Capitalism* (Cambridge: Polity).

Mintzberg, H. (1985) *The Structuring of Organisations* (London: Prentice-Hall).

Peters, T. (1990) 'Towards the Entrepreneurial and Empowering Organisation', paper presented at conference at Royal Lancaster Hotel, London, 13 February.

Ramsay, H. (1977) 'Cycles of control: Worker participation in sociological and historical perspective', *Sociology*, vol. 11, pp. 481–506.

Ravetz, G. (1973) *Science and its Social Problems* (Harmondsworth: Penguin).

Reich, R. (1991) *The Work of Nations: Preparing ourselves for 21st century capitalism* (London: Simon & Schuster)

Scarbrough, H. and Burrell, G. (1994) 'From down-sizing to de-managing: The prospects for radical change in middle management roles', paper presented at the British Academy of Management's Annual Conference, Lancaster University.

Semler, R. (1993) *Maverick* (London: Century).

Townsend, R. (1970) *Up the Organisation* (Harmondsworth: Penguin).

Touraine, A. (1970) *The Post-Industrial Society* (New York: Wildwood).

Toffler, A. (1970) *Futureshock* (London: Bodley Head).

White, L. and Taket, A. (1994) 'The death of the expert', *Journal of the Operational Research Society*, vol. 45, no. 7, pp. 733–48.

CHAPTER 3

Consultancy expertise: a post-modern perspective

Brian Baxter

Consultancy practice offers an outstanding illustration of the issues posed by current trends in the management of expertise. Specifically, the incursion of market forces into professional functions in the private and public sector has not only benefited consultants directly, but has established the consultancy model as an increasingly popular way of organising expertise. That model is profoundly ambivalent in its meaning, however. Consultancy involves forms of expertise that are close to the market and subject to all the pressures of commodification, including those of supply and demand. For some, therefore, this closeness to the market actually means that 'consultancy' no longer denotes a coherent vocation, but a new category of professional unemployment.

But the economic attrition of consultancy expertise is only one of the factors that separate it from traditional models of professionalism. Another is the vexed question of the knowledge base for consultancy expertise. Some areas of consultancy, notably the highly lucrative IT area, do involve specific technical skills. In mainstream management activities, however, not only are professional forms of quality control weak but managerial knowledge itself is so tacit and contingent (Whitley, 1988) as to make formalisation and generalisation problematic. These factors suggest to some authors that the role of consultants centres on surveillance and control over other managerial groups (Sturdy *et al.*, 1990). Alternatively it can be argued that constant market pressures have tended to condense the most critical forms of consulting knowledge into the surface elements that aid the marketing process: impression management, the careful nurturing of reputation, the construction of 'success' by manipulating problems and processes.

Whatever knowledges are applied by consultants, it is clear that their services place the client relationship under unique stress. From the client's standpoint this relationship not only defines the economic nexus, but also, in a prospective sense, has to bear the extra burden of the evaluation and monitoring of the consultant's expertise. Moreover, although market forces are customarily seen as neutralising the exercise of power in favour of efficiency and utility, their effect is actually to sublimate rather than erase political processes. Thus the client–consultant relationship is itself a political one. This is not only in the sense of an agreed covert agenda, such as the role of corporate hatchet man, but more insidiously in terms of the consultant's claims to privileged and objective knowledge.

By calling into question the market's role as a mechanism for organising expertise, these points serve to highlight the links between its various political, economic and epistemological dimensions. In this chapter, these links will be examined through the lens of both modern and post-modern perspectives.

Consultancy and the uses of knowledge

The purpose of this chapter is to explore some of the changing conceptions and practices of management consultancy. The growth and diversification of consultancy services in organisations may serve as an exemplar of the shifts taking place in the nature – and dilemmas – of what constitutes expertise.

Management consultancy regularly experiences criticisms of its people, methodologies and philosophies. 'Whores in pin-stripe suits' sums up many of the more printable descriptions used about consultants (Jackall, 1988). The portrayal is accurate to a degree because it implies an exploitative cynicism that some consultants manifest towards their clients. Others have described consultants as the twentieth century's witch doctors: 'recommending half-baked, theoretical, expensive and unsuccessful remedies to problems they have mis-diagnosed in the first place' (Peet, 1988, p. 6).

It is obviously unfair to stereotype all consultants in this mould, because there are many who form mature relationships – based on mutual trust – with their clients. This broad group is, for the purposes of this chapter, the one I wish to focus on, because these consultants believe themselves to be applying sustained expertise rather than quick tricks. They also genuinely believe that they are helping their clients, and are sincere in their endeavours to make people and processes more effective, strategies more dynamic and the nature of work more rewarding.

This sincerity and commitment, I suggest, is one of the more troublesome issues lying at the heart of consulting expertise in business today. In many cases consultants appear to support a view of organisations – and indeed their own processes of engagement – that privileges (puts as foremost in importance), first, the organisation's goals and ethos above other less-articulated 'minority' goals, cultures and voices, and second, the pursuit of knowledge about an organisation as the 'systematic' uncovering of 'deeper truths' about its people, the marketplace, business processes and the like.

There is, however, another type of consultant who supports a different perspective. This type believes that the quest for 'deeper truths' creates a tension between requirements of an organisation – as a pragmatically oriented transformer of resources – and the needs and expectations of the individuals who make up the organisation, with their hopes, fears and self-development aspirations. The challenge for these consultants as they see it is to attain a balance of their humanitarian and social perspectives with the more functional demands of their 'masters' – the paying client.

The sincerity underlying the business endeavours carried out by both these groups of consultants is problematic because, in my view, their practices and belief-systems – and those of their clients – are, to a large degree, resting on questionable views of the world – those of, *humanism*, the *quest for enlightenment* and *modernism*.

'Humanism' as a practice and philosophy has a long heritage. It flourished originally in Renaissance Italy with the aim of directing attention away from theoretical speculation about God's supremacy towards that of studying the works of mankind as revealed in history, literature and art. Its core premise was based on a repositioning of individuals over God as the prime locus of attention. This evolved into a concern to understand the development of the whole individual – mind, body and spirit – so that the 'inner man' could grow in richness of understanding *vis-à-vis* the world 'out there'. The legacy of humanism today is the widely taken-for-granted notion of *inner* self-development through the understanding, use and conceptualisation of reality *outside* the individual. Consultancy work in the field of humanistic psychology for instance, centres its efforts on ensuring that individuals in organisations can achieve their own personal growth and self-enrichment towards an autonomous, 'self-actualised' state.

The 'quest for enlightenment' – the Enlightenment project developed during the nineteenth century – was based on the view that through effort, rational thought and a belief in the universal ordering of things, all knowledge could be discovered about the world and its attributes. Progress – a key enlightenment notion – was the result of freeing society from the arbitrary actions of nature, superstition and religion through the pursuit of knowledge in order to control and order the world in a rational fashion to benefit humanity. The focus of this agenda became increasingly difficult to sustain in the social, political and fiscal turbulence of the mid-nineteenth century. By the early twentieth century the humanitarian aspects of the Enlightenment project had become caught up in the conditions of modernity then prevailing.

'Modernity' was characterised on a societal level by the compression of time and distance through rapid transport and communication methods. In the realm of ideas of reality, modernity manifested itself through an awareness of a sense of fragmentation and disunity exemplified, for instance, by the emergence of 'relativistic' theories of knowledge and perception in mathematics (non-Euclidean geometry), science (Einstein's work on relativity theory), language (Saussure's work on structuralism) and art (cubism/perspectivism). As Harvey has commented, modernism 'took on multiple perspectivism and relativism as its epistemology for revealing what it still took to be the true nature of a unified, though complex, underlying reality' (Harvey, 1989, p. 30).

Furthermore, whilst the modernist view of the world destroyed the conventional perspectives of distance, time and communication, so that social processes of engagement and communication could be speeded up to augment productivity, for instance in Henry Ford's car assembly lines, this meant that the enlightenment project could be revitalised into a project of universal emancipation, united through mechanisms of social intervention and communication. If external and public space could be organised, it was believed that the interior and private space – the consciousness and psyche of the individual – could grow and develop, in that the focus on efficiency and functionality could serve individual liberty and welfare. This became one of the underpinning beliefs of modernist thinking. This optimism of modernism with a human heart was reflected in an 'extravagant expectation that the arts and sciences would promote not only the control of natural forces, but also understanding of the world and of the self, moral progress, the justice of institutions, and even the happiness of human beings' (Habermas, 1981, p. 9).

From a somewhat different perspective Max Weber (1958) has argued that the consequences of the enlightenment project was the creation of a 'purposive-instrumental rationality', that is, a kind of functional, impersonal goal-oriented state that, contrary to expectations of it leading to universal freedom, establishes an 'iron cage' of bureaucratic rationality from which it is very difficult to escape. This rationality is based on the modernist activities of the corporate business environment, with its emphasis on the concept of structural differentiation (Clegg, 1990). Rationality, functionality, the primacy of technology, and the universalisation and globalisation of processes that unite to place a structure on social action, all result in a positivistic, rationalistic and technocentric practice of business life that, in turn, still seeks to incorporate the enlightenment beliefs of development for progress and the liberation of humanity.

Lyotard – a post-modernist – has argued that these forms of 'grand narratives' (for example the liberation of humanity and the creation of wealth) are a characteristic of modernism. He believes that the modernists' reference to a 'meta-discourse', which they use to 'explain' goals is only to be seen as a legitimising and privileging set of unquestioned assumptions that deny the presence and validity of alternative 'discourses' or views on why we do things. In the context of some of the well-known theories (or narratives) that have supported consultancy thinking and practice, Gergen (1992) has identified that a modernist perspective underpins each of the following: scientific management theory and its derivatives, general systems theory, the contingency theory of Lawrence and Lorsch (1967), cybernetic theory, trait methodologies (which presume a stability of individual patterns of behaviour) and cognitive theories of individual behaviour.

In fact it may be seen that consultants use models, processes and interventions – like the techniques of other kinds of expert – as tools to aid the grand narrative of enlightenment and modernist projects. With these tools they can learn more about a client's competitors – people, organisational processes and so on – in a way that gives the client, as an organisation, power. Power to get the right product to the right marketplace, at the right time, with the right people in the right way, for the right money. Inevitably it may not be quite 'right', but, as many consultants argue, at least it is better than before, and these modernist–based tools provide a method of getting it 'more right' next time. This is a rather summarised view of what actually occurs in organisations, but it is the spirit underlying much action and management energy today. What is problematic here is not so much management's actions and energy *per se*, but the modernist spirit that motivates and sustains them. In summary, this spirit has a twofold aspect. First there is the goal of 'essential rightness', a transcendental state of either knowledge or existence to which our endeavours must – ought to – be directed. Second, the clarity of the point to which our directed actions must go – the corporate vision, in business terms – is complemented by a corresponding clarity of actions, processes and information (Weber's purposive-instrumental rationality) that will enable us to get there. This clarity of actions is achieved in business organisations through the extensive use and development of rationalistic surveillance systems; that is, methods and technologies designed to track people and processes. The work of the French philosopher Michel Foucault has enabled some consultants to understand the significance of what is meant by surveillance in an organisation.

One piece of Foucault's research that now receives almost as many citations in organisation literature as Thomas Kuhn's work on paradigm shifts is that of his analysis of panopticism (1977). The panopticon is a building design, as Foucault has told us, derived from Jeremy Bentham's model for a prison. In this, an unseen observer sits in the central tower surrounded by an outer ring of cells full of miscreants, one per cell, with large windows facing only the central tower. Those in the cell cannot see the central observer, and if that were not anxiety-inducing enough, they cannot see each other either.

The panopticon is thus also a model of organisation that Bentham believed could be 'a great and new instrument of government', one that, he argued (quoted in Foucault, 1977) makes it possible to note the aptitudes of each worker and compare the time he takes to perform a task. The director (in the central tower) can 'spy on all the employees that he has under his orders, he will be able to judge them continuously, alter their behaviour, impose upon them the methods he thinks best' (Foucault, 1977, p. 227).

Those in the panopticon cells are subject to continual scrutiny – the gaze – of those in the observation tower – or they *think* they are, and the fact that they think they are keeps them in order. Panopticism is therefore, in Foucault's understanding, an exercise of power relations, operating through hierarchy, surveillance, observation and the writing or documenting of records on those surveyed, and indeed on those surveying. Power is therefore located not in a particular person, but in particular practices. These practices, in many cases in business, are a major product of the activities and services of consultancy.

Although the idea of a bricks and mortar panopticon is echoed only in old-style businesses and factories, where the supervisor sits above the workers in a glass-walled room and surveys all below, nowadays the actual gaze is supplanted with the 'virtual' gaze of consultancy-derived reporting systems: financial management information, time sheets, performance management systems, computer usage or whatever, which are all rationalist instruments to make visible every facet of an organisation's life to those within the organisation. Striving towards the corporate vision is thus augmented by all aspects of business being illuminated to the gaze of senior management, either directly through 'management by walking around', or indirectly through information and reporting systems.

Unlike the panopticon, the gaze in business is now often two-way – a sort of double gaze – in that management's actions are subject to the scrutiny of those they gaze upon. This raises another problematic issue for consultancy expertise: the visible reduction or distortion of the data and information they provide.

Marx said in his preparatory notes for *Das Kapital* – the *Grundrisse* (1973) – that one of the problems with capitalism is that it takes the products of people's labour and *uses it against them*: the alienation (*entausserung*) of their activities to their organisation leads to the individuals' estrangement (*entfremdung*) from that which they produce and the context wherein they produce it (Baxter, 1982). The resultant 'fetishisation' of the products is an outcome, as Marx said, of the masking of the social relationship between producers (for example the consultants) and consumers. The observation I wish to make is that the fetishisation of consultancy expertise is supplemented by a further unmasking of the social relationship between the consultants and the users of their work, because it is subjected to the 'double gaze' that exists in modern organisations: the scrutiny by management of the consultants' actions, and the consultants' own awareness of what management is doing with the products of their expertise.

This, in my experience, is an increasing concern of consultants, particularly those offering detailed functional and technical services. Whilst they may produce a subtle, nuanced view, couched in caveats and conditionals, with multiple perspectives maintained in the spirit of the more pluralist, multifaceted assessment of the situation, they then see management, and others in the organisation, stripping away much of the subtlety and using the information in a rather black-and-white fashion. The management of a large British organisation describes those who provide a subtle response to their problems as 'techno-nerds' – people who are bogged down in and fret over tedious micro facts that the busy, pragmatic manager need not and should not have to be bothered with. Subtlety and plurality of perspectives derived from consultancy work is thus dismissed as detail, obscuring the clarity and functionality of the deliverable. In this sense the quest for rationality and enlightenment can render invisible the alternative voices and views offered by the consultant.

This may be contrasted with a post-modern approach to consultancy, which depends on the acknowledgement of multiple voices and a plurality of perspectives, none of which is privileged into one paradigm over another. The functional suppression of alternative voices and views is often reinforced by hiring only consultants who can shape all the multiplicity of views into a coherent, single-voiced, multiple-choice picture, with spelt-out implications for a given course of action. Other consultants in the market place quickly realise that in order to survive, they must contain the plurality of 'this and this and this' to a few 'either this or that', to meet the functional demands of a pragmatic board of directors as it serves the modernist imperatives of the business.

From modern to post-modern consultancy practice

How can consultants work with the post-modern recognition of multiple voices, plural readings of faceted, linked and echoed realities in an organisational context where people believe that a modernist perspective and purposive-instrumental approaches offer the only ways to understand and carry out their business activities? I believe that consultancy, an external privileged and privileging form of expertise, could, potentially at any rate, begin to enable organisations to rethink in a fresh way some of the fundamental issues at the root of these conflicts and multiple voices.

Exploring what I mean by this requires a closer look at what consultants actually *do* in organisations. It also requires a setting-out of some of the qualities of post-modernism – as something with its own distinctive characteristics and methodologies. In order to provide an understanding of what consultants have done and are doing in organisations I wish to highlight some of the main themes and preoccupations that have emerged in this profession over the last 80 or so years.

In the 1920s and 1930s consultancy was a relatively new profession or body of practice. One of the earliest consultancies was Booz, Allen and Hamilton, which started in New York in 1914. However management consultancy took a notable step forward through the work of James O. McKinsey. Many good and even interesting books have been written about both the man and his business (for example Wolf, 1978). The general drift of these is that 'Mac', as he was known, was a workaholic who balanced his various career activities (as professor of business policy at the University of Chicago and chairman of Marshall Field & Co.) with establishing a first-rate consultancy practice. He died in his late forties of pneumonia, which had been exacerbated by his continuing to work while fighting the illness. His dedication to work and his insistence on in-depth, logical analysis of organisations (against a checklist of questions, in fact) set the seal for generations of enthusiastic business graduates who were either employed by the firm or created lookalike consultancies.

Other kinds of consultancy practice also existed during this period, but with a different provenance: they did not always describe themselves as *management* consultants, but they nonetheless provided consultancy services to help businesses to become more efficient and effective. The work of Lieutenant Colonel Urwick in the UK reflects stereotypes one might associate with the man's title: 'rigorous, analytic, scientific' were terms proliferating in the work of his people; purposive instrumentality was the underlying belief system in the activities of his firm.

A further range of consultancy-services for business problems and issues – particularly to do with understanding people, their motives and modes of working – became popular through the work of the National Institute for Industrial Psychology, started by Charles Myers in 1921 in the UK, and the writings of Elton Mayo in the USA. Anyone interested in pursuing these areas must refer to Wendy Holloway's excellent book (1991) for a more detailed overview and critique.

The common theme of consulting up to the 1950s was the rationalist pursuit and explication of facts. These were either facts that enabled an understanding of the 'reality' of an organisation and its problems, or facts based on applying a humanistic understanding to how people worked and how working life could be made more dignified, involving and satisfying, within the context of business demands and expectations. Inevitably, in the 1960s and 1970s consultants realised that the process of fact-gathering and analysis to find the real meaning or 'truth' of organisations was not always effective, so instead, they began to model and create scenarios of possibilities based on their clients' relative positions to other organisations. For example the Boston Consulting Group started in 1963 by Bruce Henderson and focusing on the provision of strategic advice, may be described as one of the first 'model-based' consultancy firms. Positioning where an organisation's products were in relation to those of its competitors, for instance, using a decent model, and then mapping out different strategies and actions to exploit that position was a breakthrough for businesses wanting action-oriented solutions to problems. As relativistic modelling developed, consultants realised that they had no need to gather a large number of facts; just by checking out the key indicators underlying the model they could ascertain where their client was in relation to other organisations and were able to provide effective advice on this basis.

Implicit in this consultancy work was a growing awareness of the inappropriateness of searching for a meaning based on 'out there' pure facts waiting to be uncovered. In its place consultancy practice (or some parts of it) shifted to the realisation that the meaning of activities, processes and strategies in an organisation was to be found in treating 'facts' as originating in positional relationships rather than absolutes. Although this was not commonly appreciated in business circles at the time, it paralleled a development that had already taken place in philosophy – the emergence of 'structuralism'.

Structuralism as a facet of the modernist project had many variations, but the distinctive doctrine upon which it was based was that any part of a system only has meaning by virtue of its relationship to another. So, for instance, the word 'bar', which is an example of what structuralists call a 'sign', has meaning only in that it is not 'bat', 'far' or whatever. Its difference from these other words creates a possible meaning that can be affirmed slightly further when it is located in relation to other signs: 'I went to the bar for a drink of beer'. Thus truth – the meaning of something – does not have a substantial 'out there' meaning, only a relational one. Structuralism occupied itself with analyses that tried to isolate underlying sets of laws by which individual 'signs' become 'signifiers'; that is, are combined into meanings. Structuralists believed that, because meaning is functional in the strict sense of the term, one can analyse an organisation as a system of signs. So a structuralist analysis of the organisation will try to identify the objective structure that underpins the arbitrary relationship between these signs and gives them meaning. Consultancy based on organisation systems theory in the 1970s was a practical example of this approach.

As consultancy in the 1960s became involved in what were in effect structuralist analyses, consultants (and their clients) believed that, by getting to the fundamental structures of the organisation and the relationship between structures/departments/people, the 'true' nature of the relationships that create meaning will emerge. The subsequent visibility of those relationships and the laws that govern them will inform business practice. Whilst I can trace no explicit recognition that consultants wrote about what they were doing in relation to what was going on in structuralism, or whether it was dismissed as philosophical wordplay, consultancy's preoccupation with the organisation's structure, systems and the relativistic modelling tools show it to be preeminently structuralist in its sentiments and approach.

Of course structuralism was not the only philosophy underpinning consultancy in the late 1960s and 1970s. The enlightenment and humanist interests in the human worth of individuals against the 'monolithic Other' that represented big business, stimulated a strong body of consultancy expertise with its origins in psychological and sociological practices. This was particularly the case in the field of organisational development (OD), which has been defined as 'the long-range effort to improve an organisation's problem-solving and renewal process, particularly through more effective and collaborative management of organisational culture . . . . with the assistance of a change agent or catalyst and the use of the theory and technology of applied behavioural science, including action research' (French and Bell, 1973, p. 19).

Organisation development, as a consultancy practice, drew upon the work of industrial and human relations, notably that of the Tavistock Institute in the UK and the Michigan University Institute for Social Research in the USA, which was based upon the research of Kurt Lewin. Workgroups, roles, leadership styles, satisfaction of the various kinds of individual needs, different management styles, working participation and so on, were all legitimate foci for consultants in this period. French and Bell's definition captures the essence of the consultancy role – that of a change agent or catalyst. No longer were consultants 'experts' in the sense that they knew more than others about facts, structures and data. Instead they knew about group dynamics, about what makes people tick; they could bring a group of people together from within an organisation and, through skilful under-standing of the processes occurring within a group – or a series of interacting groups – guide or facilitate the group to achieve its own solutions at both the collective and personal levels.

Not surprisingly perhaps, these consultants represented the antithesis of objectivity. Although they might have believed that they were standing to one side of the group processes they were facilitating, the humanist tone pervaded their work, in the sense that they felt it was right to encourage people to overcome conflict, that members of a group should aspire towards fulfilling the goals of the organisation *and* be able to pursue self-development as self-aware, growing individuals. That is, their belief system, as consultants, was centred on a philosophy that, as Heidegger once said, 'rests in the need to establish an authentic relation to our still-to-be-realised possibilities of being' (Heidegger, 1978, p. 352).

Perhaps understandably, these humanistic consultants felt a certain contempt towards the activities of their structuralist colleagues because of the latter's focus on systems and structures as somehow more important, fundamental and objective than the soft stuff of organisations – yet both actually fed off each other. By this I mean that business people could 'intuitively' see both that their people needed special attention as human beings, and that at the same time their organisation needed adequate understanding as a system. Different specialist consultants grew up to serve these apparently different needs, each affirming that there was both a hard, objective side to business and a soft, subjective side.

So by the late 1970s consultancy work tended to fall into two broad camps: consultants as 'relative fact' gatherers and analysers of marketing, business planning and financial management, and those who focused their expertise on understanding and facilitating people and group processes, working with businesses to select people, organise them and develop their talents through training and the like. Also around this time a new consultancy service emerged. Consultants became 'business solution providers' offering *integrated* solutions to business problems. Business solution provision was (and is) most noticeably practised by one-time accountancy firms such as Arthur Andersen, later Andersen Consultancy. This kind of consultancy arose initially out of clients' need to install computer systems into organisations running specialist applications to meet given requirements, for example a financial management system. Doing this effectively required an understanding of the particular business, how it worked, its purposes and expectations of how it should work – which is what a structuralist perspective would provide. But it also required insight into how to get people within the business to work with the computer system, the data it generated and the requirements and working practices it needed. Furthermore consultants recognised that if people were to start doing something different, they had to stop doing what they already did – a rather obvious point, but it led to the emergence of consultancy expertise in managing change within a business, both structurally and at the level of the individuals and groups within the organisation.

This interest in managing change was also fuelled from an independent source in the 1980s, when the giant bureaucracies needed to 'down-size' and become more able to dance to the tune of the market place, as Kanter (1989) and many others have said. Thus it was no longer appropriate for consultants to treat organisations from either a structuralist or a humanist perspective, each needing but apparently despising the other – consultancy now incorporated both these into a focus on the *culture* of organisations. This new area tied together structuralist preoccupations with deep structures and humanist concerns for attention to people and processes. Consultancy services in the culture field were based on a recognition that values and beliefs that circulated among people in organisations could be seen as 'belief-systems', and that the 'deepest structure' of all was not some objective network of relationships within or between business activities; it was actually the philosophies, ideologies, values, beliefs, assumptions and norms that existed within an organisation. So in order to change an organisation, whether this was to provide an integrative solution to a problem or to restructure the business, consultants began to develop mechanisms and processes to gain an understanding of the culture of their client and to help them identify the 'culture goals' they should be working towards.

The surfacing of 'culture' as an area of interest for management stimulated the politicisation of new kinds of consultancy expertise. Thus, for instance, consultancy in manufacturing systems, quality management and purchasing/

contracts management, areas that in the 1970s would not have been seen as proper management consultancy, now helped to drive organisations' restructuring activities, culture change programmes and strategic business relationship realignments. Each of these areas of consultancy expertise depended upon incorporating, and treating as integrated, the structuralist and humanist perspectives on business. As a result the traditional humanist consultancy emphasis on teamwork, consensus development, conflict management, personal authenticity and the like now resurfaced as a focus on understanding and developing clients' values and belief-systems to create people who would feel able to endorse the desired corporate culture, in a way that fulfilled simultaneously their personal aspirations and business necessity. These are the same goals that modernists advocated back in 1910.

Much effort and ingenuity was devoted by consultants and their business masters to create and implement culture change programmes aimed at making organisations into more flexible, customer-responsive, market-alert entities. Because these movements peaked around the late 1980s, the time when the business recession occurred in the West, culture change programmes became known by more cynical employees and managers as FIFO workshops (fit in or faze out). FIFO crudely but accurately sums up the privileging philosophy underlying the focus on culture as an organisation tool. Serious debate in business about the existence of alternative cultures, so-called 'weak cultures', was directed not at their merits or validity in themselves, but at reframing and repositioning them to bring them into line with organisation culture, the one that mattered.

From one perspective, these efforts at subsuming diffuse cultures and practices within one dominant organisation culture may be seen as a natural outcome of what consultants, and of course the senior management, are striving towards – making visible a previously invisible quality of organisational life. It is, after all, part of their modernist, enlightenment perspective of the world, a project whose goals may never be obtained in reality, but the focus it gives to people's endeavours is sufficient to ensure that, as the dreadful cliché has it, 'we are all singing from the same hymn sheet' – a phrase that in my experience is particularly favoured by chairmen of organisations. Business leaders, aided by consultants, showed that the creation of a clear, singular culture – manifest in a set of sensitively written goals – could be a conduit through which organisations could transform themselves and thrive on the 'chaos' that existed in their market place. Mobilising employees through a cult of personal charisma and entrepreneurial drive was seen as one of the best ways of supporting the validity of these culture goals.

It couldn't last of course; the arbitrariness and the idiosyncrasies demonstrated by business leaders, in the guise of charismatic culture-creating, could not be tolerated elsewhere in the organisation – or if it was emulated lower down, it led to a disruption of the processes and practices that many managers felt were necessary to providing effective services and products for their customers and to managing their business.

Organisations thus struggled to balance the desire for charismatically endorsed flexibility (with its associated culture goals), and the need to retain some grasp on the necessary processes and parameters deemed appropriate to enable people to work effectively together in the business. In the continuing economic difficulties of the 1990s a 'new' reality emerged: shareholders, and the demands of the marketplace, required organisations to reassess and retune the effectiveness of the processes they employed to design, develop, produce and deliver their products and services.

As a result a new wave of consultancy services arose, for example in the areas of business process re-engineering (BPR) and total quality management (TQM). The changes brought about as a consequence of these sorts of service have created what amounts to a 're-bureaucratisation' of business; in that they encourage organisations to develop clearly defined and documented processes supported by behavioural frameworks, all of which are established to produce swift, tangible outcomes or deliverables carried out by empowered individuals who can take initiatives within an established context.

In this rebureaucratisation of business, the 'iron cage' traditionally perceived as a characteristic of bureaucracy is less obvious because there is the illusion of the viability of an empowered subjectivity – that is management and staff – who are encouraged to act within an 'objective' framework (Frug, 1984). This illusion has led some management 'gurus' such as Handy (1989) to assume that the emergence of federalised, shamrock-like organisations will result in a post-bureaucratic business environment. This view is perhaps true at the macro-organisational level, in that the traditional source of power and control is now dispersed in many organisations, but at the operational levels current business practice tells a different story.

These movements have been complemented by consultancy services that lead to a similar rebureaucratisation in the way organisations deal with the people side of business:

- The rise, for instance, of performance management processes (PMP) that focus on personal performance according to agreed business objectives and cultural requirements.
- The search for behaviourally oriented 'competencies' or characteristics thought appropriate in an individual when doing a given job in a given organisation culture.
- The new special attention given to people assessment and development, which turns formerly intuitively guided activities into formalised processes.

Undoubtedly some consultants in these fields would disagree that their earnestly and sincerely conducted activities represent part of an implicit rebureaucratisation programme. Others are more honest with themselves and acknowledge that, whilst they are emphatically not seeking a return to the degraded bureaucracies of old, their consulting services are directed towards producing sharper clarity, visibility and consistency in business practices, processes and outcomes. Today the consultancy profession is dominated by these sorts of activity, along with standard strategic consultancy, business enterprise solutions services and other 'boutique-type' consultancy services (marketing, manufacturing processes, financial management, for instance), all of which are directed at providing their particular kind of 'symbolic analyst' expertise (Reich, 1991) to clarify and further the organisation's goals. A distinctive feature emerging in the 1990s is that consultancy services are generally provided through a 'partnering' or alliancing relationship between consultant and client, rather than the older, hands-off, pseudo-objective approach.

A less documented consequence of the emphasis on organisation culture has been the dissatisfaction of some consultants and business people with 'culture' being treated as a singular noun. These consultants have begun to take account of the rise of post-modern principles and to use them in their work. This is not an easy task because (1) they are surrounded by those who uncritically accept modernist beliefs and perspectives, (2) their own professional heritage is distinctly modernist in beliefs and practices and (3) the nature of the term post-modern is subject to a certain amount of confusion and misunderstanding.

This confusion may be felt because the words post-modern, post-modernity, post-modernism, the *condition* of post-modernity, have either been used in a loose way by those in 'pop-management fields' – and indeed in some areas of organisation literature by people who ought to know better – or in a restricted way that privileges to an extraordinary degree an infatuation with technology and the apparent desire to sustain what amounts to a technically determinist vision of networked, information-based organisations.

Post-modern analysis

To resolve some of this diversity of meaning, it is useful to distinguish between the post-modern *condition* and post-modern *analysis*. Baudrillard (1983) saw the former term as describing the condition or characteristics of today's (Western) society: one that is dominated by the ever-greater acceleration of time and motion in production, exchange and consumption; the ephemerality and volatility of images; the emphasis of effect over cause. As a consequence of this Lyotard (1984), in a less extreme fashion, saw the *temporary contract* becoming the predominant feature of the post-modern condition.

A post-modern analysis, on the other hand, is a possible response to the post-modern condition. This response is informed by thinkers and practitioners who believe that attempting to remain with a modernist analysis will restrict the opportunity for pragmatic insights into our organisations and society. A further concern is that a modernist analysis of the post-modern condition can reinforce the legitimising, privileging and reification of concepts and practices into a complex 'out-there-reality' that apparently requires more sophisticated analytic tools to uncover and predict.

A post-modern analysis, in contrast, questions business concepts and practices – in a way I shall consider shortly – in order to identify and understand their inherent undecidability and their supplementarity (or built-in dependencies and oppositions) with other less-privileged concepts. A post-modern analysis would add a powerful, critical tool to the work of practical management writers and consultants. For instance the work of Tom Peters (1987, 1992) represents an extraordinary effort of energy. His observations of what is really going on in organisations are first-class – he describes numerous organisations' attempts to cope with the post-modern condition that now prevails in the business world or, as he describes it, the fast-paced, fashionised, disorganised, paradoxical, transforming, telecommuting, project-based business environment of today. Yet the solutions he proposes as a result of these observations show him to be still tied up in modernist beliefs. For example he approvingly quotes the work of the anti-interventionist economist Friedrich Hayek: 'On the one hand, Hayek argues persuasively that rules are imperative to progress (in a very small number: private property, enforceability of contracts). On the other hand freedom is maximised – as in wealth and the fruits of civilization in general – precisely because these rules are impersonal' (Peters, 1992, p. 500). Despite his clear attachment to a modernist analysis, Peters' books, although often viewed with contempt in the writings of organisation theorists, are at least produced by a man willing to explore the major issues occupying business today, unlike much of the self-referential and pretentious babble that currently exists under the rubric of organisation thinking.

In Chapter 2 of this book Gibson Burrell presented some views on the characteristics of post-modernism as they manifest themselves in our organised world. I would like to pick this up and attempt to identify what a post-modern analysis means in consultancy practice. For this, the writings of Jacques Derrida (1976, 1978, 1981) are at the core of my thinking. Derrida is probably the most systematic and least apocalyptic exponent of post-modern analytic thought, in both how he writes and what he says. So, too, is the work of Bob Cooper (for example, 1987, 1988, 1989; Cooper and Burrell, 1988), whose subtle and insightful writings show what is possible in the field of organisation thinking. Through the application of Derrida's works, a post-modern analysis for consultancy could, I believe be characterised by the following condensed list:

- A recognition that the meaning of things, concepts, people and so on is *endlessly deferred*.
- An understanding that *process is primary to structure*; (that is, process creates structure, not the other way round).
- The *quest against the privileging* of something over another, for example one culture over another.
- Avoidance of conceptual closure, or ultimately fixable frames of reference through the *continual application* of *reflexivity*, or the need to be critical of our intellectual assumptions.
- The existence of a continual interplay or double movement within concepts, so that opposites merge in a constantly undecidable exchange of attributes.
- An understanding of the necessary *supplementarity* of meanings in the relationship of 'opposite' terms. For example managers tend to talk of 'old paradigm' versus 'new paradigm', whereas each should be seen as both necessary to and yet simultaneously threatening to the identity of the other.
- Acknowledgement that the factual is replaced by the *representational*; that is, that there is no 'genuine order of things'.

As a basis for a post-modern analysis, Derrida uses the special term 'différance' to suggest at the same time the impossibility of closing off the *differing* aspects of meaning, and the perpetual *deferral*, or postponement, of meaning. He argues that the 'movement of différance' undermines our desire or need to achieve a coherent and singular meaning in a given concept.

What is important for us in the consulting context is that Derrida sees 'différance' not as a word or a concept, but as a force of *continuous absence*; that is, where the meaning of something cannot be attained without a continuing recognition of the meaning it defers. In other words, the processual nature of meaning is embedded as the continuous movement of différance within any term or concept. The challenge of a post-modern analysis in consultancy is to uncover and explore that différance within a concept, belief system, culture, paradigm or culture, in an endeavour to see more clearly the concept's presuppositions, dependencies, qualities and implications.

Of paramount importance, therefore, in a post-modern analysis is the drive to question things, to deconstruct the constructions and structures around us – not in a bored teenager, nihilistic way, but more as an interested child might – yet, unlike the child, not necessarily accepting anything the grown-ups say. The questioning is done with rigour and precision – first to disrupt or overturn the given, which all consultants do at the microlevel anyway, for example when they question the strategies and directions of an organisation, and second to ensure that the questioning, even if fundamentally or ultimately ludicrous/playful, does not then lead to the erection of a singular new alternative. The hallmark of deconstruction is this second stage: the attempt to go beyond hierarchies of oppositions and to sustain the perpetual double movement *within* the opposition to acknowledge their mutual definition and contradictions. This should not just be seen as a complicated way of talking about relationships between one concept and another, but as an effort to focus on (1) the concepts themselves and where they might derive their power and influence, (2) the privileging and inadequately questioned meanings attributed to them, and (3) their supplements – covert or otherwise – which both support and supplant the concept's meaning.

Many business people give up at this point, seeing a post-modern analysis as something dangerously destructive, with no purpose other than to dismantle processes, structures and people's views on the world. They point out that to expect people to live in a kind of fuzzy, ever-questioning and analysed place where things have no pin-downable meaning is frankly daft and counterintuitive. Consultants who practice in the field of change management would recognise this reaction as a classic Stage II resistance/ rejection phase on the 'transition curve', which all people go through in the face of unwelcome or threatening insights drawn from an unfamiliar frame of reference.

However, as difficult as this might be to accept at first glance, a post-modern analysis is first and foremost a pragmatic, action-oriented approach intent on enriching an organisation's understanding of itself and its actions. The process of deconstruction is fundamental to a consultancy operating within a post-modern analysis. Deconstruction begins with setting up – but not staying with – a kind of dialectic of difference: a to-ing and fro-ing reflexive debate about the privileged existence of something, for example a dominant paradigm. This first step in deconstruction can only take place if a concept's contexts, oppositions, components, supplements and constitutive processes are recognised in a way that maintains a continuous state of difference and thereby a deferral of final meaning. When the debate about a concept's worth dies, the potential to motivate social action – through, for instance, a reoperationalisation of that concept – dies too.

This might sound somewhat abstract and removed from the concerns of pragmatic business life, but a respected practitioner in the business world, Richard Pascale, has taken some of these points in his book *Managing On The Edge*. He disagrees with the conventional modernist view of management as a process of shifting old paradigms to new ones, which are then consolidated. He argues that the 'ultimate and largely ignored task of management is one of creating and breaking paradigms. The trouble is, 99% of managerial attention today is devoted to techniques that squeeze more out of the existing paradigm – and it's killing us' (Pascale, 1991, p. 14). He further says – and devotes a whole chapter to it – that 'the question is the answer', and the book's subtitle is 'How Successful Companies Use Conflict To Stay Ahead'. Finally (and this must be a first for a mainline management text) he uses a simplified version of the Hegelian dialectic – thesis, antithesis and synthesis – to underpin his analysis.

Hegel, as a metaphysical philosopher, used the dialectic as the process through which being becomes Being; that is, the process whereby an individual works through a process of dialectical reversals and syntheses, eventually to attain a transcended authenticity – a perfection beyond the merely subjective. But Pascale, unlike Hegel, does not seek a transcended state of perfection, he focuses our attention on the dialectical *process*, one that continually welcomes conflict, based on questioning the dominant thesis of the day, and putting in its place the antithesis before letting the synthesis emerge, which in its turn has another antithesis, and so on.

Of course, as we have seen, the dialectical process is *not* deconstruction, because the latter is not about a synthesis emerging from a reversal of categories. Furthermore, whilst deconstruction undoes the given sense of priorities, it also questions the very system of hierarchical conceptual opposition that makes that order possible. However the fundamental point is that Pascale and post-modernists alike never rest by allowing the privileging of one thing, one paradigm, over others – this feature is one significant characteristic that differentiates deconstruction from the modernist notion of incisive criticism.

Thus deconstruction, far from being a negative, destructive process, is actually a liberating one because it does not confine itself to asking 'is this "fact"?' but addresses the issue 'how could this come to be considered as a fact – and what are the consequences of this?' Thus the deconstructive approach to facts and meanings of concepts can serve as a basis for consultancy action because it helps to unravel clients' 'phenomenological ambivalence'; that is, the uncertainties and vagaries that surround and characterise us as people in a world of mixed and conflicting messages. It is an awareness of this ambivalence that serves as the motive to organise and to make temporary sense of the world. So it is the special role of deconstruction, as the process of defamiliarisation, to ensure that the motive to organise does not attain enclosure into an encompassing, rigid paradigm.

In the context of post-modern analysis, phenomenological ambivalence has its location not in the psychology or sociology of the individual – as the humanists contend – but, as Derrida argues, in the concept of the *text*.

His understanding of text is not just as a book or magazine, but as (1) the result of an interplay of discourses – regulated systems of statements that inform and are informed through beliefs and practices, for example social, organisational, political acts – and (2) the stage upon which the process of deconstruction is enacted. Moreover these texts – for example an organisation – are dislocated from authorial intent, and so open to deconstruction by all. That is, no one person or group 'writes' the text. 'Writing' for Derrida has special significance, although his commentaries on the nature of writing lie beyond the scope of this chapter. For him it is the process through which people 'inscribe' organisation and structure on their environment and through which a consciousness of a sense of self develops: 'we are written as we write' is his noted aphorism to describe the origins of subjectivity, self-awareness and the presence of a decentred subject.

In more prosaic contexts we can acknowledge that no one person or group 'writes' a particular business organisation, although all contribute to its discourse and are in turn written upon by that organisation to inform their beliefs, values and actions.

Thus, for post-modernists, creating a business culture or establishing particular strategies are to be seen as legitimising processes of organisational writing, serving to supplant one reading of the text – that is, one paradigmatic view – over another in business. Supplanting one reading over another can actually obscure and deny the necessary logical undecidability that resides at the core of social action in an organisation. In the consultancy context this means that analysis is to be understood as applying their own readings of organisation texts. Subsequent modernist implementations overwrite the old paradigms to establish the new, yet according to post-modern consultants this 'new' paradigm would simultaneously disempower and stifle the actions of those in the organisation and therefore reduce its viability. This is because attempts to introduce a paradigmatically based set of practices and beliefs, new or otherwise, presuppose (among other things) the need for an effective shared meaning – which, in the post-modern context, is not possible. As Linstead (1993, p. 60) has noted, 'shared meaning is nothing more than the deferral of différance'. His view is based on Derrida's notion of supplementarity which indicates that meaning exists in a continual resonance or interplay, with its own negation or oppositions, so to talk about a sense of shared meaning denies the paradox and ambiguity inherent in that meaning. The net effect, therefore, of attempts by modernist consultants to develop shared meaning in organisations is the realisation by people in organisation that they are being subject to the FIFO syndrome.

I am aware that modernist consultants – and many business people – have a certain amount of trouble with the language used by post-modern consultants, especially with its emphasis on writing, discourse and texts. These terms are not used as metaphors to replace modernist notions (for example, inputs, processes and outputs), but serve to indicate the *processual* nature of what goes on in organisation life. It is incidental that they do have a metaphoric quality in that they allow us to see, think about and understand organisations in fresh ways.

By understanding organisations processually in terms of writing, discourses and texts we can retain the post-modern suspicion of our own intellectual assumptions. This suspicion rests not on paranoia but on the notion of 'reflexivity', where we can recognise that all modernist propositions, paradigms/viewpoints/beliefs/values that remove and treat as 'out there' reified concepts or structures are themselves simply representations transient and arbitrary in nature, if 'useful'.

So the post-modern message to modernist consultants is not that meaning in the post-modern context is inexhaustible, but rather that any final specification of meaning can only function as a self-defeating attempt to stabilise and restrain the 'dissemination' of the text. Whereas the modernist analysis of the world is based on the belief that meaning is gradually uncovered through learning and the critical questioning of things, meaning in a post-modern analysis can never be retrieved from apparent un-meaning, but instead actually consists in the repression and suppression of un-meaning – or other meanings, alternative readings and supplements.

The issue of the meaning of things in a business context is one of the basic preoccupations of consultants. To explore this further, the writings of Foucault in the area of understanding the nature of power can once again help consultants to see the mechanisms and processes that suppress meaning into un-meaning. Foucault emphasised that objects of knowledge are not natural or 'out there', but are ordered and constructed by discourse based on the *a priori* assumed parts of knowledge that determine what is the 'seeable and the sayable' (Foucault, 1970). Yet all discourse creates practices and concepts so that they appear, in certain points of history, as natural, self-evident and indispensable. It was his task to unravel, to deconstruct, the nature of these discourses to see how these so-called 'natural truths' emerged.

We have already touched on his use of the panopticon as an exemplar of organisations. The panopticon he sees as an example of a *discipline* – a series of techniques to observe, monitor and control behaviour. A discipline is thus a type of power based on knowledge – a view with which both consultants and experts would readily concur. Foucault develops this concept of the power/knowledge connection through his term 'governmentality' – derived from the words government and rationality. Government is about 'the conduct of conduct', a form of activity aiming to shape, guide or affect the conduct of some person or persons (Foucault, 1979). So programmes of government, like business, require vocabularies – that is, ways of representing that which is to be governed – and mechanisms to supervise and administer individuals and groups. Rationality is a recognition that before something can be governed or managed it must first be known. So governmentality refers to processes through which objects and people are made amenable to intervention and regulation by being formulated in a particular conceptual way.

For Foucault, then, the act of knowing something – giving meaning to something – is in fact to create a new power relation where power exists as a condition, rather than the property of something or someone. This is an important concept for consultancy and business. Traditional views of power treat it as a commodity, to be held by an organisation or group or individual; so power is to be acquired, and one group holds power over another. Thus modernist consultants tend to ask 'where or with whom does the power reside?' This presupposes a central organising power locus, which consultants then try to trace, to see how it is passed down from a particular point, person or process in the organisation. This 'descending' analysis of power tends to involve searching in a dualistic way for determinants and constraining factors that either sustain or undermine the organisation's power. Much of the current consultancy preoccupation with empowerment of individuals in organisations is located in this perspective of power. Foucault proposes an alternative view when he talks of power as a condition that reproduces specific organisational discourses, which in turn have the effect of constituting knowledge in that organisation. Consultants applying this point in a post-modern analysis of an organisation can, therefore, only proceed by under-standing the mechanisms, practices, techniques and procedures of power relationships within and around a business.

Thus power is not a commodity or possession to be 'passed' to people lower down in the organisation; it exists as an integral feature of knowledge relations, sustained and expressed through practices or disciplines of governmentality. That is why Foucault sees power as productive in the sense that it produces reality, produces domains of objects and rituals of truth. The implication of this constitutive nature of power is that post-modern consultants can shift their attentions from modernist examinations of the who and why of power, with its presupposition that power is something to be tracked to its source, to a concern with the *how*; that is, not how it is manifested, but how power is exercised through the relational discourse that exists in an organisation. A deconstruction of what 'empowerment' means would therefore require an examination of these discourses, the knowledge and assumptions they produce, the supplementarities and deferrals they imply and the effects (intended or otherwise) that they produce. That is, taking the 'how' approach in post-modern consultancy involves tracing knowledge production and its power effects, so it is thus an 'ascending' analysis of power, starting from the tiny mechanisms and events that constitute it in everyday business life.

These insights may be combined with those of post-modern thinking based around recognising the importance of avoiding conceptual closure, so that post-modern consultancy can go beyond helping a business in the traditional modernist ways of establishing privileged goal-oriented processes that create a disciplining of the organisation's interior to serve a turbulent market place. For instance, some strategic consultants now explicitly recognise the post-modern condition by acknowledging the arbitrariness and transitory nature of the meanings they have placed on an organisation's interactions with customers, suppliers and other people. Consultants' former emphasis on long-range planning has given way to the devising of temporary (project-based) processes that enable strategically flexible responses to be made to the unpredictable situations of the post-modern condition. Complementary efforts are now directed at creating 'learning organisations' that are ready to respond to sudden ruptures of the given, whether it is the marketplace or the activities of competitors. Some consultants are also attempting, through a deconstruction of the concept of 'alliancing', to rethink traditional power relations between contractors, suppliers and the organisations with whom they work. More consultants are now concerned with notions of disorganisation, multiple views and voices within business settings, and are working with organisations to help them to live with structural chaos, ambiguity and the ability to react to inherent uncertainty and disorder in localised contexts. Some writers have described the post-modernist organisation as characterised by a series of temporarily sited 'tents', rather than palaces, each encampment based on transitory structures with no single centre of power (Berg, 1989). Consultants in the field of organisation restructuring, acquisition management and culture change are beginning to acknowledge the tent theme in their work.

First steps

Yet these endeavours are but first steps – because, although they may be conducted in the spirit of genuine acknowledgement of the plurality of voices, cultures and diverse outcomes that constitute the post-modern condition, they can also be seen as late modernist attempts to incorporate and subsume within its practices a networked organisational environment that still serves the old power relations and discourses sustaining the supremacy of the organisation and its drive towards a financial return on investment. This modernist gloss on post-modern conditions in business is particularly evident in the fields of current consultancy activity that focus on people in organisations, where two modernist assumptions still prevail: a reworking of the humanist perspective, and the consolidation of mechanisms of visibility. On the first point, the insights of Gareth Morgan (1986) and his work on the presence and potency of metaphor in organisations has inspired many in business to rethink how they see and act within their organisations. The practical application of his ideas (Morgan 1993) has enabled people to see things – power relations, paradigms of beliefs, each other, and themselves – in fresh ways. Seeing things in new ways thus empowers them to act. The problem, however, is that Morgan's work accidentally elevates metaphor creation into a 'special task' rather than enabling managers to realise that the 'truths' about their organisational processes and beliefs are but old metaphors. In my experience and that of other consultants I have talked to, metaphors are seen by managers as just useful ways of interpreting a 'reality' that is still 'out there'. If too extreme a reading of the organisation emerges as a result of these metaphor-creating exercises, the response of the managers is to dismiss it through laughter or cynicism.

So in this sense – unintended by Morgan – the application of specific metaphors and the personal meanings that they can unfold is only legitimised if and when they empower employees to overcome resistances or difficulties in the organisation. The hegemony of the organisation, its demands and its adherence to particular cultural goals is not challenged or deconstructed in any fundamental way. But because metaphor enactment can, in a humanist spirit, 'help' people in an organisation, it is often used in management circles as the way to address the needs of individuals and allow them to voice their concerns and beliefs as a prelude to action. It is perhaps unfair to single out the problematics of metaphor creation in this way because other techniques – team building, individual excellence programmes, coaching for performance, developing the empowered, authentic individual, and the like – operate in much the same organisation-legitimising fashion, with a humanist subtext. Consultancy in the field of personal counselling within a business setting, although humanist in orientation, is one of the few exceptions to the business-legitimising type of consultancy as it actively encourages the finding of 'one's own voice' as one equally viable voice among many, both within and beyond the organisational context. But this is an area not yet readily recognised as management consultancy.

On the second modernist assumption still prevailing in consultancy, the consolidation of *mechanisms of visibility* is the other broad area in which consultancy is active in 'helping' individual people in organisations. Here we have a curious irony: people are the ostensible focus, yet much of the consultancy emphasis is on setting up surveillance systems, procedures and frameworks for competent behaviour, all with the intention of managing and tracking employees' actions within the business. This modernist agenda for control is reinforced by, for example, performance management processes, objective-setting programmes, job descriptions, and hierarchically based pay scales (Townley, 1993).

One reason why consultancy in the people side of business is particularly prone to the modernist susceptibility is, I think, due to the unquestioned beliefs they hold about the nature of individuality; individuals are seen as autonomous subjects, with their own 'essence' and integrity. Derrida's questioning of this assumption about the 'essential' nature of subjectivity, I mentioned earlier but this may be a good point at which to expand further on this issue.

If we take Foucault's understanding of power relations, Lacan's work on psychoanalytic theory, and some feminist writings (for example Cameron, 1992) as but three starting points, they support the view that the 'self' is an actively constituted reality – a site of 'intertextuality' as Derrida puts it. That is, the individual, from the perspective of a post-modern analysis, cannot be seen as an entity possessed of an essential personal identity consistent across time and circumstance; individuals are continually constituted through social relationships and discourses that play on them and in which they play a part. If power/knowledge produces reality, as Foucault said, then the individual, and the knowledge that may be gained of him or her, belongs to this production. Indeed post-modernists believe that the individual is one of power's prime effects, a heterogeneous and variable outcome of the language, social expectations and norms placed on him or her. Self-introspection and a sense of the body merely reinforces a feeling of the essential self – it is not the result of an autonomous subject.

Thus consultancy work that centred on knowing the individual through, for instance, competency analysis and assessment techniques is simply reducing the individual to an object of knowledge within the consultant's sets of meanings – legitimised in and through behavioural language acceptable to business. This reduction thereby denies the movements of différance, supplementarity and deferral of meanings that are inherent in an under-standing of self.

Thus if we acknowledge a post-modern understanding of the de-centring of the self – that is, there is no essential reality 'inside' a particular individual, – then consultants who deal at the individual level need to recognise more explicitly in their activities that subject-positioning statements are, in fact, given by the language through which they work. This means that the emphasis of their work must move away from interpretative and comparative strategies of analysis, towards an identification of supplementarity and representational processes that shape a particular individual. Some interesting moves in this direction have been made by consultants who choose to explore managers' own structures of meaning, using variations on the repertory grid technique from construct theory. Although this has been around for some time, it is now enjoying a revival as a practical method that can elicit a non-privileging plurality of voices, which is the first step in beginning the deconstruction process to understand some of the movements of différance and supplemen-tarity that make up the individual's self-perception (Fransella and Porter, 1990).

However, much of consultancy in the popular fields of personal assessment and psychometric testing is still particularly embedded in humanist and rationalist belief systems. Although sophisticated assessment centres that explore managers' reactions to very diverse situations are emerging in the profession, the data they generate are often reduced to narrowly defined and closely tracked attributes, so rendering irrelevant much of the subtlety and plurality of managers' responses.

Nonetheless there are other glimmers of light. Management education and development – which is increasingly seen as a service within the management consultancy field – is also in the early stages of applying a post-modern analysis in their work. Education and development programmes now exist to help managers go beyond the limits of just making themselves more competent or more resourceful. Consultants have been involved in develop-ment work with managers to enable them to become more sensitive to difference, ambiguity and uncertainty; to acknowledge and deconstruct the constitutive nature of the language they use in business; to stop playing with metaphors and start thinking about metonyms – the symbolic presences and representations of organisational power relations and language games – and their impact on organisational discourse.

This consultancy work is now developing further to help senior people in organisations to understand the multiplicity of 'narrative fictions', the acts of writing that make up organisational life, their strategic plans, ways of interacting and doing business. These approaches explore the 'bricolage' of conscious managerial decisions, data from experts, market information and straight intuition, where none of the parts is sufficient to account for the outcomes and consequences reached. By guiding management through a process of exploring the narrative fictions that allow them to make a strategic response, there is a greater feeling that decisions – whilst much harder to make – are less likely to privilege one voice over others, even if they are still subject to what Lyotard has called 'performativity'. The consequence of this consultancy is that it is helping managers to stop being limited to thinking in terms of paradigm shifts, and to begin the process of 'syntagmatic relationship' development. This small field of consultancy takes the spirit of the post-modern intertextuality of meanings, the supplementary oppositional relationships between one process and another, or one culture and another, and tries to help clients re-present their organisations as discourses that are not 'either/ or' but 'and/also'. This approach enables clients to see that all the cultures existing in their organisation have their meanings simultaneously supported and denied by the existence of separate, diverse and intertextually linked belief systems, the presence of which constitutes the organisation. This insight has enabled people to rethink their approach particularly to management of change strategies, organisation 'culture goals' and strategy formulation. Sadly this practical application of post-modern thinking is rather handicapped by the continuing flow of pop-management books that evangelise on the power of 'paradigm shifting' as the way forward.

The practice of post-modern consulting may be patchy and only partly understood, but I believe that it offers the potential of an ethically oriented approach, based not on tired enlightenment ambitions or modernist privileging, but on a genuine, if necessarily erratic, desire to rethink what business organisations are about – to deconstruct the practices, belief-systems and preoccupations of what it is to live in an organised, consumer-oriented and consuming society. If consultants can help business to understand the implicit ambivalence in everything they do and strive for and cut through some of the deeply embedded privileging that simultaneously supports and handicaps business life, then their work may be transformational. At worst, it might even be useful.

References

Baudrillard, J. (1983) *In the Shadow of the Silent Majorities . . . or, the End of the Social and Other Essays* (New York: Semiotext(e)).

Baxter, B. (1982) *Alienation and Authenticity: Some consequences for organised work* (London: Tavistock).

Berg, P. (1989) 'Postmodern Management? from facts to fiction in theory and practice', *Scandinavian Journal of Management*, vol. 5, no. 3, pp. 201–17.

Cameron, D. (1992) *Feminism and Linguistic Theory* (London: Macmillan).

Clegg, S. (1990) *Modern Organisations: Organisation studies in the post-modern world* (London: Sage).

Cooper, R. (1987) 'Information, communication and organisation – a post-structural revision', *Journal of Mind and Behaviour*, vol. 8, no. 3, pp. 395–416.

Cooper, R. (1989) 'Modernism, post modernism and organisational analysis 3: The contribution of Jacques Derrida', *Organisation Studies*, vol. 10, no. 4, pp. 479–502.

Cooper, R. (1992) 'Formal organisation as representations', in M. Reed and M. Hughes (eds), *Rethinking Organisation* (London: Sage).

Cooper, R. and Burrell, G. (1988) 'Modernism, post-modernism and organisational analysis: an introduction', *Organisation Studies*, vol. 9, no. 1, pp. 91–112.

Derrida, J. (1976) *Of Grammatology* (Baltimore: The John Hopkins University Press).

Derrida, J. (1978) *Writing and difference* (London: Routledge & Kegan Paul).

Derrida, J. (1981) *Dissemination* (London: Athlone Press).

Derrida, J.(1982) *Margins of Philosophy* (London: Harvester).

Foucault, M. (1970) *The Order of Things* (London: Tavistock).

Foucault, M. (1977) *Discipline and Punish* (Harmondsworth: Penguin).

Fransella, F. and Porter, J. (1990) 'Using Personal Construct Psychology in development', in M. Pedler *et al.*, *Self Development in Organisations* (Maidenhead: McGraw-Hill).

French, W. and Bell, C. (1973) *Organisation Development: Behavioural science interventions for organisation improvement* (Englewood Cliffs, NJ: Prentice-Hall).

Frug, G. (1984) 'The Ideology of Bureaucracy in American law', *Harvard Law Review*, vol. 97, no. 6, pp. 1276–388.

Gergen, K. (1992) 'Organisation Theory – the post-modern era', in M. Reed and M. Hughes (eds), *Rethinking Organisation* (London, Sage).

Habermas, J. (1981) 'Modernity versus Postmodernity', *New German Critique*, no. 22.

Habermas, J. (1983) 'Modernity: an incomplete project', in H. Foster (ed.), *The Anti-aesthetic: Essays on post-modern culture* (Washington: Port Townsend).

Habermas, J. (1987) *The Philosophical Discourse of Modernity* (Oxford: Oxford University Press).

Handy, C. (1989) *The Age of Unreason* (London: Business Books).

Harvey, D. (1989) *The Condition of Post-modernity* (London: Basil Blackwell).

Heidegger, M. (1978) *Being and Time* (London: Basil Blackwell).

Holloway, W. (1991) *Work, Psychology and Organisational Behaviour* (London: Sage).

Jackall, R. (1988) *Moral Mazes: The world of corporate managers* (Oxford: Oxford University Press).

Kanter, R. M. (1989) *When Giants Learn to Dance* (London: Simon & Schuster).

Lawrence, P. R. and Lorsch, J. W. (1967) *Organization and Environment* (Cambridge, Mass.: Harvard University Press).

Linstead, S. (1993) 'Deconstruction in the study of organisations', in J. Hassard and M. Parker (eds) *Post Modernism and Organisations* (London: Sage).

Lyotard, J. F. (1984) *The Post Modern Condition: A report on knowledge* (Manchester: Manchester University Press).

Morgan, G. (1986) *Images of Organisation* (London: Sage).

Morgan, G. (1993) *Imaginization* (London: Sage).

Marx, K. (1973) *Grundrisse* (London: Allen Lane).

Pascale, R. (1991) *Managing on the Edge* (London: Penguin).

Peet, J. (1988) 'Management Consultancy; the new witch-doctors', *The Economist*, 12 February 1988).

Peters, T. (1987) *Thriving on Chaos* (New York: Knopf).

Peters, T. (1992) *Liberation Management* (London: Macmillan).

Reich, R. (1991) *The Work of Nations: Preparing ourselves for 21st century capitalism* (London: Simon & Schuster).

Sturdy, A., Nicholls, P. and Newman, I. (1990) 'Management expertise, agency and practice: A case of management consultants', Annual Labour Process Conference, Aston University.

Townley, B. (1993) 'Performance appraisal and the emergence of management', *Journal of Management Studies*, vol. 30, no. 2, pp. 221–38.

Weber, M. (1958) *The Protestant Ethic and the Spirit of Capitalism* (New York: Scribner).

Whitley, R. (1988) 'Social science and social engineering', Working Paper 171, Manchester Business School.

Wolf, W. (1978) *Management and Consulting: An introduction to James O McKinsey* (Ithaca, NY: Cornell University).

PART 2

EXPERTISE AND TECHNOLOGICAL INNOVATION

Designing jobs with advanced manufacturing technology: the negotiation of expertise

J. Martin Corbett

Prompted in part by the advent of IT networks and software packages, we no longer think of technology in terms of machines and hardware but as the outcome of a social process. Some writers have viewed this process in terms of the 'contested terrain' (Edwards, 1979), defined by the conflicting interests of managers and workers at the workplace. Managers are seen as pursuing objectives centred on efficiency and control, while workers seek to retain a degree of control over the work process. This political model of technological change is attentive to motives and interests and defines functional issues as a facade for such interests. Its analytic drive is upwards and outwards, pointing to the – largely unspecified – effects of the wider social context as the ultimate determinant of workplace events.

In contrast, the following study views technology as a process of social construction that is shaped by the distribution of different forms of expertise and knowledge. This study does not discount political influences, but rather sees power and knowledge as closely intertwined in the expertise of particular groups. This has the distinct advantage of allowing us to track technological outcomes back through the shaping and interaction of different forms of expertise. Instead of the self-conscious exercise of power, the technology process is seen as bodying forth expert thinking, social relations and technical potential into specific machine systems and job designs. This avoids ascribing *a priori* interests to particular groups, or translating technologically complex issues into crude political terms. More importantly, it avoids reproducing the stark dichotomy of technical and social domains (Latour, 1987), which is a far more insidiously political influence on the technology process than any of the interest-group issues mentioned above.

The social construction of technical systems is thus seen as a quiet and undramatic affair, which is influenced by the structural interpenetration of management and engineering expertise and by the dependencies built into firm–supplier relationships. It unfolds not through the negotiation of interests, but rather of expertise, meaning that the interpretation of technical options and the assertion of influence are jointly invoked by the same process of innovation.

Introduction

This chapter explores the relationship between the design and use of advanced manufacturing technology (AMT). It is based on an evaluation of recent empirical and theoretical research using knowledge and expertise as its focus of analysis. The chapter is in six sections. In the first the nature of AMT is outlined. This is followed by a brief summary of the technological determinism or organisational choice debate, which has dominated research into the relationship between AMT and shopfloor job design. In the third section, a theoretical approach that goes beyond these two competing perspectives is introduced. This forms the basis for an analysis of the AMT production chain from design through implementation to its use on the shopfloor in terms of the structures of knowledge and expertise that are negotiated between (and prioritised by) key actors and afforded by the artifacts and procedures they construct. Section 4 examines the nature of the knowledge, values and assumptions held by the designers of one particular form of AMT; namely, computer numerically controlled (CNC) machine tools. Section 5 then describes a case study of the negotiation of expertise within a CNC user organisation. In section 6 the results of research outlined in the previous two sections are analysed to reveal that CNC job design decision making is dominated by technical and engineering knowledge structures that simultaneously enframe and legitimate this process throughout the AMT production chain.

The nature of advanced manufacturing technology

In examining the impact of AMT on job design, two forms of application can be distinguished. The first comprises direct applications, for example CNC machine tools, robotics and automated guided vehicles. Such AMT incorporates the information storage, manipulation and retrieval capabilities of computer and microprocessor technology to control machinery that physically transforms or transports materials, or assembles components. The second form of AMT utilises computer technology to support the coordination and management of production. Applications include computer-aided production planning and scheduling, and inventory control.

The focus of this chapter is on the direct forms of application, with particular emphasis on CNC machine tools. These machines are most commonly found as 'stand-alone' technologies, although they have the potential to be integrated with other types of direct technologies to form flexible manufacturing systems. When such systems are integrated through the use of additional types of direct and indirect AMT, highly automated computer integrated manufacturing systems are possible. It is this potential that gives rise to the vision of the peopleless factory of the future (Corbett 1990). CNC machine tools represent the building blocks of such a future.

Despite talk of an 'information technology revolution' in UK manufacturing (for example Forester, 1980), the diffusion of AMT has not been widespread. For example, by the late 1980s CNC machine tools accounted for less than 8 per cent of the 746000 machine tools used in UK industry. However the use of CNC is on the increase, and by 1990, 38 per cent of total machine tool investment by UK industry was in CNC technology (Corbett, 1995a). Indeed, whilst the average age of the machines used in UK industry is 12 years, 70 per cent of all CNC machines in use in 1987 were less than five years old (Metalworking Production, 1987). CNC is therefore still very much a 'new' technology in the UK.

The impact of AMT on job design: determinism or organisational choice?

Within the social sciences, two perspectives have dominated theoretical and empirical research on the impact of AMT on shopfloor job design in recent years. One perspective views the development and diffusion of AMT as a process by which jobs are increasingly deskilled. This view was given a new impetus in 1974 with the publication of Braverman's *Labor and Monopoly Capital* (1974). Braverman's thesis argued that AMT embodies a more effective means of simplifying jobs and enhancing managerial control over the production labour process.

Braverman notes that the expertise and skills required to operate manual machine tools are qualitatively different from those required by CNC. With manual machines, parts are produced by highly skilled machinists using general-purpose machine tools. The machines provide the mechanical power, whilst the machinist utilises knowledge of the required cutting speeds of different metals, the depths and angle of cut and so forth to control the machine in realtime through the manipulation of hand-operated wheels and controls.

With the introduction of numerical control and CNC the mechanical aspect of the work remains the same, but is now under the control of a computer program:

> Decisions on how to machine a given part are pre-recorded and embedded into the program. This defines precisely the sequence, location and depth of the cuts to be made. In effect, the knowledge and skill required to make a part has been permanently captured in the program. The program controls the entire machining cycle without the need for human intervention (Wall and Kemp, 1987, p. 9).

Thus computer control provides the opportunity to deskill the job of the machinist, who merely loads, monitors and unloads parts. Further support for what has become known as the 'deskilling hypothesis' has come from the research of Shaiken (1980), Noble (1984) and others.

The main thrust of the argument employed by researchers sharing this determinist perspective is that the design of AMT is shaped and legitimated by the interests of capitalists (for example the owners and directors of business organisations) who desire to minimise labour costs and maximise management control of the production process. Executives of organisations in which AMT is produced and of organisations in which AMT is used are assumed to hold this interest in common. This view tends to either read social implications such as job design directly from attributes of technological design or read technical design as a direct expression of social interests.

This deskilling hypothesis smacks of excessive technological determinism to many researchers, and Braverman's book heralded a tide of case studies that shows no immediate signs of abating. Conclusions drawn from these studies lend support to quite a different perspective on the impact of AMT on shopfloor job design. Case-study research (for example Buchanan and Boddy, 1986; Child, 1985, 1987; Rhodes and Wield, 1985) suggest that the context of technology adoption (particularly management strategy and organisational custom and practice) is a crucial intervening or moderator variable in the relationship between AMT design and job design. In this view, technological imperatives are weak, whilst organisational choices are crucial.

In most academic texts the determinist and choice perspectives are treated as paired opposites akin to the philosophical dichotomy of determinism and free will. Bourdieu (1989) argues that such dichotomies are little more than 'colluding adversaries' that 'tend to delimit the space of the thinkable by excluding the very intention to think beyond the divisions they institute' (Bourdieu, 1989, p. 87). However, if one views the determinism–choice division as mutually constitutive perspectives it is possible to expand the region of the 'thinkable'. For example neither perspective offers much insight into unanticipated consequences of AMT adoption on job design. Both view AMT job-design decision making as a fairly unproblematic management prerogative (either through influencing technological design or through the design of shopfloor work organisation). Yet consider the results of a survey of 276 UK manufacturing works managers carried out in 1984 as part of a larger survey by researchers at the Policy Studies Institute (see Daniel, 1987). These showed that 34 per cent of survey respondents felt that their ability to organise shopfloor work in relation to AMT was constrained by technological and organisational factors beyond their control; that is, outside the bounds of management choice. Such results do not sit comfortably with either the determinism or choice perspectives. Whilst the determinists have tended to ignore the role of workplace resistance, the advocates of organisational choice have tended to ignore the ways technology may act effectively to constrain both management's power to choose and the type and extent of user knowledge afforded by technological design. As Scarbrough and Corbett note:

> Far from containing or controlling the technology process, the formal boundaries and managerial hierarchies of organisation may themselves be restructured by it . . . Indeed on occasions, the transformational power of technological knowledge may escape the intentions of the powerful and undermine, and not simply reproduce, existing social and economic structures (Scarbrough and Corbett, 1992, p. 23).

This chapter will argue that findings from research within both the determinist and choice camps can be gainfully analysed if one views AMT job design as a process of negotiating and renegotiating expertise. The key variable in this perspective is not social or technical forces, but knowledge itself.

AMT job design as process

A processual perspective on AMT job design overcomes many of the problems associated with the determinist and organisational choice camps discussed above by emphasising the mutuality of technological and organisational possibilities and knowledges. According to this view: 'although particular technological and organisational forms may be shaped initially by different sets of sectoral contingencies, we find that at the level of design and use technological and organisational knowledges are combined to produce distinctive configurations of machines and work organisations (Scarbrough and Corbett, 1992, p. 13).

Applying this perspective to the world of manufacturing, Barnes argues that

> neither the crude raw materials used in production, nor the objective character of the given tools of production, can be held to determine production itself. They are the raw materials and tools only because they are conceptualised and operated upon in a certain way, only because, that is, of the meaning imputed to them and the knowledge of them which people possess. Production is necessarily the accomplishment of cognitively competent, knowledgeable, socialised groups of men [*sic*] (Barnes, 1977, p. 71).

Barnes further argues that the potential for successful action of any social group will depend upon its skills and competencies (its knowledge in the sense of knowing how), and upon its knowledge of what appertains in its social and physical setting (its knowledge in the sense of knowing what). It will depend also on the general distribution of knowledge within the broader sociocultural milieu.

When we apply this view of knowledge to the design of shopfloor jobs involving AMT, we may view design decisions as an on-going process of negotiation between a variety of knowledgeable actors and social groups, each attempting to further their perceived interests. As we shall see later, the structures of knowledge (and their justifications) concerning the propagation of principles and maxims of conduct that are utilised in these negotiations are of key importance as they serve to validate certain types of knowledge and expertise (and invalidate others) within the decision-making process.

AMT job design: key actors in the negotiation of expertise

As discussed above, researchers in the determinist camp argue that the design of AMT is shaped and legitimated by the interests of the owners and directors of business organisations who desire to maximise their control of the production process. However it is clear from research located in the organisational choice camp that other parties play an important role in shaping AMT job design. The social character of design tends to be the outcome of the interplay between diverse forces, rather than the unilateral imposition of power or interest. Hence AMT job design needs to be examined as a decision-making process involving social actors and interest groups who bring their own distinct expertise and structures of knowledge to bear during negotiations.

Who then are the key actors and groups in this process? Case study researchers have identified a veritable host of participants, including executive managers, engineering designers, AMT suppliers/producers, engineering and production managers, financial and management accountants, technical specialists, personnel management, and users (see Corbett, 1995a; Francis and Grootings, 1989; Scarbrough and Corbett, 1992).

Figure 4.1 places these major decision makers in the context of the broader forces shaping AMT job design. The figure forms the conceptual basis for an analysis from a processual perspective whereby jobs with AMT are designed through a reciprocal sequence of activities organised within an interdependent chain of production. The chain is constituted as a network of intra- and interorganisational activities linking each phase of AMT design, development, implementation and use: 'From this vantage point, innovation appears not as a discrete location (R&D) or function (scientific research) within separate

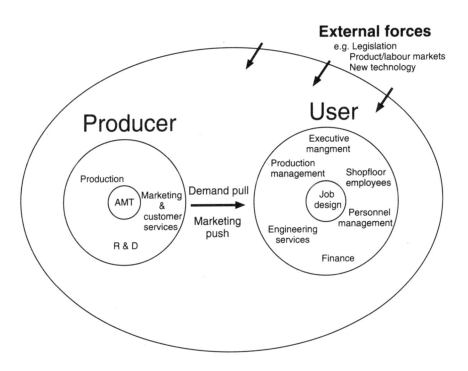

FIGURE 4.1 The shaping of job design: spheres of influence in the AMT production chain

organisations but as an accumulation of knowledge and the transformation of practice occurring throughout the production chain' (Gordon and Krieger, 1991, p. 2).

Figure 4.1 concentrates on key actors and decision makers within this chain of production and combines the determinist and choice perspectives without being restricted to one or the other. For instance determinists have tended to focus their attention on the unity of interests between AMT producers and executive management within user organisations, whilst researchers in the choice camp have virtually ignored this relationship in favour of the interactions within the user organisation. The approach favoured here does not give precedence to either perspective, but opens up the decision-making process to a wider-ranging empirical investigation of the AMT production chain.

The shaping of AMT job design: the influence of the AMT producer

It is beyond the scope of this chapter to examine the range of external forces shaping innovations in and the diffusion of AMT (the interested reader is directed to the work of Clark and Staunton, 1993; Landes, 1969; Rosenberg, 1982; Scarbrough and Corbett, 1992; and Swan, Chapter 5 this volume). Of primary interest here is an examination of the knowledge, assumptions and values shared by actors and groups engaged in AMT design and production. We begin with a brief summary of the theoretical work in this area.

The dominance of engineering specialists in the design and production of AMT is well documented (for example Cressey, 1985; Ehn, 1988; Noble, 1984; Wilkinson, 1983). Many commentators and researchers (for example Hampden-Turner, 1970; Noble, 1984; Cooley, 1987; Willcocks and Mason, 1987) argue that 'hard systems thinking' predominates the design practices of these specialists. Hard systems thinking involves the imposition of a clear-cut problem definition on a relatively unstable (that is, 'soft') organisational reality. It also means the adoption of systematic, orderly, rational procedures that restrict research and design in a very complex organisational reality. A further implication is an overriding concern for technical design and the by-passing of the organisational context in which the system is to operate and the social implications of the system. More fundamentally, it leaves the engineering experts to decide the extent to which user participation is useful and permissible.

As part of this 'hard' approach to AMT design, the design expert will make (often implicit) assumptions about the way the technical system will be used. For AMT, where technical considerations are paramount and a high level of automatic computer control is emphasised, the role of the user can only be readily understood and modelled if operating tasks are predictable and well defined. A narrow view of human potential and worth is folded into these assumptions about human nature and specifications for job design. Research conducted by Taylor (1979) and Salzman and Rosenthal (1994) lends further support to the view that, for engineering specialists, users tend to be reduced to the status of 'noise' in a technical system.

Recent research on CNC machine tool design, carried out by a team of researchers under the auspices of CAPIRN (International Research Network on Culture and Production), reveals a more complex picture of the ways in which producers construct and define their products and users (see Corbett, 1995b; Kaneko, 1991; Ruth, 1994). This research – a questionnaire survey of 91 randomly selected CNC producers (17 from the UK, 29 from Germany, 45 from Japan) – concentrated on two key areas of interest, namely producer perceptions of the forces influencing the design and development of their CNC products, and their perceptions of the relative importance of technical and social criteria for optimal CNC machine tool design. Survey questionnaires were completed by company managing directors.

Survey results collated by Corbett (1994) show that 76 per cent, 71 per cent and 51 per cent, respectively, of German, UK and Japanese producers regarded customer demand as the chief development impulse for their CNC products. When asked to outline the nature of this demand, all survey respondents cited customers' desire to reduce lead times, to achieve higher quality machining and increase production flexibility. On first reading these results suggest a strong customer/market orientation in CNC machine tool design and the development practices of producers in all three countries. However, on closer analysis the data reveal that, whilst the survey sample of CNC producer companies sell their products in quite different market sectors and to different customers, there are marked similarities in their perceptions of optimal CNC design (indeed statistical analyses indicated no significant cross-national differences in these perceptions). Although 43 per cent of producers regarded meeting customer requirements as a key design criterion, 26 per cent of producers regarded the reduction of user's direct labour costs as an 'extremely important' CNC design criterion and 27 per cent saw the automation of mental work (that is, the embedding of planning and operational decisions into CNC software) in a similar light. This compares with only 18 per cent of producers who saw the utilisation of user skills as 'extremely important'. Also note that none of the Japanese producers perceived direct labour cost reduction as a customer priority and yet 28 per cent of them viewed such a reduction as an 'extremely important' CNC design criterion (see Corbett, 1994). This lends support to the view that despite the rhetoric of meeting perceived customer demands, a hard engineering approach to CNC design remains discernible. The fact that only eight of the sample of 91 CNC producers made provision for customer participation in joint conceptual design suggests that customer requirements are only met within narrow producer-defined limits (see Corbett, 1994).

Indeed, far from taking a lead from users in CNC design and development, producers appear to encourage user dependency on their knowledge and expertise. For example, many CNC-user companies need to take full advantage of the training services offered by producers because their own skill and knowledge base is not fully commensurate with the skill and knowledge requirements of the purchased machines. Responses to the CAPIRN questionnaire reveal that 69 per cent of producers engage regularly in after-sales training courses for both the office and shopfloor users of their products – a trend that Dohl (1992) sees as evidencing both a lack of user-centredness in AMT design and an increasing user dependence on producers who have to assume training, financing and other services in addition to their usual technological services.

> This dependency enables the manufacturers (i.e. producers) to force the user companies into adopting systems that correspond best to the manufacturers' own production, development and financing conditions. This does not mean to say that such systems are ineffective as a means of solving flexibility and cost problems, for they are developed with precisely these ends in mind; however, it cannot be denied that the user companies have to pursue their rationalisation strategies with techniques and technologies which do not fully correspond to their conditions and needs and which, above all, prevent them from trying out other alternatives. Moreover, the difficulties and problems that the user companies experience in attempting to master these suboptimal solutions increase their dependency on the manufacturers, due to the continual need for their intervention when difficulties arise. This leads to a further weakening of the user company's position, for example in terms of their skill potential (Kohl, 1992, p. 91).

Results from the CAPIRN research demonstrate that the survey sample of CNC producer companies shared very similar perceptions of optimal CNC design. Whilst there was a strong consensus amongst the 91 managing directors who participated in the survey that marketing should drive product design, many of them argued that, in practice, the limited technical knowledge of marketing personnel restricted their contribution to the development process (a finding echoed in the research of Salzman and Rosenthal, 1994). Hence the orientations and values expressed by product design engineers remained a key driving force in the design and development process. When embodied in CNC design, criteria such as the reduction of direct labour costs and particularly the translation of shopfloor expertise and knowledge into technical artifacts result in the embodiment of technological knowledge, which is then transferred to the user organisation. This is not to say that assumptions embedded in CNC design determine how that technology is used and operated. Technical design must fall prey to situated interpretation. As Brown, Duguid and Nunberg (1991) argue, CNC design (as well as the marketing rhetoric associated with it) cannot determine what structures of knowledge and legitimation are employed by user organisations. However technological designs inevitably attempt to cue relevant structures of knowledge and to dismiss others through the structures of user knowledge they afford.

As CNC designs become more complex (for example live tooling and direct numerical control facilities), higher levels of technological knowledge (that is,

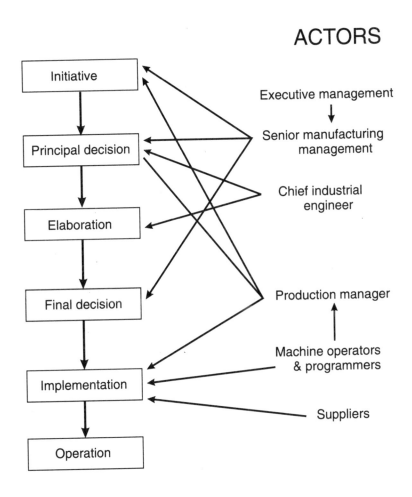

FIGURE 4.2   Flow chart of AMT job design decision making in a Belgian manufacturing company

Source: Based on Kesteloot, 1989.

concerning systems architecture and design of integrated production processes) are afforded. If, as the CAPIRN survey results suggest, CNC design is shaped by hard systems thinking this may lead to both an increase in user dependence on producer company technical expertise and a corresponding decrease in user discretion regarding how CNC is implemented and used.

The shaping of AMT job design: the influence of the AMT user

Field survey and case study research alike lends support to the notion that CNC job design options are constrained to a greater or lesser extent by the choices made at the level of technical design, and that options chosen are shaped, at least in part, by customer demands; that is by decision makers located in user organisations. The next stage of our analysis is to uncover the nature of user influence on CNC design and use.

Figure 4.2 illustrates a useful start point for the study of this process. The example is based on one of Kesteloot's (1989) excellent case studies of the introduction of CNC machine tools into Belgian manufacturing companies. The strength of these studies lies in the fact that they demonstrate the ways in which a variety of actors are involved in the decision process.

Kesteloot's case studies show how user involvement is often minimised and how certain types of knowledge and expertise tend to dominate decision making in CNC user organisations:

> In general we can say that the introduction of CNC technology in the firms we have studied can be analysed in terms of a multiple logic of action complex in which the perception of (new) structural requirements by management and, accordingly, the technical and economic rationalisation efforts with which they want to meet them, are intertwined with mainstream 'pro Hi-Tech' attitudes, with power relations – and thus with control – and with the technical orientations of the major decision-makers themselves (Kesteloot, 1989, p. 279).

A couple of points are worth stressing here. First, Kesteloot's research indicates that representatives from CNC producer/suppliers may be involved in AMT job-design decision making at the implementation stage (Figure 4.2). This involvement centres around the solving of emergent problems at the interface between the technology and the organisational context in which it is to be operated. In practice such efforts are usually restricted to user training and are required because the structures of user knowledge afforded by the CNC machine tool design do not accurately map onto the structures of user knowledge within the user company. A second point arising from Kesteloot's work is the dominance of the technical orientations of AMT job design decision makers. Notice that senior engineering management are key actors in this process (Figure 4.2).

Research by Mueller *et al.* (1986) exposes a certain bias in the way senior engineering managers evaluate choices of CNC job design. The researchers asked all middle and senior managers within a large UK computer manufacturing company to express their CNC job design preferences. The researchers found that, with the exception of quality and test engineering

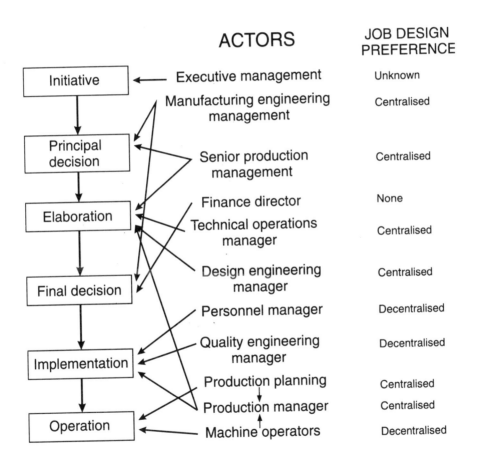

FIGURE 4.3   Flow chart of AMT job design decision making in a UK manufacturing company

management, all engineering managers expressed a strong preference for the more centralised option of CNC office programming. In contrast personnel management preferred the more decentralised option of shopfloor CNC programming. Financial management and production supervisors expressed no particular preference (see Figure 4.3 and discussion below).

CNC job design: a case study of Apollo UK

The present author's own research within the company in which Mueller *et al.*'s work was conducted (hereafter called Apollo UK) offers the opportunity to examine the dynamics of the negotiations that led to the company's subsequent decision to choose a centralised job design option a year after the completion of Mueller *et al.*'s research. The flow chart in Figure 4.3 outlines the key actors in the AMT job design decision process and their respective job design preferences ten months prior to involvement in the process.

The initiative for investment in AMT at Apollo UK was taken at board level. The board members were eager to establish a state-of-the-art computer assembly utility employing the latest CNC technologies in the manufacture and assembly of computer boards. Two broad sets of objectives for introducing new technology were cited. The first set comprised strategic objectives. The board members were keen to upgrade process and assembly technologies to meet changing market conditions. They wished to establish two interconnected flexible AMT systems: a flexible process system (manufacturing bare printed circuit boards) and a flexible assembly system (for the automatic insertion of electronic components onto the boards). The ideal systems would reduce lead time and improve product consistency and price relative to competitors.

The second set of objectives related to shopfloor operations. The board was intent on reducing production costs and to increasing flexibility (allowing batch sizes of between one and 800 to be manufactured). The flexible assembly system should also be designed to increase production efficiency through the removal of bottlenecks in the present assembly area and the production of defect-free boards. No objectives relating to the control of the two systems were articulated.

For their part, the senior manufacturing engineering and production managers believed that automation was the key to the development of a high-efficiency, high-quality assembly system. They viewed the present generation of CNC component insertion machines as nearing obsolescence (despite being only six years old) and, in collaboration with two senior design engineering managers, looked to ways in which the design of the company's computer circuit boards could be altered to take advantage of the latest 'surface-mount'

CNC technology. This particular form of AMT enables boards to be manufactured more cheaply as surface-mount boards do not require components to be inserted through drilled holes as at present, but soldered automatically to the surface of the board (the drilling process being seen as both expensive and a bottleneck in the production process by this group of Apollo UK managers).

As a result of this collaboration, senior engineering management recommended the purchase of highly automated CNC surface-mount assembly machines with robotic parts-transfer capabilities. At that time the only producers of such machines were Japanese. These machines were designed to facilitate off-line programming via a direct numerical control (DNC) link to computer aided design (CAD) technologies. The machines had no provision for shopfloor programming and editing.

Thus, at Apollo UK, product innovation became an integral part of the process innovation. Once this decision was made, the control of the system came up for discussion and it was only then that job design issues entered the technical decision frame. Four management groups – senior production management, technical operations, design engineering and production management (collectively known as the management development team) – were involved at this stage and all favoured centralised control of the two systems (Figure 4.3). Line management, personnel, programmers and machine operators were not consulted as, according to the technical operations manager, 'the issue was one of robust systems engineering – not job-design'.

Issues of financial justification were also excluded from negotiations at this system elaboration stage (Figure 4.3). Indeed the members of the management development team felt that formal justification of the planned capital expenditure on surface-mount technology compared with alternative technologies and systems configurations was unwarranted. During one interview with the author the senior manufacturing engineering manager even went so far as to argue that 'a highly automated system based around surface-mount is the only systems configuration that will meet the board's requirements specification'. What is interesting here is that the specification he referred to was actually drawn up by the development management team according to the broad set of objectives stipulated at board level. Note also that personnel from the customer services division of the CNC producer company made numerous visits to the user site during this period. They were eager to supply systemic software to integrate the CNC surface-mount machines, but the manufacturing engineering manager argued that sufficient engineering expertise and accumulated control system design know-how existed within Apollo UK for them to design and development their own. Nevertheless both groups agreed that shopfloor CNC programming was not a viable option.

The purchase and systemic configuration of the CNC machines were based solely on technical considerations and Apollo UK's engineering management gave little or no consideration to the social aspects of the new systems. Essentially, their approach to the technical systems design was as 'hard' as that taken by the CNC producers discussed earlier.

In due course the finance director signed off the investment despite the fact that no accurate measures of productivity and quality gains or of comparative improvements in efficiency were presented to him. The only 'hard' measure in evidence was based on cost savings associated with the closure of the drilling department and the sale of the eleven 'obsolete' CNC drilling machines. Other case studies of CNC design and implementation suggest that this lack of measurement is by no means unusual (for example Majchrzak, 1988; Wilkinson, 1983).

At Apollo UK it was only at the implementation stage that any dissenting voices were raised. Both the quality engineering manager and the personnel manager felt that the proposed new systems would fail to utilise the full range of skills possessed by the direct labour force. Indeed, two years previously the company had invested considerable sums of money in quality awareness training and skills development for all shopfloor personnel. To quell the concerns of the personnel and quality engineering managers, the two were given responsibility to oversee the implementation of the new systems (in collaboration with the production department management team and the producers). In practice the role of the personnel department was restricted to redundancy counselling, liaison with the training department and allaying trade union concerns relating to the real-time work-monitoring capabilities of the new technologies.

The management development team and the personnel manager both wanted to achieve the goals set by the board, but gave quite different emphases to how these should be achieved. The management development team (and the producer representatives) did not regard decentralisation as appropriate because the machines were not designed to facilitate such a mode of operation. Indeed the senior production manager argued that productivity and quality would be enhanced only if the most efficient use was made of the CNC technology. On the other hand the personnel and quality engineering managers saw the same goals being achieved only if the most effective use was made of the skills and knowledge of the shopfloor operators.

We discussed earlier how technical design may cue relevant structures of knowledge and dismiss others through the structures of user knowledge it affords. In the case of CNC surface-mount technology, much of the expertise accumulated by shopfloor CNC operators was based around less technically sophisticated CNC machines. The latter technology enabled operators to see the insertion process clearly and to make simple yet effective quality checks, for example checking that the pins on a microchip had gone through the correct holes in the printed circuit board. In contrast the operation of the surface-mount machines was less visible and simple visual quality checks were no longer possible. Indeed it was this lack of visual access that senior engineers and producer company representatives felt necessitated (and justified) the distancing of shopfloor operators from control of the machine. It was argued that the technology itself would take care of any quality issues through utilisation of the inbuilt automated continuity checking facility.

As a corollary, senior engineers argued that expert office-based programmers should be put in control as, given that component misplacements were difficult and time consuming to correct manually, it was vital that programming errors did not occur in the first place. Although no evidence was available to support the implied superior expertise of office programmers in terms of error detection and recovery, this circular argument was employed by the members of Apollo UK's management development team to justify their preference for centralised job design. Producer representatives were employed on two occasions to add their weight to this argument. Political factors are indicated here. As Lee and Smith (1992) point out, senior engineers within CNC user companies are particularly well placed to make explicit the choices to be made when implementing such technologies as their command over the technology knowledge base affords them considerable expert power.

Ironically (perhaps inevitably) within six months of the flexible assembly system going into operation on the shopfloor the company was forced to decentralise control to the extent that operators, programmers and the line manager were put into programming teams in an attempt to overcome persistent quality problems with the new surface-mount technology. Operators learned the peculiarities of the machines very quickly through observation, and it was not uncommon for the office programmers to request access to the minutes of the shopfloor quality-circle meetings in their efforts to understand why the machines did not always function as predicted. This reflected earlier experiences with the CNC insertion technology where informal working practices developed by operators to overcome machine downtime problems had become institutionalised at the request of the technical operations manager. Interestingly, despite the success of this shift towards decentralisation (documented in Wall *et al.*, 1990), the technical operations manager expressed no desire for a similar shift in the operation of the new surface-mount machines. Indeed he was extremely unhappy about the emerging decentralisation of control of the latest technology as he felt it undermined the efficiency of the system. He was particularly concerned about what he called 'shopfloor tinkering' with the surface-mount machines. Although he did not dispute the evidence that decentralisation had brought improvements in productivity on both occasions, he felt that even greater improvements were achievable through centralisation. He told the author on one occasion:

> Management here keep losing their nerve. Just because we have had a few teething problems with surface-mount technology doesn't mean we should have to give up. Anyway, and this is the bottom line as far as I'm concerned, the whole thing

[decentralisation] is self-defeating. You lose flexibility once the workers start taking responsibility for machines . . . I mean, it took the company nearly six months to get them to agree to basic changes in working practices on the assembly line. A machine will do it in a matter of seconds!

Apollo UK and the negotiation of expertise

What, then, does this case study tell us about the negotiation of expertise within AMT job design decision making? First, it is clear that important decisions were taken at each step in the production chain. The design of the CNC surface-mount technology was shaped by technical experts within the producer organisation and a similar bias informed user company choice of the technology. In Apollo UK it was senior engineering management's reinterpretation of their board of directors' strategic and operational objectives in strictly engineering terms that led to the formulation of centralised job design objectives. Yet as Wilkinson (1983) argues:

> The important point is that the ambiguous and imprecise nature of the measurement of performance means that choices between alternative available designs and the way they are used (the way work is organised) cannot be explained simply in terms of technical and economic advantages. Where engineers and managers do use these explanations one must remain suspicious and expect to find additional motives (Wilkinson, 1983, p. 83).

Apollo UK followed a 'hard' approach to the design and implementation of the flexible assembly system. Once interpreted within such a structure of knowledge, labour becomes a problem ('noise') as it does not lend itself readily to simple and precise measurement. The members of the Apollo UK management development team, in their search for system robustness, effectively ignored the social context in which the system was to be embedded as this brought too many uncontrolled variables into their decision frame. In fact assumptions about job design were implicit in their decision making and alternatives to centralisation were constrained by the very nature of the technology chosen. When job design options were explicitly considered later, the very way the concept of efficiency had been defined meant that decentralisation was not a valid option as it would lead to under-utilisation of the machines' technical capabilities. It was only when the engineers' concept of efficiency was challenged by the realities of shopfloor operation that such an option came into the decision frame.

Analysis of the management development team's decision making revealed a cognitive disjuncture between the team members' technical expertise and the knowledge and expertise accumulated by shopfloor users in the operation of the previous generation of CNC insertion technology. The team utilised structures of engineering knowledge that were reflected in the assumptions made during design and implementation. These assumptions align closely with the list of assumptions identified by Pacey (1983) that are commonly made by technical design experts. These include:

- Assumptions based on academic specialism and the desire to maintain professional boundaries and demarcation lines.
- A tendency to overlook opportunities for improvements in the way a particular technology is used and to go for technical fixes instead.
- A failure to recognise the invisible and informal organisational aspects of technology invariably developed by users, which may often contribute to the more effective use of the technology.
- A failure to recognise the conflicts of values and interests that specific technological projects may entail.

Certainly technological innovations evoke opportunities and pressures to change established patterns of intraorganisational power relations. But since organisations vary in their cultural and political make-up, the types of opportunities and pressures for change will vary also. Given that the control and use of AMT (such as CNC surface-mount technology) is shaped not only by design but also by the social rules and knowledge structures embedded in an organisation, the relationships between technology and the preexisting balance of power in organisations is of key analytical importance. In the case of Apollo UK, the encroachment of worker on-the-job expertise into the operation of the CNC component-insertion technology was clearly seen as a threat by the technical operations manager – hence his resistance to the emergent decentralisation of control of surface-mount CNC. However the logic of efficiency employed during the design and implementation of the technology broke down six months after the technology was introduced and managerial pragmatism rapidly displaced engineering expertise. That said, most senior engineers were unhappy with the resultant job redesign and continued searching for a technical solution to the 'teething problem' of poor quality output.

It is possible to analyse these actions in political terms. Consider Layton's (1971) analysis of the rise of the mechanical engineering profession. This reveals how members of a professional group may seek to create a monopoly of knowledge and expertise in order to increase senior management dependence on their expertise, thereby increasing their autonomy and independence from management control. The freedom given to senior engineers at Apollo UK in the way they interpreted the board's broad set of objectives, and their resistance to the countervailing views of personnel and quality managers, may be interpreted in such a way. The exclusion of shopfloor users from the management development team can be seen as further evidence of the 'hard' approach taken by the user company engineers,

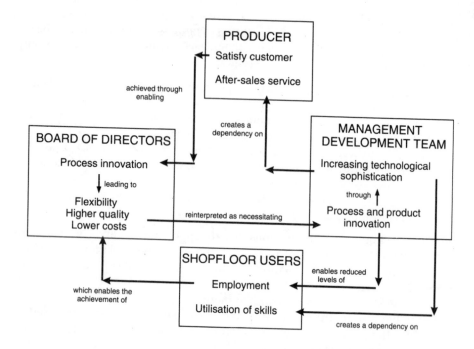

FIGURE 4.4   The web of dependency in Apollo UK

with shopfloor users being separated from the processes of design, organisation, management and control of the AMT system. As Burns and Flam argue:

> Such structuring processes are in the hands of relatively small elite groups. Of course, designers and producers in many instances, but certainly not consistently, shape and develop such systems according to their perceptions of the needs or demands of users and potential users as well as in terms of their own interests and organising principles (Burns and Flam, 1987, p. 301).

Yet there are limits to engineers' power to shape systems in terms of their own interests and expertise. As Figure 4.4 illustrates, engineers within both producer and user organisations become enmeshed in a broader web of dependency within the AMT production chain. An interpretation of Figure 4.4 starts with the assumption that the introduction of CNC at Apollo UK was a process of negotiation between a variety of knowledgeable actors and social groups, each attempting to further their perceived interests. The interests of the Apollo UK board of directors centred around successful process innovation leading to higher flexibility, higher quality and lower costs; whilst those of the management development team were more aligned to the need for higher levels of technological sophistication. The latter group's reinterpretation of the board's collective interest ultimately led to the board becoming more dependent on the technical expertise of the management team. Ensuing production problems also made the management team more dependent on the expertise of shopfloor users and the machine producers. The nature and implications of this dependency are explored in the final part of this chapter.

Discussion: technical enframement as constraint

In piecing together the accumulated field survey and case study evidence presented in this chapter, it is clear that decision making within the AMT production chain is enframed by structures of engineering knowledge and expertise that obscure the socio political underpinnings of AMT job design. This is not to suggest, in support of a technological determinist line, that engineering designers and managers in producer and user companies somehow collude to remove control from the shopfloor – the case of Apollo UK clearly illustrates the limits of such an undertaking. As Scarbrough and Corbett suggest:

> Even in minor applications, existing power structures will be disturbed by the introduction of new technology and, as a consequence the implementation process will reproduce (and amplify) existing strains and conflicts within the organisation. Hence, although management will often attempt to incorporate their production goals into the design of hardware and software, when such designs encounter the local and social realities of the use process, management objectives – and sometimes even the design configurations of the hardware itself – may become fragmented. This may lead to a further series of adjustments and 'sub-strategies' (Clark *et al.*, 1988) as front-line managers try to rescue the original goals of the technological change (Scarbrough and Corbett, 1992, p. 58–9).

By the same token, the evidence does not support the notion of weak technological imperatives and strong organisational choice. The picture that emerges is a process of design, development, implementation and use within which engineering knowledge and expertise predominates. It is only during the final use stage that different structures of knowledge become influential – by which time the choices of job designs may be severely constrained by social and political choices embedded in the technology during the technical design phase. As Marcuse (1968, p. 223) states, political interests are 'not foisted upon technology 'subsequently' and from the outside; they enter the very construction of the technical apparatus'. What is particularly interesting in the Apollo UK case is both the autotelic nature of the senior engineering managers' high-technology/centralised control argument and the way they would often justify their stance by reference to what the CNC technology itself would or would not permit.

Research by Clegg and Corbett (1986), Clegg and Kemp (1986), Cressey (1985) and Daniel (1987) reveals that a sequential approach to AMT design and implementation (whereby technical aspects are designed, with the social and organisational aspects considered too little and too late), as exemplified in the Apollo UK case, is the common approach taken by AMT-adopting companies both in Europe and the USA. What these researchers fail to articulate is the extent to which this represents a conscious political strategy (as many determinists would claim) or an inevitable consequence of the dominance of engineering expertise. Evidence presented here tends towards the latter interpretation, given the important role played by engineers' assumptions, values, expectations and knowledge about the context and role of AMT technology in influencing its design, implementation and use.

These values and assumptions, along with the technological artifacts themselves, are the formative aspects of structures of knowledge, or what Hill (1988) and Orlikowski and Gash (1994) term 'technological frames'. Such frames are actors' taken-for-granted definitions of organisational reality relating to the purpose, context, importance and role of technology. In the case of CNC producers, CAPIRN survey results suggest that, despite the rhetoric of customer choice created by the companies' marketing specialists, their technological frame is constructed around hard systems thinking that emphasises technological sophistication, the automation of mental work and the reduction of direct labour costs. Such a view was congruent with that held by the engineers within the management development team at Apollo UK. For the members of this group the value of the new technology was obvious, hence their failure formally to justify their investment and implementation decisions or to consider implications for job design and training at an early phase of the design and implementation process. The Apollo UK case reveals how technological frames are self-reinforcing to the extent that the management development team members refused to 'see' the benefits ultimately gained from the decentralisation of CNC programming. This accords with Dougherty's (1992) view that frames are resistant to change and may even reject knowledge that does not fit their system of meaning.

The technological frame of the shopfloor operators and personnel manager at Apollo UK was incongruent with that of the engineers insofar as the former's knowledge of technology-in-use was based on a less sophisticated technology and was mainly tacit and informal in nature. Within the engineers' technological frame, such subjective knowledge was, at worst, noise to be designed out of the technical system and, at best, knowledge in need of formalisation and codifying into software. Ultimately, of course, the engineers' frame saw technology-in-use as relatively unproblematic and of secondary importance to design and implementation (Orlikowski and Gash, 1994). This in part explains why technical experts in CNC producer companies resist the intrusion of marketing experts into the design process.

We have seen how the negotiation of expertise around the design, implementation and use of CNC technology incorporates political, processual and knowledge dimensions of social action. The technological knowledge afforded by CNC design has a political dimension insofar as it reinforces the expert power of engineers and engineering management at the expense of marketing experts in producer companies, as well as direct users and their support staff, who possess a more pragmatic and subjective knowledge of technology-in-use. This power has both structural and conceptual components (see Markus and Bjorn-Andersen, 1987). Technical experts exercise structural power over users by virtue of the former group's creation of technologies that prescribe systems architectures and routine operating procedures that give them formal authority over users or foster user dependence on them for important resources. This would appear to be true especially in producer–user relations. Technical experts also exercise conceptual power through their prioritisation of a 'hard' technological frame embodied within the artefacts they design and develop.

Ironically, of course, technical experts find themselves dependent on expertise derived from operators' frame of reference once the technology goes into operation on the shopfloor. Typically this then puts the onus on production line management to solve problems created by the internal inconsistencies of the technological frame that shaped the design and implementation of AMT. Despite the fact that operational problems are an inherent part of technological change, from a 'hard' technological frame of reference these represent a misuse of technology by operators and line management, rather than any failing on the part of engineers. Yet within the web of dependency associated with the introduction of new technology (see Figure 4.4), line managers who experience difficulties in resolving the resultant problems of technology-in-use are often tempted by technical solutions offered by the engineering experts themselves. CNC machines offer the capability of capturing data not only on machine performance (tool wear, spindle speeds, cycle times and so forth), but also on operator performance (time taken to load/unload parts, batch completion rates, calibration errors and so on). Such information can be obtained invisibly (that is, without the knowledge of the operator) whilst rendering the behaviour of the machine operator more visible and measurable to management. Although not taken up by Apollo UK's line management, such a technical fix is proving irresistible to many AMT user companies (see Sewell and Wilkinson, 1992; Shaiken, 1985).

The use of electronic surveillance thus broadens the web of dependency to enmesh virtually all key actors in the AMT job design decision making process within a systems engineering technological frame that defines their role and requisite level of expertise.

With regard to the processual dimension of technological change, evidence here reveals that the CNC production chain may not be as tightly coupled as researchers in the determinist camp maintain. Despite the rhetoric of customer-led innovation within CNC producer companies, there is little evidence to show that customers (or even the producers' own marketing personnel) have a direct influence on CNC design. Conversely producers do appear to influence user companies insofar as CNC designs prioritise and reinforce an engineering technological frame upon users' choice of systems architecture and job design. The resulting dependency on technical experts can lead to companies restructuring their operations simply to get the technology to function properly, rather than as part of a planned strategic choice. Small wonder, then, that the strategic management of expertise has become a key item on the agenda of many a corporate board meeting in recent years!

Yet strategic technological change, if it is to be successful, would seem to go beyond a rallying call for the judicious management of engineering expertise. Along with Pacey (1983) we have noted a consistent tendency for engineering experts to see only those parts of what Francis Bacon (1605) called 'the globe of knowledge' that are of direct technical interest. They reduce the globe to an 'expert sphere', which they know in detail, leaving a completely different view – a 'user sphere' – which they effectively ignore. Solving the problems this professional misperception creates is no easy task. For not only are engineers' professional identities predicated on this disintegration of the globe of knowledge, in pursuing their professional interests engineers seek to enrol others to their agency by positing the indispensability of their 'solutions' for their definition of other groups' 'problems' (see Callon, 1986). Over time this creates a web of dependency in which corporate executives themselves are caught.

Within the dominant technological frame that shapes and reflects the design and use of AMT, the solution of organisational problems that new technology produces must be handed over to technical experts, for it is they who are defined as possessing the technological efficiency to filter information and to command what constitutes the appropriate knowledge structures that can be applied. In this context, the key to strategic technological change must unlock the technological frame that bounds the negotiation of expertise. Indeed this imperative lies at the heart of the work carried out by those engaged in the development of 'human-centred' AMT (see Badham, 1991; Cooley, 1987; Corbett *et al.*, 1991). Perhaps, as Hill (1988) maintains, the reshaping of what constitutes valued technical knowledge is beyond the scope of business corporations (or isolated examples of experimental human-centred

AMT systems) and lies in a fundamental reorientation of secondary, and especially tertiary, education practices towards an integration of wider cultural, critical and historical perspectives into the education of the experts of the future.

References

Bacon, F. (1605) *The Advancement of Learning*, reproduced in R. M. Hutchins (ed.), 'Great Books of the Western World Series', vol. 30, (1978) (Chicago: Encyclopaedia Britannica, 1978).

Badham, R. (1991) 'The social dimension of computer-integrated manufacturing: an extended comment', *International Labour Review*, vol. 130, no. 3, pp. 373–392.

Barnes, B. (1977) *Interests and the Growth of Knowledge* (London: Routledge).

Bourdieu, P. (1989) 'Scientific field and scientific thought', in S. Ortner (ed.), *Author meets critics: reactions to 'Theory in Anthropology since the Sixties'*, CSST Working paper No. 32, (Ann Arbor, Michigan: University of Michigan Publications).

Braverman, H. (1974) *Labor and Monopoly Capital* (New York: Monthly Review Press).

Brown, J. S., Duguid, P. and Nunberg, G. (1991) *Design as Communication* (Palo Alto, Cal: Xerox PARC Publications).

Buchanan, D. and Boddy, D. (1986) *Organisations in the Computer Age* (Aldershot: Gower).

Burns, T. R. and Flam, H. (1987) *The Shaping of Social Organisation* (London: Sage).

Callon, M. (1986) 'Some elements of a sociology of translation: domestication of the scallops and the fishermen of St. Brieuc Bay', in J. Law (ed.) *Power, Action and Belief: A new sociology of knowledge?*, Sociological Review Monograph 32, (London: Routledge & Kegan Paul).

Child, J. (1985) 'Managerial strategies, new technology and the labour process', in D. Knights, H. Willmott and D. Collinson (eds), *Job Redesign: Critical perspectives on the labour process* (Aldershot: Gower).

Child, J. (1987) 'Organisational design for advanced manufacturing technology', in T. D. Wall, C. W. Clegg and N. J. Kemp (eds), *The Human Side of Advanced Manufacturing Technology* (Chichester: Wiley).

Clark, J., McLoughlin, I., Rose, H. and King, R. (1988) *The Process of Technological Change* (Cambridge: Cambridge University Press).

Clark, P. and Staunton, N. (1993) *Innovation in Technology and Organisation* (London: Routledge).

Clegg, C. W. and Corbett, J. M. (1986) 'Psychological and organisational aspects of computer aided manufacturing', *Current Psychological Research and Reviews*, vol. 5, pp. 189–204.

Clegg, C. W. and Kemp, N. J. (1986) 'Information Technology: personnel, where are you?', *Personnel Review*, vol. 15, pp. 8–15.

Cooley, M. J. E. (1987) *Architect or Bee?* (London: Hogarth Press).

Corbett, J. M. (1990) 'Factory of the future', in D. C. Wilson and R. H. Rosenfeld, *Managing Organisations: Text, readings and cases* (London: McGraw-Hill).

Corbett, J. M. (1994) 'Cultural aspects of the design of advanced manufacturing technologies', in P. T. Kidd and W. Karwowski (eds), *Advances in Agile Manufacturing* (Amsterdam: IOS Press).

Corbett, J. M. (1995a) 'The cultural and social shaping of factory automation: towards a new research agenda', in L. Rasmussen and F. Rauner (eds), *Industrial Cultures and Production: Understanding competitiveness* (London: Springer-Verlag).

Corbett, J. M. (1995b) 'The social shaping of machine tool design and manufacture in the UK: some preliminary findings', in L. Rasmussen and F. Rauner (eds), *Industrial Cultures and Production: Understanding competitiveness* (London: Springer-Verlag).

Corbett, J. M., Rasmussen, L. B. and Rauner, F. (1991) *Crossing the Border: The social and engineering design of computer integrated manufacturing systems* (London: Springer-Verlag).

Cressey, P. (1985) *Consolidated Report on the Role of Parties in the Introduction of New Technology* (Dublin: European Foundation Publications).

Daniel, W. W. (1987) *Workplace Industrial Relations and Technical Change* (London: Frances Pinter).

Dohl, V. (1992) 'The role of manufacturing technology markets in systemic rationalisation processes', in N. Altmann, C. Kohler and P. Meil (eds), *Technology and Work in German Industry* (London: Routledge).

Dougherty, D. (1992) 'Interpretative barriers to successful product innovation in large firms', *Organisation Science*, vol. 3, pp. 179–202.

Edwards, R. (1979) *Contested Terrain* (London: Heinemann).

Ehn, P. (1989) *Work Oriented Design of Computer Artifacts* (Stockholm: Arbetslivscentrum).

Forester, T. (ed.) (1980) *The Microelectronics Revolution* (Oxford: Blackwell).

Francis, A. and Grootings, P. (eds) (1989) *New Technologies and Work: Capitalist and socialist perspectives* (London: Routledge).

Gordon, R. and Krieger, J. (1991) 'Industrial culture, technological change and competitiveness: the US machine tool building industry', paper presented at the EC–Japan Conference on the Future of Industry in the Global Economy, Tokyo, November.

Hampden-Turner, C. (1970) *Radical Man* (New York: Schenkman).

Hill, S. (1988) *The Tragedy of Technology* (London: Pluto Press).

Kaneko, S. (1991) 'Technology bunching and development-oriented enterprise in machine tool industry: a study of a questionnaire in Japan', paper presented at the EC–Japan Conference on the Future of Industry in the Global Economy, Tokyo, November.

Kesteloot, R. (1989) 'Introduction of computerised numerical control and the rationalisation of production: the Belgian case', in A. Francis and P. Grootings (eds), *New Technologies and Work: Capitalist and socialist perspectives* (London: Routledge).

Landes, D. (1969) *The Unbound Prometheus: Technological change and industrial development in Western Europe, 1750 to the present* (London: Cambridge University Press).

Latour, B. (1987) *Science in Action* (Milton Keynes: Open University Press).

Layton, E. T. (1971) *The Revolt of the Engineer* (New York: Case Western Reserve University Press).

Lee, G. L. and Smith, C. (1992) 'British engineers in context', in G. L. Lee and C. Smith (eds), *Engineers and Management: International Comparisons* (London: Routledge).

Majchrzak, A. (1988) *The Human Side of Factory Automation* (San Francisco: Jossey-Bass).

Marcuse, H. H. (1968) *Negations* (London: Routledge & Kegan Paul).

Markus, M. L. and Bjorn-Andersen, N. (1987) 'Power over users: its exercise by system professionals', *Communications of the ACM*, vol. 30, pp. 498–504.

Metalworking Production (1987) *The Sixth Survey of Machine Tools and Production Equipment in Britain* (London: Morgan-Grampian).

Mueller, W. S., Clegg, C. W., Wall, T. D., Kemp. N. J. and Davies, R. T (1986) 'Pluralist beliefs about new technology within a manufacturing organisation', *New Technology, Work and Employment*, vol. 1, pp. 127–139.

Noble, D. (1984) *Forces of Production* (New York: Alfred Knopf).

Orlikowski, W. J. and Gash, D. C. (1994) 'Technological frames: making sense of information technology in organisations', *ACM Transactions on Information Systems*, April, pp. 25–41.

Pacey, A. (1983) *The Culture of Technology* (Oxford: Basil Blackwell).

Rhodes, E. and Wield, D. (eds) (1985) *Implementing New Technologies: Choice, decision and change in manufacturing* (Oxford: Basil Blackwell).

Rosenberg, N. A. (1982) *Inside the Black Box: Technology and economics* (New York: Cambridge University Press).

Ruth, K. (1994) 'Industrial culture and machine tool industries: competitiveness and innovation trajectories', in L. Rasmussen and F. Rauner (eds), *Industrial Cultures and Production: Understanding competitiveness* (London: Springer-Verlag).

Salzman, H. and Rosenthal, S. (1994) *Software by Design: Shaping technology and the workplace* (New York: Oxford University Press).

Scarbrough, H. and Corbett, J. M. (1992) *Technology and Organisation: Power, meaning and design* (London: Routledge).

Sewell, G. and Wilkinson, B. (1992) ' "Someone to watch over me": surveillance, discipline and the just-in-time labour process', *Sociology*, vol. 26, pp. 271–289.

Shaiken, H. (1980) 'Computer technology and the relations of power in the workplace', *Research Report 43* (Berlin: International Institute for Comparative Social Research).

Shaiken, H. (1985) *Work Transformed: Automation and labour in the computer age* (New York: Holt, Rhinehart and Winston).

Taylor, J. C. (1979) 'Job design criteria twenty years later', in L. E. Davis and J. C. Taylor (eds,) *Design of Jobs*, 2nd edn (Santa Monica: Goodyear Books).

Wall, T. D., Corbett, J. M., Martin, R., Clegg, C. W. and Jackson, P. (1990) 'Advanced manufacturing technology, work design and performance: a change study', *Journal of Applied Psychology*, vol. 75, pp. 691–697.

Wall, T. D. and Kemp, N. J. (1987) 'The nature and implications of advanced manufacturing technology: introduction', in T. D. Wall, C. W. Clegg and N. J. Kemp (eds), *The Human Side of Advanced Manufacturing Technology* (Chichester: Wiley).

Wilkinson, B. (1983) *The Shopfloor Politics of New Technology* (London: Heinemann).

Willcocks, L. and Mason, D. (1987) *Computerising Work: People, systems design and workplace relations* (London: Paradigm Press).

CHAPTER 5

Professional associations and the management of expertise

Jacky Swan

This chapter highlights two factors that give the management of expertise its contemporary significance. The first is the increasingly rapid diffusion and turnover of technological innovations in industry. Although it seems trite to begin with this oft-stated fact, the associated proliferation of specialist knowledges poses important new demands on management while creating niches for the formation of expertise. Secondly, the empirical study reported here shows the critical role of the professional networks that spring up around technological innovations; ostensibly to supply the needs of management but simultaneously promoting particular bodies of expertise in doing so. Such networks defy easy classification into the standard categories of professional formation. Their knowledge base is specialised and mundane, even esoteric, and exerts little 'disciplinary' force (Foucault, 1979). Nor do they convey much of the mystique associated with the classical professions. Indeed, part of their success is the normative espousal of a demystifying technical rationality. In this context their official role is usually defined as the disinterested transmission of neutral techniques through the liberal connectivity of the marketplace.

Yet despite their weak readings on the usual indices of professionalism, and even their denial of ideological or political ends, these diffusely organised social groupings may be extremely important structural influences on the social construction of knowledge within organisations. They may appear to be held together by nothing more than surface tension, but these floating knowledge networks are certainly capable, for instance, of reinforcing internal divisions of knowledge by importing interprofessional conflict into organisations. As innovation processes demand the application and recombination of different knowledge bases, this can aggravate political barriers with cognitive ones. More importantly, as outlined below, the so-called 'diffusion' of particular techniques also incorporates social choices and social shaping of the knowledges that guide innovation processes.

Introduction

With rapid technological change and increased complexity of knowledge, many organisations face demands for new types of efficiency based on adaptability and innovation (Bolwijn and Kumpe, 1990). In particular, competitive advantage can depend on an organisation's ability to design technological solutions to its problems (Clark and Staunton, 1989; Hayes and Wheelwright, 1984). This necessitates the presence of people within organisations who have the expertise needed to think about and develop technological solutions. Crucial to the innovation process are both the diffusion of knowledge among experts working within particular organisational fields and the appropriation of this knowledge into firm-specific solutions. Thus it is important to understand the networks through which knowledge relevant for technological innovation is socially constructed, shaped and diffused among communities of firms and across societies (Rogers, 1983). This chapter explores the roles of professional association networks in this process. A primary goal of professional associations is to disseminate knowledge and information about new developments to specialists in particular professional domains. Specialists who work in industry thus have the potential to act as 'technological gatekeepers' who, through their involvement in relevant professional associations, learn about new developments in their field and translate this knowledge into firm-specific solutions.

This chapter will consider the ways in which the social networks formed through professional associations play a role in constructing (and constraining) the knowledge and expertise that is relevant for innovation in particular problem domains, and it will illustrate how this role may differ across societies. Throughout the chapter these issues will be explored using examples from research carried out with professional production and inventory control (PIC) associations. Production and inventory control deals with problems of handling material flow around factories so that materials required for production are available without holding unnecessarily high levels of inventory. Production and inventory controllers face complex logistical problems in the timing and sequencing of production runs and inventory levels, usually in manufacturing industry although similar problems exist also in service industries (for example room bookings in hotels). In the past, PIC was carried out using manual systems that relied heavily on the tacit knowledge of PIC personnel. The case of PIC is interesting because recently there have been major technological developments in this area, with the introduction of complex information technologies that formalise the process using computer hardware and software to network the information used across different functional areas of the firm. Appropriation of these technologies (collectively referred to here as production and inventory control systems – 'PICS') has proved problematic.

Our research examined the professional PIC associations as networks relevant for the diffusion of innovation in Britain (the British Production and Inventory Control Society – BPICS) and in North America (the American Production and Inventory Control Association – APICS – and the Canadian Association of Production and Inventory Control – CAPIC). These associations concern themselves with similar areas of expertise in the different countries. Not only are they concerned with the same problem domain, but they are also related organisations. BPICS is a licensee of APICS, which means that it operates fairly autonomously but pays a fee to APICS so that it can use APICS publications and administer APICS-owned certification exams. CAPIC has a closer relationship with APICS and is one of its eight geographical regions. But CAPIC also maintains some independence by having its own rules and bylaws – a result of a merger of the two associations in the 1950s (Swan and Newell, 1995). Thus all three associations use APICS-owned certification programmes and literature but they also concern themselves with nationally-specific issues through their own unique dissemination activities. The empirical work began in 1989/90 and involved interviews with key players in these associations as well as surveys of BPICS members (1989 = 262 – see Newell and Clark, 1990) and CAPIC members (1992 = 189 – see Swan and Newell, 1995), and comparisons of these data with an earlier survey of APICS (Newell and Clark, 1990; Swan and Newell, 1993).

This research highlighted a series of interrelated issues concerned with (1) the roles of boundary spanners, who involve themselves in professional associations and therefore have the opportunity to monitor and translate the body of knowledge that they are concerned with; (2) the channels through which professional association networks shape knowledge and expertise in particular problem domains in different societies; (3) the roles of these professional associations in shaping the design of PIC technologies in Britain and North America by promoting technological solutions to industry; (4) the extent to which knowledge disseminated by these associations may be useful for developing technological solutions; and (5) the extent to which professional associations constrain knowledge and expertise that is relevant for technological innovation. These issues are discussed later in the chapter.

Innovation design and diffusion: the relevance of expertise

In the innovation diffusion literature, 'innovation' has been defined variously, but basically along the lines that it is 'an idea, practice or object that is perceived as new by an individual or other unit of adoption' (Rogers, 1983, p. 11). This approach distinguishes innovation from invention, which refers to the original creation or discovery of a new idea by suggesting that as long as the idea is perceived as new by the people involved, then it is an innovation, even though it might already exist elsewhere (Rogers, 1983). The emphasis, therefore, is on how new ideas are communicated through certain channels to a community of firms over time so that members of those firms can decide to adopt and implement that new idea; that is, innovation *diffusion* (Rogers, 1962; Rogers and Rogers, 1976). Thus models of innovation diffusion have emphasised the importance of social networks through which new ideas and expertise can be diffused to organisations that belong to the social system.

In the past the most influential models of innovation diffusion tended to focus on networks that forged links between suppliers of new technologies and users (Clark, 1987). These models showed central diffusion agents (for example software suppliers) how to get targeted audiences (that is, users) to adopt new 'best practice' technologies (for example Rogers, 1962). Broadly, this represents a 'broadcaster–receiver' approach, whereby users tend to be treated as recipients of knowledge and the problem of diffusion focuses on the need for suppliers to make users aware of available technologies and their advantages. This places the requirements for expertise squarely on the shoulders of the suppliers of new technologies, since it is they who need to be able to communicate the relative advantages of the technology they offer. Diffusion research has looked for ways of facilitating this process, for example by identifying which characteristics make some organisations more likely to adopt a new idea, and therefore more likely targets for suppliers, than others.

These models have been useful for understanding and encouraging the spread of new ideas where there is an identifiable 'best practice', for example the diffusion of family planning products to countries in the Third World from US relief agencies. Further, they have highlighted the importance of interorganisational social networks for the innovation process. However they have also been subject to a number of criticisms (see Clark, 1987). Among these (recognised by Rogers himself) is the risk of 'pro-innovation bias'; that is, 'the implication of most diffusion research is that an innovation should be diffused and adopted by all members of a social system' (Rogers, 1983, p. 93). In other words the models tend to assume that there is always an identifiable, single 'best practice' solution – a technological 'fix' to the user's problems. Typically the technological solution is comprised of both hardware (the tool itself) and software (information on how to use it – Rogers and Rogers, 1976), configured in a particular way. The only choice that the user needs to make, then, is to adopt this technological solution when it is relevant to do so. Innovation tends to be measured in terms of adoption, whereby organisations that have adopted more technologies are seen as more innovative, and problems with innovation are attributed to users implementing the best practice solution badly.

More recent research on innovation has suggested that the idea of a best practice technology with fixed parameters is oversimplified (for example Clark and Staunton, 1989; Leonard-Barton, 1988; Scarbrough and Corbett, 1992; Rogers, 1983). Instead it is more useful to see technologies as multifaceted bundles of knowledge that are socially constructed and designed, or configured, in various ways by organisations facing unique problems within unique organisational and societal contexts. Clark and Staunton (1989), for example, describe technology as knowledge that is manifested in the design of hardware, software, languages, organisational procedures, physical layout and so on. They emphasise the importance of appropriation; that is, typically, usage of technology will involve the configuration and reconfiguration of new ideas about both technical and organisational processes. They argue that supplier interests are focused on adoption (that is, rate of sales) and not appropriation. Suppliers may simplify technological solutions, playing up their chances of success and playing down their complexity. The problem for users is to unpack and reconfigure technologies that are presented by the supply side as best practice. Similarly, Berniker describes technology as 'knowledge that can be studied, codified, and taught to others' (Berniker, 1987, p. 10). Weick (1990) suggests that technology is an 'equivoque' (that is, something that can be interpreted in a variety of different ways) and therefore is something that requires sense-making on the part of the user in order to be managed. These approaches to technological innovation emphasise innovation as a process rather than an entity, during which knowledge is socially constructed (and reconstructed) and ultimately manifested as new technical and organisational procedures. This means that technology is inseparable from the knowledge and expertise of the social actors within the using organisation. Innovation and expertise are therefore inextricable.

These approaches have been supported by research findings that suggest that problems with technological innovation often occur before implementation during the time when firms are considering their problems and outlining potential solutions (that is, during agenda formation – Newell, Swan, and Clark, 1993). During this episode in the decision-making process firms may be persuaded to adopt technologies that they are simply unable to implement effectively. Thus outcomes of the innovation process have been found to depend crucially on *choices* on behalf of the user about how to design technological solutions so that they are appropriate for their problems. In making these choices, users need to access relevant knowledge and expertise by involving themselves in social networks with others both within and outside the boundaries of the organisation.

However, it is not simply a question of accessing a fixed body of knowledge because, through their engagement in social networks of various kinds, users will develop new expertise and play a role in constructing and reconstructing the body of knowledge itself. For example, a manufacturing firm may access knowledge about new systems by developing links with a software vendor, but may then reconfigure the software when it is implemented in the firm. This new knowledge could then be further diffused to others firms through, for example, user groups or via the supply side (Fleck refers to this as 'innofusion' – see Fleck, 1987). This is the approach taken in this chapter. It is reflected in a definition of innovation as 'the development and implementation of new ideas by people who over time engage in transactions with others in an institutional context' (Van de Ven, 1986). This definition both represents innovation as a process and recognises the importance of a variety of inter- and intraorganisational networks in the development of new ideas and expertise.

Inter- and intraorganisational networks in the innovation process.

Recently the literature on innovation has focused more on the role of interorganisational networks in the diffusion process (for example Abernathy *et al.* 1983; Rogers, 1983; Alter and Hage, 1993). The assumption is that networks between different organisations can encourage innovation because through such networks firms can exchange knowledge and, in some cases, the resources needed for innovation (Alter and Hage, 1993). The development of networks is seen as particularly important in the current competitive environment because demands for flexibility have led many large, vertically integrated firms to decentralise and shift their emphasis towards adaptiveness and innovation (for example Bolwijn and Kumpe, 1990). Through collaboration, organisations can benefit by gaining access to the knowledge and expertise needed to develop innovative ideas that are lacked internally (Alter and Hage, 1993). Later in this chapter these assumptions will be questioned, as it has become evident from other research that interorganisational networks, and in particular professional association networks, can also constrain the development of new ideas.

Some interorganisational networks link different firms in industry. These might include formal contracts between suppliers and customers, affiliated companies, interfirm collaboration on a project that is perceived to offer mutual benefits when completed, user groups and so on. These types of network may link firms that are competing in the same sectors of industry (competitive networks – Alter and Hage, 1993) or in different sectors (symbiotic networks). For example, a cartel may protect competitive firms in the same sector, whereas a borrower–lender arrangement offers mutual benefits to firms in different sectors. Much of the innovation literature has focused on these types of network, looking at formal contracts between firms. Alter and Hage cite several examples, including Japanese firms such as Hitachi who are linked to a network of suppliers involved in the creation of solutions to shared technical problems. Kabi in Sweden forged links with Gentech in the USA to develop and produce a new growth hormone, which was approved for sale only seven years after the project started. The formal contract between them allowed Gentech to produce the hormone for the North American market, and Kabi for the European market, but the two firms still continued to work together on research projects (Laage-Hellmen, 1989).

These interorganisational networks do not always involve formal contractual agreements among the organisations involved. Recently our research looking at interorganisational networks in the manufacturing industry has suggested that 'user groups' may be important for firms that are trying to discover new ideas. These user groups tend to develop on a fairly *ad hoc* basis and are driven by manufacturing firms, either in the same or different industrial sectors, who realise they are facing similar manufacturing or software problems. For example, the Business Excellence Club (BEC) in the UK has a fee-paying membership of around 80 manufacturing organisations across a variety of industries (including product and process manufacturing). Two representatives from each member firm, usually at middle or senior management level, are entitled to attend a series of four full-day BEC meetings a year, where they hear papers and attend workshops that are run by other BEC members. The emphasis is very much upon practitioners in industry learning about innovative solutions through hearing about the first-hand experiences (both good and bad) of other practitioners during presentations and workshops.

There is also the expectation that a lot of the most useful networking activity takes place outside the formal sessions and four days are scheduled to encouraged this. Open exchange of information is encouraged but members of this particular user group may come from firms that are in competition with each other so that protection of information that would give competitors an advantage is still an issue. Other user groups address this problem by excluding more than one company from the same sector from joining. Although the user firms themselves decide the agenda for the BEC meetings, the administration for the user group is carried out by an independent consultant (MRP Ltd) and membership is generally restricted to firms that have used MRP's courses. The benefits for the consultancy lie in the potential to develop new business through the group. Thus, although MRP does not directly dictate the content of the knowledge disseminated through the BEC, it does have some indirect involvement by being in a position to introduce or restrict membership.

Other types of network link firms in industry with a variety of other types of organisation, such as independent consultancies, educational institutions, government bodies, research institutions and so on. These types of interorganisational network have received relatively less attention in the literature, but are also potentially important for diffusing and shaping knowledge and expertise in the innovation process. The Business Excellence Club, above, is one example. Although the emphasis is on firms in industry learning from one another, the club would not have been founded and would be unlikely to continue without the involvement of the consultancy. Another example of this type of network is the consortium established by the White House Science Council in the USA which brought together firms in industry (for example AT&T) and provided a government-funded laboratory in an attempt to maintain competitive advantage in the semiconductor industry. In return for their investment in research, firms in industry are helped by university researchers and government laboratories to develop commercial products; in turn, as the product is developed and sold, the universities and laboratories receive additional staff posts and funding (Alter and Hage, 1993).

These types of interorganisational network may evolve for a variety of reasons and involve different types of social-exchange relationship, both formal and informal. Professional associations represent this type of network because they typically involve members from a range of occupational sectors. Their role in the innovation process and in the shaping of knowledge and expertise is the main focus of this chapter.

The literature cited above suggests that it is important for organisations to form networks of a variety of types with other organisations in order to share knowledge and resources and acquire the expertise needed to develop new ideas and innovative solutions to problems. The development of interorganisational networks occurs through individuals who are active in such networks and involve themselves in the process of constructing new forms of expertise through their social interactions. Individuals who are active in this way are referred to in the literature as 'boundary spanners' (Tushman and Scanlan, 1981). Through their networking activities outside the boundaries of their organisations, these individuals are able to acquire and shape knowledge and expertise in their particular field. Boundary spanners can then act as technological 'gatekeepers' by acquiring new forms of knowledge and expertise and then translating this into firm-specific technological solutions. However boundary spanning involves a two-step process of communication that necessitates the development of not only interorganisational networks but also *intra*organisational networks. That is, if boundary spanners are to be effective, they need to be able to develop internal networks so that they can disseminate knowledge within their own firms and, in doing so, influence the innovation process (Tushman, 1979). Thus the role of professional association networks in constructing and shaping knowledge relevant for innovation depends crucially on the body of knowledge that they promote, but also on the networking activities and occupational profiles of their members, who are able to construct and deconstruct this body of knowledge and translate it into firm-specific solutions.

Professional association networks and the social shaping of expertise

Professional associations see themselves as a crucial component of inter-organisational networks for encouraging the development of knowledge and expertise in particular problem domains (Lynch, 1989). They typically involve specialists who work, or have worked at some time, within those problem domains, although often across different occupational sectors, for example industry, academia, consultancy and so on. Members of professional associations have the opportunity to shape expertise in their field by acting as boundary spanners who construct and monitor a body of knowledge that is relevant to their particular area of specialism, and then translate this knowledge into their own industry (Allen, 1977; Tushman and Scanlan, 1981; Newell and Clark, 1990). To have an impact as boundary spanners, these members need actively to involve themselves in the professional association, to have developed communication networks within their own organisations, and to have an occupational status whereby they can influence decisions about technological innovation within their own firms. The role of a professional association will also depend on the body of knowledge that it promotes and the extent to which this knowledge is relevant for helping firms to appropriate innovative solutions. These issues are discussed next, using the example of professional PIC associations. A theme throughout is that the role of professional associations in shaping knowledge and expertise depends on their social and historical contexts and therefore differs across national boundaries.

Boundary spanners in professional PIC associations and their role in shaping knowledge and expertise

Our research[1] with PIC associations examined both the occupational status of members and the extent to which members were more or less actively involved in these different associations (Newell and Clark, 1990; Swan and

Newell, 1995). This suggested differences across countries in the nature of boundary spanning activity. One important difference in occupational status is that BPICS tends to attract members that are somewhat older, further on in their career path, and who stay with the association longer than do members of APICS or CAPIC (Newell and Clark, 1990; Swan and Newell, 1993). This is in part because BPICS restricts full membership to people that already have several years' experience in the production control area. In contrast, anyone with interests in production control who pays the appropriate fee can become a member of APICS or CAPIC. The knowledge diffused via these different national professional associations is aimed, therefore, at a qualitatively different audience and this is reflected in the content of their organised events.

In general, the activities organised through the British association are more oriented towards continued development of experienced production controllers, whilst the focus in North America is more on basic education. For example a large proportion of the APICS/CAPIC budget comes from providing and developing educational course materials. Members tend to join APICS/CAPIC at fairly junior operational levels so that they can take courses that will help them to pass exams leading to the Certificate of Production and Inventory Management (CPIM). The CPIM is administered by APICS and is recognised in North America as a basic qualification in production control. CAPIC has also developed a series of even more basic 'Principles' courses for training operators on the shop floor who have no prior knowledge or experience of production control, do not necessarily intend to enter careers in this area, but may need to know a little about it. Having passed their CPIM, or attended courses, many APICS/CAPIC members see no reason to remain with the association, with the result that the membership tends to rotate over a two- or three-year cycle, and tends to focus on more junior operational levels. This rotating membership is seen as problematic by APICS/CAPIC because it serves to perpetuate the image of these associations as low-status providers of basic educational materials.

Although BPICS offers CPIM qualifications, in Britain there is very little emphasis on being CPIM-qualified (reflected in the fact that many more APICS/CAPIC members than BPICS members take the CPIM). Instead BPICS promotes its own advanced diploma aimed at providing continued development for production managers who already have a basic grounding in production control. In addition, other activities (for example meetings, seminars and conferences) are oriented more towards continuing the development of qualified professional production controllers in the British association than in the North American associations. This is important because the activities that are oriented towards continued development and keeping up with the latest ideas may play a more significant role in the innovation process and in creating new forms of expertise. Another consequence for the diffusion of innovation is that that BPICS disseminates knowledge to people that tend to be more senior, or with more experience, and therefore more likely to be involved in choices about the design of technological innovation in PICS in their firms than members of APICS or CAPIC.

BPICS tends, therefore, to have a more elite status as a 'professional' association than its counterparts in North America. These differences stem from the ways in which BPICS attracts and retains members, but perhaps also from differences in the historical development of notions about professionalism and broad differences in the status of professional bodies across national boundaries (see also Lee and Smith, 1992; Child *et al.*, 1983). Child *et al.*, for example, argue that institutional value systems for professionalism are highly developed in Britain (compared, say, with Germany) and are embedded in the national systems of education and work organisation. These values 'both reflect and reinforce a particular approach to education and training which leaves the specification of qualifications in the hands of specialist occupational associations' (Child *et al.*, p. 72). In contrast, in other European countries the state has taken a more central role in vocational training, rather than leaving it to the professions.

Strongly embedded notions of professionalism in Britain contribute to the establishment of occupational specialism and help to promote knowledge and expertise within these specialist areas. However it also creates boundaries between specialist functions (Child *et al.*, 1983; Abbott, 1988) and this may prove problematic for the management of innovation and expertise in Britain, where such notions are highly developed. It is increasingly the case that complex information technologies require expertise across traditional functional boundaries in order to be fully appropriated. For example, developing and using integrated computer-aided production management technologies may require information systems specialists to write and develop the software, but it also requires sales specialists and purchasing specialists to provide the data needed to plan scheduling requirements, as well as specialists in production control to operationalise the system. Functional specialisation, which is established by strong professional identities, encourages experts in different functional areas to perceive technologies in different ways, to have different sets of priorities, work to different agendas and so on. In short, specialists from different functional areas will cognitively construct and represent knowledge in different ways (Swan and Clark 1992). This can cause political infighting among different groups of experts when confronted with technologies that cross traditional knowledge domains. Some areas of expertise will also be more strongly represented in the decision-making arena of some firms than of others and this can cause problems when firms are making choices about innovation design (Swan and Clark, 1992; Scarbrough and Corbett, 1992).

Examples of this can be seen in research that has looked at cases of firms in Britain that have tried to adopt integrated PICS (Waterlow and Monniot, 1986; Swan and Clark, 1992; Bessant and Buckingham, 1989). This research has revealed that firms have frequently experienced problems in appropriating these technologies and that major problems have occurred when firms have tried to go from using modules of PICS within traditional functional areas to integrating these modules across functions. Furthermore, the production control specialists, who had a great deal of tacit knowledge that was relevant to choices about innovation design, lacked power relative to other functional specialists (Swan and Clark, 1992). As a result they were frequently not involved in decisions about the design of technological solution and only became involved when their firms came to implement the bought technologies. Instead, decisions about technology design were taken by information systems specialists who were seen as the experts by senior management and, in some cases, were brought into the firm from outside. This led to problems in implementation, either because the people needed to operationalise the system (that is, the production controllers) did not believe it could solve their production problems, and/or because the new technological solution was incompatible with existing ways of managing production control within the firm (Swan and Clark, 1992). In some cases there was open hostility and resentment between production managers and information systems experts, and this contributed to a general lack of cooperation and commitment to a technological solution that was, in any case, felt by the production managers to be the wrong choice. The situation was one of 'them' not understanding 'our' production problems. Functional specialism is encouraged by the establishment of strong professional identities through, for example, professional associations. This can create difficulties of problem ownership when traditional areas of expertise are threatened and some professional groups are marginalised from the decision-making arena, and it can make it very difficult to adopt technological solutions that require new areas of expertise that integrate across functional areas (cf. Waterlow and Monniot, 1986).

These problems are likely to be typical in Britain because production is the one arena that has been least able to establish a clear identity for itself. Child *et al.* (1983) argue that this is because, historically, it has been dominated by well-established professions in non-production areas of expertise, for example finance and accounting. This can be seen, for example, in the structure of degree programmes in management (for example the MBA), where in most cases production management is not a core subject. Thus strongly entrenched notions about professionalism have served to perpetuate production as a low-status, low-paid occupation in Britain (Lawrence, 1980) and have put constraints on innovation and the development of expertise in the production area in British industry. Child *et al.* do not address the situation in North America, but it could be argued that there the idea of professionalism is also very well entrenched, as evidenced by the status, power and segmentation of many professional groups. However the dominance and success of the manufacturing industry in the USA this century may have made the production function less of a 'poor relation' in comparison with other areas of professional expertise (cf. Child *et al.*, 1983).

These issues about professional status and identity were considered important by the production personnel in our research. Even though, in Britain, BPICS tends to have a higher status than its counterparts in North America, it still struggles for recognition as 'the' professional body for production management. Production is an area of expertise that is characterised by a large number of professional bodies to which people might belong, including BPICS, but also engineering associations (for example the Institute of Mechanical Engineers) and logistics associations (for example the Institute of Logistics). These associations fight hard to protect their particular specialist niches and tend to compete for members and recognition. Attempts to form alliances between these associations in the logistics field has, so far, not been very successful. Production control also lacks a clear career path and production control specialists tend to come from a variety of different educational backgrounds. The knowledge domain relevant to production functions is therefore highly fragmented and this fragmentation is evidenced both in the number of different professional associations to which production control specialists belong (in addition to BPICS) as well as the variety of educational backgrounds that they have. Typically, production control experts in Britain have come into careers in manufacturing on a fairly *ad hoc* basis (Robertson, 1994). The career structure is not clearly established in production functions and again, this will tend to weaken the status of production in Britain and limit the role of professional associations in this area.

National differences in the status and power of professional groups has been found in other professions as well. For example the engineering profession has evolved differently in Germany than in Britain (Lee and Smith, 1992). In Britain there are a number of different engineering institutes and there is no clear route to becoming a 'professional' engineer. Engineers in Britain have lower status in managerial hierarchies, receive less pay, and are unionised and more closely identified with manual labour than are their German counterparts. Lee and Smith (1992) argue that this is due in large part to differences in the historical development of the engineering professions in these two countries. Indeed in Germany the notion of 'professionalism' via affiliation with professional associations outside of work organisations appears to be less strongly entrenched than in the UK (Raelin and Caroll, 1992).

The role of BPICS in the diffusion process in Britain is also limited by other factors, particularly its size. BPICS is about one quarter of the size of APICS and about half the size of CAPIC, taking national population differences into account. Therefore, by virtue of size alone BPICS may have a smaller role. Comparison of the surveys also revealed that the majority of APICS and CAPIC members work in the manufacturing industry (over 85 per cent) whereas in Britain only about 70 per cent of BPICS members work in manufacturing (surveys suggest between 50 and 75 per cent, probably depending on sample bias). In contrast BPICS has relatively more members working as consultants or as suppliers of hardware and software compared with North America. This means that in Britain much of the knowledge disseminated by BPICS reaches industry via suppliers and consultants, whereas APICS and CAPIC have a more direct link to industry in North America. This may be problematic for British manufacturing because, as seen, suppliers and consultants have their own interests to consider (that is, getting sales) and tend to present a simplified view of complex PIC technologies to users so that they are persuaded to adopt them. Success for the supply side is measured in terms of sales but sales can be a very poor indicator of usage, with many instances of firms failing to implement bought technologies because they did not have the knowledge and expertise needed to make appropriate design choices (Clark and Staunton, 1989; Swan and Clark, 1992). Professional PIC associations in North America may be able to provide knowledge directly to the users at the design stage, although their usefulness will then depend on the types of knowledge they promote. The roles of professional associations networks in the diffusion of innovation thus depend on complex relationships among the different occupational groups represented in the associations, differences in their ability to influence dissemination activities within the professional association, and differences in their ability to influence decisions about innovation design.

Dissemination channels and their exploitation

Professional associations use a variety of channels to disseminate a body of knowledge and shape expertise in their problem domain. These involve both formal, organised events and informal social exchange among people who meet through these events. In PIC associations the channels for dissemination, and the content of the body of knowledge itself, are directed by the headquarters of the respective associations, which employ a few full-time staff, but mostly by the members themselves who volunteer to organise the associations' activities. The most obvious channel is the dissemination of knowledge and information about technological developments directly through organised events such as meetings, conferences, seminars, educational courses, certification programmes, journals, magazines and so on. For example BPICS, CAPIC and APICS hold regular conferences and workshops at which members who work in industry, academia, consultancy and so on can share information. Some of the activities of CAPIC and BPICS are allied to

APICS, whilst others focus on specifically national manufacturing problems. For example, the members of all three associations receive APICS *Production and Inventory Management Journal*. In addition, members receive a more popular magazine that features advertisements, notices and short articles. BPICS has its own version of this magazine that focuses on issues specific to British industry (predominantly the manufacturing industry). Other dissemination channels include conferences, national and regional seminars, 'dinner meetings', educational courses, visits to companies and occasional social events.

The surveys of BPICS and CAPIC suggest a varied orientation towards these organised activities, with some members being very actively involved in these boundary spanning activities, while others only scan a few of the journals (Swan and Newell, 1993). The extent to which members are actively involved in these associations varies according to the occupational status of the members. For example consultants and academics tend to read more than junior and middle managers. Although the majority of members of all three associations work in the manufacturing industry, the minority in consultancy, software and hardware form a relatively strong presence at formal events. For example, at the recent 1994 BPICS conference around 50 per cent of the papers were presented by consultants or suppliers. Consultants are also involved in running BPICS educational courses and training programmes. Consultants and software suppliers also have a strong presence in the administration of CAPIC, and around half of the regional 'chapters' of CAPIC are run by members from these occupational sectors. Furthermore, some of the 'Principles in Inventory Management' courses were developed in Canada by a large consultancy firm.

Again, this suggests that the body of knowledge that is disseminated through the formal activities of these PIC associations is not politically 'neutral' but is heavily influenced by technology suppliers and consultants. Whilst many of the consultants are 'independent', in the sense that they do not align themselves with particular technical systems, their involvement in professional PIC associations is still driven by an interest in developing new business and persuading firms to adopt new technologies (though these may or may not incorporate new software). This will result in a 'pro-innovation' bias, where it is assumed that a new technology should be adopted by all firms in the user community (Rogers, 1983). Firms in industry, however, have a different set of priorities, with their interests lying in appropriating and using technologies – this may include decisions *not* to adopt technological solutions when they are not appropriate for their business. It may be just as important for practitioners in the manufacturing industry to learn about situations where there have been disasters with new technologies as about successes. Because many of the formal activities organised through these professional PIC associations are led by consultants and suppliers, they tend to focus on the positive features of technological innovation, and underrepresent the negative features (Clark, 1987). It is also very difficult to get members from industry to talk publicly about failures that reflect badly on them (because they were involved in the failure) or on their firms.

Professional associations can also use formal mechanisms to influence the content of the knowledge that is disseminated in their particular field by setting formal rules and regulations that govern what is seen as acceptable practise in their field. This can be achieved by awarding professional qualifications and controlling rules about membership. For example, in order to be accredited by the Institute of Personnel Management in Britain, degree programmes in personnel management must teach a particular range of topics to students. This accreditation is seen as important in attracting students to educational programmes because it indicates that the programme has been 'approved' and is more likely to be recognised by potential employers. Thus the content of the degree programme, and therefore the development of expertise among students of these programmes, is in part specified by the professional association. Again, the influence of different professional associations in this respect will vary across different professions in different societies depending on the power and status of the particular professional body.

For example in Britain the accountancy and finance professions have a great deal of influence in this respect, whereas BPICS has relatively little influence because the qualifications it awards are not uniformly recognised by employers. In contrast the CPIM is more widely recognised by employers in North America and therefore APICS is more able to shape expertise, albeit among a mainly junior production personnel, via the CPIM route. BPICS is currently trying to raise the profile of its qualifications by structuring them to provide a clearer path for career progression in the broad area of operations management, but this strategy will only be effective if the qualifications are recognised by industry. By setting formal rules governing membership and qualifications, professional associations can promote particular types of knowledge and expertise but can also have a constraining influence in the innovation process because access to the knowledge and the content of the knowledge base, is restricted.

Professional associations also have the potential to shape the diffusion process indirectly by providing a network of relatively informal social relationships or 'weak ties' among their members (Granovetter, 1973). For example, at BPICS conferences there are usually social events where people may exchange ideas in fairly loose informal ways, as well as during the more formal activities for knowledge dissemination such as formal paper presentations. Alter and Hage (1993) argue that such weak ties may encourage innovation because they establish a feeling of trust and willingness on the part of the people involved so that they are more likely to develop collaborative forms of exchange relationships. Similarly Shearman and Burrell (1987) emphasise the importance of informal social exchange in their social model of industrial development. Here industries at the early 'community' stage of development share higher levels of trust and reciprocity: 'relationships are predominantly social, dynamic, frequent, multi-faceted and *ad hoc.* 'Geographical proximity, together with shared perceptions and common values, lend themselves to a dense and rich set of social interactions in which little sense of the economic "cost" of any transaction is apparent' (Shearman and Burrell, 1987, p. 331). In this sort of community there is relatively free exchange of information and innovations are diffused rapidly.

Social interactions among members of professional associations may take this form of exchange. For example, in Canada CAPIC holds regional events run by volunteers, many of whom also work in the manufacturing industry. Interviews with these volunteers revealed that many gave their time to these events because they valued the idea of sharing with other people their experiences of dealing with problems in the production inventory control area. One remarked that, as a junior production inventory controller, he had benefited from his membership of the professional association and wanted to 'put something back' into it. Thus at these regional events there was identification with the community of production inventory controllers, as professionals experiencing similar problems, rather than with the specific firms for which individuals worked. Individuals from different manufacturing firms would therefore share information informally (that is, 'off the record') about experiences and failures with innovation within their own firms that, under different circumstances of more formal social exchange, they would perhaps not have revealed.

Most of the members of these professional associations in Britain and in Canada who worked in the manufacturing industry, worked for large firms, in spite of the fact that small firms represent a huge section of the manufacturing industry in both countries (see, for example, Fournier and Noori, 1991). This means that these professional association networks underrepresent the problems faced by small firms in the manufacturing industry (Newell and Swan, 1993). The same is likely to be true of other types of professional association since it is often the case that small firms do not have specialists in rather narrow functional areas who would take the time to become actively involved in such associations. The lack of involvement of small firms means that these firms are unable to either access or influence, at least directly, the knowledge base that they provide. Although indirectly they could learn through consultants or suppliers who are members, this route is problematic given the interests of these occupational groups. Alter and Hage (1993) argue that small firms have the most to gain from involvement in interorganisational networks that allow them to develop expertise and share the resources needed to adopt innovative solutions, but this research suggests that these firms lack power and influence in such networks, at least in the area of PIC.

The discussion so far suggests that professional associations have the potential to play a significant role in the innovation process through the establishment of both formal and informal social networks that shape expertise in a particular area. However it also suggests that this role depends crucially on the boundary spanning activities and occupational status of members and is likely to vary across national boundaries, depending on the historical and social contexts in which different professional groups emerge. However diffusion of knowledge does not necessarily equate with the appropriation and use of that knowledge in the innovation process when designing technological solutions. The next section, then, looks at the extent to which the knowledge that is diffused through professional association networks is actually translated into technological innovation within firms in industry, again using the example of PICS.

The relationship between professional networks and innovation

Previous research has demonstrated that implementation of PICS requires a blending of technical and organisational systems and practices, and that success or failure with implementation depends heavily on the decision-making processes involved during earlier episodes of agenda formation and selection, when crucial choices about the design of PICS are made (Waterlow and Monniot, 1986; Newell, Swan and Clark, 1993). This research has revealed that the design of PICS is shaped by managerial knowledge and expertise (both organisational and technical) and societal predispositions to problem solving (for example Clark and Staunton, 1989; Swan and Clark, 1992). Adoption of PICS poses complex problems for the user, but these problems tend to be underemphasised by the suppliers of hardware and software.

At least two broad design forms of PICS have emerged since the 1950s (Clark and Newell, 1992). American visions of PIC, manifested as materials requirements planning (MRP) and later as manufacturing resources planning (MRP2), incorporated American experiences of using centralised planning to control operations on the shopfloor so that material requirements orders are kept in line with inventory depletions. This represents a closed loop system where accurate data from the shopfloor feeds into centralised computer systems, which in turn plan the material requirements on the shopfloor (Corke, 1985). The reported benefits of MRP2 are reduced inventory, lead times and costs, better control over manufacturing practises and faster responses to market demands. Whilst some companies have achieved these benefits, many have not (Wilson *et al.*, 1994) and there are now questions about the extent to which the MRP2 'ideal' can exist in practise. Nevertheless MRP2 is still recognised by PIC personnel, especially by those who have completed professional courses in the UK and the USA. A second variant, just-in-time (JIT) emerged in Japan (Schonberger, 1982). Japanese firms (for example Toyota) facing pressure brought about by lack of space and small batch size reinterpreted American visions and produced an alternative based on simpler operations with production being controlled at the shopfloor level (Clark, 1987). This represents an open system such that components are only produced when they are pulled through the system by customer orders from outside.

Professional associations have been key players in shaping the design of PICS by promoting one variant or another to industry. In the USA, major suppliers (for example IBM) used academics and consultants who were also members of APICS to promote their vision of MRP/MRP2 to industry via the APICS network (Clark and Newell, 1992). The involvement of APICS was important because it meant that suppliers could relate their message to industry through a network that was perceived as politically neutral in their promotion of best practise. In this way, it could be argued that APICS actually constrained ideas about the design of PICS by promoting only one vision of best practice – MRP2 – as the fixed solution. However, as seen above, an important feature in appropriating technology is that firms consider alternatives when designing innovative solutions to their problems. Later, having witnessed Japanese successes with JIT, APICS again played a role when it sent members to Japan to learn about these new developments. APICS then used this information in a mid-1980s 'crusade' espousing the benefits of JIT, which led to some firms integrating their existing MRP2 systems with JIT philosophies.

In Britain the development of PICS has been heavily influenced by American visions, and even JIT appears to have come to Britain from Japan via the USA. Again, professional associations have played a role, with BPICS – because of its licensee arrangement with APICS – disseminating APICS material to industry. However BPICS is relatively small and thus appears to have had relatively less influence in the diffusion process. This, together with the absence of major firms in industry developing and promoting British solutions to PIC problems, has made the development and design of PICS in Britain somewhat more confused (Clark and Newell, 1992).

In Canada the development of PICS has paralleled that in the USA. The majority of Canadian manufacturing lies along the border with the USA and most of Canada's trade is with the USA, therefore it is not surprising that Canada should mimic US approaches to PIC problems (and vice-versa). CAPIC has also played a role in disseminating and promoting APICS-owned materials. However Canadian firms have generally been slower to adopt PICS technologies (Fournier and Noori, 1991). There may be a number of reasons for this. CAPIC has a smaller membership than other APICS regions and so has had a relatively lower potential to influence the diffusion process. CAPIC is also unique in that it is in the largest and least densely populated region of APICS territory. One of the difficulties that CAPIC faces, then, is that members may have to travel long distances to attend CAPIC-organised events. This makes attracting members difficult. Thus the CAPIC network is more widely dispersed than that of other APICS regions. This may contribute to the relatively slow rate of diffusion of PICS technology in Canada.

The same argument could apply to a variety of other interorganisational networks that are perhaps important for innovation in Canada and may be less likely to develop due to the geographical spread of firms. For example mimetic processes such as benchmarking, whereby firms observe and mimic structures and processes that are seen to be successful in other firms, occur less easily between firms that are physically distant (see, for example, DiMaggio and Powell, 1983). When such mimetic processes do occur in Canadian firms, they are likely to be between Canadian and neighbouring US firms on the Canada–US border as well as between different firms within Canada.

The above discussion shows that professional PIC associations can play a role in shaping the design of PIC technologies in Britain and North America. The studies of CAPIC and BPICS also provide support for the notion that expertise acquired through these professional association networks is used in practise for developing technological solutions in PIC. In particular, members who are more active in these professional networks are more likely to be involved in decisions about PICS within their firms and to work in firms that have developed their PICS to a greater extent (Swan and Newell, 1995). Of course it could be the case that firms that have developed more technologies in PIC tend to employ specialised production control personnel who are members of professional associations in this area. However respondents also perceived the professional association to be a more useful network for learning about technological developments in their field than other types of interorganisational network that link them to specific occupational groups (government, academia, other firms in industry, consultants and hardware/software suppliers). Through the professional association members can establish links with most of these other occupational groups when it is helpful to do so.

The surveys of BPICS and CAPIC found that development of technologies in PICS was predicted by involvement in the activities of these professional associations and also suggested that the activities oriented towards continued professional development were more important in the innovation process than those oriented towards basic education (Swan and Newell, 1995). This again suggests a source of difference in the roles of professional associations in different countries, with BPICS being more involved than CAPIC in the kinds of activity that seem to be relevant for developing technologies in production control. The surveys also found that technological development is more likely when members of an association have good communication networks with others within their own organisation. This supports the idea that knowledge promoted through a professional organisation only influences innovation in firms to the extent that it is translated within the organisation by members with well-developed intraorganisational networks; that is, that inter- and intraorganisational networks are important for boundary spanning (Swan and Newell, 1994).

Constraints on innovation through professional association networks

The previous section suggested that professional associations can be active in shaping and promoting knowledge and expertise in specialist areas, and that this knowledge is used to develop and design technological innovation, at least in relatively large firms. With evidence like this it is tempting to conclude that the role of a professional association network is to encourage innovation through the sharing and development of expertise, and that this translates into productivity gains for industries who have more professionals. However this is too simplistic. The remainder of this chapter will attempt to show that in some senses professional associations also constrain the development of new forms of expertise and innovation.

First, supply-side involvement in professional associations is important because it supports the perspective that professional associations are not homogeneous communities of individuals, but rather comprise individuals with different values and interests with different opportunities to shape the body of knowledge that is promoted through that professional association (Drazin, 1990). Drazin suggests that the structural–functional perspective, which has dominated the study of the role of professionals in the innovation process, is fundamentally flawed. This is because it assumes that all professional groups collectively share values and motivations towards contributing to the development of knowledge within their particular field (see, for example, Merton, 1967). Thus professional values are for richness of experience, for seeking external sources of knowledge, for contributing to standards of professionalism, for advancing the field and so on. These values are assumed to encourage and promote innovation and expertise within employing organisations. Professionals are seen as 'role incumbents who serve as transfer agents to facilitate the movement of information between the profession and the employing organisation' (Drazin, 1990, p. 249), thereby ensuring innovativeness in organisations that have more professional employees. This structural–functional approach does not distinguish between the interests of different professional groups, nor does it address hetero-geneity of interests and expertise within the professional group itself. Professionalism simply becomes another feature of an organisation that makes it more likely to adopt innovative ideas (much as spending on research and development, or investment in training might). The structural–functional perspective, then, makes the organisation and its professional subgroups the unit of analysis rather than the profession itself (Drazin, 1990).

The discussion earlier in this chapter shows that the structural–functional approach is too simplistic. For example, in highly fragmented knowledge domains such as PICS, professional groups compete with other professional groups for membership and status. Differences of interest also vary among different stakeholders within professional groups themselves. Drazin (1990) suggests that a radical–functional perspective on the role of professionals in the innovation process is more useful (cf. Child *et al.*, 1983). This recognises heterogeneity both between and within professional groups. Professional groups are seen as consisting of multiple social segments with divergent political interests oriented towards maintaining power, status, and control over particular knowledge domains (Abbott, 1988). According to this perspective, a positive relationship between professionalism and innovation is not automatic because innovation entails changes in the social system, threats to power and status, and redefinition of tasks and responsibilities. Where innovation threatens to undermine the status and power of a particular profession, the members of that profession may be motivated to preserve the status quo.

For example, in Britain and North America the professional PIC networks have been fairly active in promoting computer-aided technologies such as MRP2. These rely heavily on the knowledge and expertise of production controllers to input accurate data into the systems. They also depend on the development of computer software systems and open opportunities for system suppliers. These forms of production control technologies could therefore serve to enhance the status of members of the professional PIC associations. They also maintain the management of production as a centralised planning activity. Alternatively, production control systems designed around the philosophies of just-in-time (for example Kanban) do not necessarily rely on developments in software and may serve to simplify the production control function. It is feasible that this is one reason why professional PIC associations have not, at least until fairly recently, promoted JIT solutions. Perhaps the development of these types of solution are just not in the interests of their members (some of whom are system suppliers) because they threaten to undermine their roles as experts. With the apparent success of the Japanese it is now impossible to ignore alternative forms of production control, but these are being promoted through the associations as systems for further streamlining and complementing existing MRP2 systems. Whilst professional associations promote the development of new technologies, they promote some types of technology and not others (Drazin, 1990), whereas research on innovation (discussed above) suggests that alternative designs are possible and that these need to be considered, unbundled and reblended in order to be appropriated in particular organisational contexts (Clark and Staunton, 1989). Only then are gains in productivity likely.

The development of professional association networks may also serve to constrain innovation through a process of 'isomorphism' (DiMaggio and Powell, 1983). This is a process whereby organisations operating within highly interconnected fields come to resemble one another, but not necessarily for reasons of improved efficiency. The argument is that when organisational fields are highly interconnected and have well-established social networks, innovation diffusion occurs more rapidly. Although, initially, innovations are adopted because they result in efficiency gains, they soon become established ways of working so that other firms adopt these 'best practice' ideas, not because they offer efficiency gains, but in order to maintain power and credibility within their field. Professional associations, whilst encouraging more rapid diffusion of new ideas, also help to establish norms of acceptable behaviour and best practice. Once these norms are established, the development of further new ideas that fall outside these accepted ways of operating are constrained and organisations come to resemble each other.

DiMaggio and Powell (1983) describe three mechanisms through which isomorphism can occur – normative, mimetic and coercive – and professional associations could have an influence on any or all of these. Professional associations could encourage isomorphism through normative mechanisms whereby members of a profession develop similar ideologies, values and expertise. Professional association networks may also encourage isomorphism through mimetic processes whereby firms mimic other firms in the same sector. For example they arrange company visits and seminars whereby members can learn from other firms about 'leading edge' best practice. Finally, coercive mechanisms are possible through the establishment of formal rules about membership and qualifications.

The concept of isomorphism is particularly interesting because it explains how technically inefficient innovations can become diffused (Abrahamson, 1991). For example, as seen earlier, failures with technological innovation are rarely discussed during the formal events organised by professional associations. Instead these events tend to focus on successes and thereby simplify complex and potentially inefficient technologies. Similarly there are examples of manufacturing firms that have chosen new and complex computer-aided technologies, not because they improve efficiency, but because they need to have a 'high technology' image among customers (Swan and Clark, 1992). In other instances firms have been forced to adopt particular types of software system because their customers have demanded it or because they are subsidiaries of parent organisations that have demanded it, even though the new software is actually incompatible with their systems and actually reduces their own technical efficiency (Swan and Clark, 1992; Webster and Williams, 1993). The process of isomorphism explains how interorganisational networks such as professional associations may simultaneously encourage the diffusion of innovation and the development of new forms of expertise, whilst constraining the design of innovative solutions that are diffused or the types of expertise that is developed. Again their role in shaping (and constraining) expertise will be dependent on the national and organisational contexts in which these interorganisational networks develop.

Summary and conclusions

This chapter has examined the ways in which professional associations, as interorganisational networks, have a role in the social construction of knowledge and expertise in particular problem domains. It has been suggested that the knowledge base available through a professional association can be very useful in developing and diffusing new forms of expertise and in designing technological solutions. However the role of professional associations in the innovation process depends on the boundary spanning activities and occupational status of their members, who are involved in constructing (and deconstructing) this knowledge base and translating it into firm-specific solutions.

The case of PIC suggests that it is too simplistic to assume a positive relationship between involvement in professional associations and the degree to which firms appropriate innovative solutions. Professional associations are not politically 'neutral' networks and may, in some cases, serve to constrain the development of new ideas within knowledge domains. Again this depends on the body of knowledge that they promote and on their membership. For example professional PIC associations, under the influence of the supply side, have tended to adopt a proinnovation bias and have promoted only a limited vision of PICS design to industry. This is problematic given that there is now a lot of evidence that innovation design is crucial to subsequent implementation and usage of technological solutions.

The status and power of professional groups varies across societies, in part due to differences in the historical development and importance of professionalism. An important conclusion here, then, is that national context must be taken into account when assessing the roles of professional associations in shaping knowledge and expertise. Strategies for the management of expertise through the professional association route may be more appropriate in some societies than in others. In Britain, for example, expertise in the broad area of logistics might be further developed if the relevant professional associations could find a way of providing a clearer path for careers in logistics. This could enable their members to increase their status, relative to other strongly established professional groups, and have more influence in decision arenas. In Germany, where the concept of professionalism is different, this approach might not be relevant. Further comparative work is needed if the role of professional is to be more fully understood.

Although there are important opportunities for developing and diffusing expertise via professional association networks, there are also constraints on innovation by establishing such networks. Professional associations could help to fragment knowledge domains so that innovation requiring expertise that crosses professional boundaries of different becomes more problematic. Further, the development of professional association networks could constrain the development of new ideas through processes such as isomorphism, or encourage the diffusion of inefficient technologies. It is clearly important to address these issues if professional association networks are to play a useful role in the development and management of expertise in the future.

Note

1. This research was carried out with Sue Newell, University of Warwick, and Peter Clark, University of Aston, and compared the roles of professional PIC associations in Britain, the USA and Canada.

References

Abbott, A. (1988) *The System of Professions* (London: University of Chicago Press).

Abernathy, W. J., Clark, K. and Kantrow, A. M. (1983) *Industrial Renaissance: Producing a positive future for America* (Cambridge MA: MIT Press).

Abrahamson, E. (1991) 'Managerial fads and fashions: the diffusion and rejection of innovations', *Academy of Management Review*, vol. 16, pp. 586–612.

Allen, T. J. (1977) *Managing the Flow of Technology* (Cambridge MA: MIT Press).

Alter, C. and Hage, J. (1993) *Organisations Working Together* (Newbury Park CA: Sage).

Berniker, E. (1987) 'Understanding technical systems', Symposium on Management Training Programs: Implications of New Technologies, Geneva.

Bessant, J. and Buckingham, J. (1993) 'Innovation and organisational learning: The case of computer-aided production management', *British Journal of Management*, vol. 4, pp. 219–234.

Bolwijn, P. and Kumpe, T. (1990) 'Manufacturing in the 1990s – productivity, flexibility and innovation', *Long Range Planning*, vol. 23, pp. 44–57.

Child, J., Fores, M., Glover, I. and Lawrence, P. (1983) 'A price to pay? Professionalism and work organisation in Britain and West Germany', *Sociology*, vol. 17, pp. 63–78.

Clark, P. (1987) *Anglo-American Innovation* (New York: De Gruyter).

Clark, P. and Newell, S. (1992) 'Societal embedding of production and inventory control systems: American and Japanese influences on adaptive implementation in Britain', *International Journal of Human Factors in Manufacturing*, vol. 3, pp. 69–81.

Clark, P. and Staunton, N. (1989) *Innovation in Technology and Organisation* (London: Routledge).

Corke, D. (1985) *A Guide to CAPM* (London: Institute of Production Engineers).

Di Maggio, P.J. and Powell, W.W. (1983) 'The iron cage revisited: Institutional isomorphism and collective rationality in organized fields', *American Sociological Review*, vol. 48, pp. 147–60.

Drazin, R. (1990) 'Professionals and innovation: Structural–functional versus radical–structural perspectives', *Journal of Management Studies*, vol. 27, pp. 245–63.

Fleck, J. (1987) Innofusion or diffusation? The nature of technological development in robotics', Edinburgh University PICT Working Paper No. 4, Edinburgh.

Foucault, M. (1979) *Discipline and Punish: The birth of the prison* (Harmondsworth: Penguin).

Fournier, B. and Noori, H. (1991) 'Technology Adoption: How Canadian Companies are Measuring Up', ASAC Conference, Niagara Falls, Canada.

Granovetter, M.S. (1977) 'The strength of weak ties', *American Journal of Sociology*, vol. 78, pp. 1360–80.

Hayes, R.H. and Wheelwright, S. (1984) *Restoring Our Competitive Edge: Competing through manufacturing* (New York: Wiley).

Laage-Hellmen, J. (1989) *Technological Development in Industrial Networks* (Uppsala, Sweden: University of Uppsala Publishers).

Lawrence, P. (1980) *Managers and Management in West Germany* (London: Croom Helm).

Lee, G.L. and Smith, C. (eds) (1992) *Engineers and Management: International comparisons* (London: Routledge).

Leonard-Barton, D. (1988) 'Implementation as mutual adaptation of technology and organisation', *Research Policy*, vol. 17, pp. 251–67.

Lynch, J. (1989) 'Looking overseas for new members', *Association Management*, May, pp. 110–15.

Merton, R.K. (1967) *On Theoretical Sociology* (New York: Free Press).

Newell, S. and Clark, P. (1990) 'The importance of extra-organisational networks in the diffusion and appropriation of new technologies: the role of professional associations in the USA and UK', *Knowledge: Creation, Diffusion, Utilization*, vol. 12, pp. 199–212.

Newell, S. and Swan, J. (1993) 'The potential role of a Canadian professional association in the dissemination of knowledge', *British Journal of Canadian Studies*, vol. 8, pp. 241–259.

Newell, S., Swan, J.A. and Clark, P. (1993) 'The importance of user design in the adoption of new information technologies: The example of production and inventory control systems (PICS)', *International Journal of Operations and Production Management*, vol. 13, pp. 4–22.

Raelin, J. and Caroll, W.E. (1992) 'Cross-cultural implications of professional/management conflict', *Journal of General Management*, vol. 17, pp. 16–30.

Robertson, M. (1994) 'The role of networks in the diffusion of innovation', unpublished MA dissertation, University of Warwick Business School.

Rogers, E. M. (1962, 1983) *Diffusion of Innovations* (New York: Free Press).

Rogers, E. M. and Rogers, R. A. (1976) *Communication in Organisations* (New York: Free Press).

Scarbrough, H. and Corbett, M. (1992) *Technology and Organisation: Power, meaning and design* (London: Routledge).

Schonberger, R. J. (1982) *Japanese Manufacturing Techniques: Nine hidden lessons in simplicity* (New York: Free Press).

Shearman, C. and Burrell, G. (1987) 'The structures of industrial development', *Journal of Management Studies*, vol. 24, pp. 325–45.

Swan, J. A. and Clark, P. (1992) 'Organisational decision-making in the appropriation of technological innovation: cognitive and political dimensions, *European Work and Organisational Psychologist*, vol. 2, pp. 103–27.

Swan, J. A. and Newell, S. (1993) 'The role of professional associations in the diffusion and shaping of production management technologies: A comparison of Britain and North America', in A. Bramley and T. Mileham (eds), *Advances in Manufacturing Technology VII*, pp. 191–5 (Bath: Bath University Press).

Swan J. A. and Newell, S. (1995) 'The role of professional associations in technology diffusion', *Organisation Studies*, vol. 16 (in press).

Tushman, M. (1979) 'Managing communication networks in R&D laboratories', *Sloan Management Review*, Winter, pp. 37–49.

Tushman, M. and Scanlan, T. (1981) 'Boundary spanning individuals: Their role in information transfer and their antecedents', *Academy of Management Journal*, vol. 24, pp. 289–305.

Van de Ven, A. H. (1986) 'Central problems in the management of innovation', *Management Science*, vol. 32, p. 5.

Waterlow, G. and Monniot, J. (1986) *A Study of the State of the Art in Computer-Aided Production Management*, ACME Research Directorate Report (Swindon: SERC).

Webster, J. and Williams, J. (1993) 'The Success and Failure of Computer-Aided Production Management – the Implications for Corporate and Public Policy', Edinburgh PICT Research Report No 2., Edinburgh.

Weick, K. E. (1990) 'Technology as an equivoque: sensemaking in new technologies', in P. S. Goodman and L. S. Sproull (eds), *Technology and Organisations* (San Francisco: Jossey-Bass), pp. 1–45.

Wilson, F., Desmond, J. and Roberts, H. (1994) 'Success and failure of MRPII implementation', *British Journal of Management*, vol. 5, pp. 221–40.

CHAPTER 6

Strategic IT in financial services: the social construction of strategic knowledge

Harry Scarbrough

Our analysis of the management of expertise has begun to highlight the problems and contradictions of the managerial process around expert groups. Clearly, expertise is not simply available 'on tap' to be inserted into decision-making processes at management's discretion. Nor do its implications boil down to the carrot and stick issues of motivation and control. In contrast, we have developed a framework that highlights the role of expertise in the social construction of knowledge. This chapter applies that framework to managerial attempts to apply information technology (IT) to strategic organisational goals. It focuses on the financial services sector and in that context deals with questions such as the role of information systems (IS) in shaping corporate strategy, and more broadly with the possibility of organising expert knowledge to support the strategic agendas defined by top management.

Strategising IT

In the literature, the question of 'strategic IT' is addressed from two major standpoints, one optimistic and one sceptical. The optimistic view is to be found in the extensive writings that deal with normative models of 'strategic IT' (for example Earl, 1989) or 'strategic information systems' (Firdman, 1991). This takes the view that strategic uses of IT are based on a rational, adaptive response to the contingencies of a changing environment. A flavour of such contingent effects on the strategic uses of IT can be gleaned from the matrix suggested by McFarlan and McKenney (1983).

The sceptical view on the other hand is reflected in an equally extensive body of critical, empirical studies of IS and IT implementation (for example Willocks and Mark, 1989; Murray, 1989). Apart from registering the comparative failure of rational approaches, this literature generally takes a *processual* approach to strategy formation around IT, highlighting the political machinations of different groups as they compete to control IT developments. The *contingency* model of strategic IT is therefore seen as a rhetorical flourish – an 'ideal-typical model' as Currie (1994) puts it – concealing political agendas.

In addressing the strategic IT debate, our study of strategic IT in the Scottish financial services sector[1] took as its focus the management of expertise. In half a dozen institutions, the development of major IT projects was related to the formation and organisation of IS expertise, focusing principally upon the management of the in-house IS function. This focus partly reflected some powerful *prima facie* evidence from both rational and processual views alike as to the importance of the distribution of expertise in shaping the practicability and success of strategic IT projects. A particular concern in both literatures

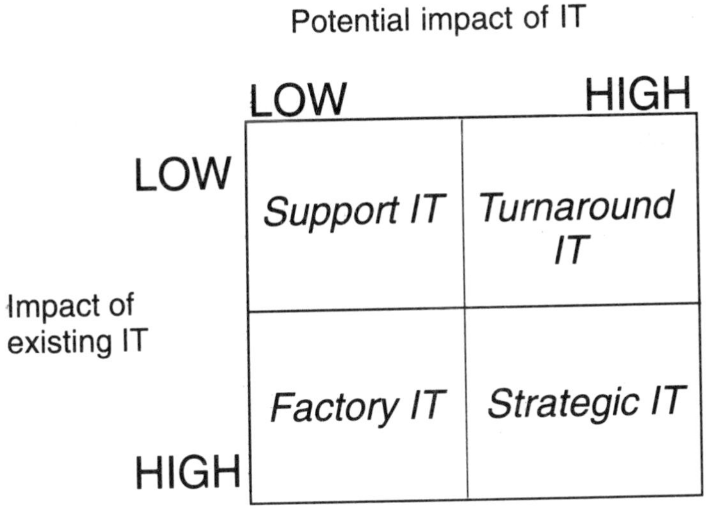

FIGURE 6.1   Potential impact of IT

Source: adapted from McFarlan and McKenney, 1983.

was the widely reported rift between the knowledge-bases of top management and IS experts respectively. Thus Currie was by no means the first to comment on 'the difficulty of fusing business awareness with technical specialism' (Currie, 1994, p. 25) as a key issue in developing IT strategies. The lack of such integration, which is widely recorded in the management literature on IT (Mumford and Ward, 1968; Dey *et al.*, 1988; Gunton, 1990), is generally seen as reflecting structural constraints: top management have privileged access to knowledge of business goals and the wider environmental context while IS specialists control detailed knowledge of the technology. This is seen as preventing the assembly of the unified knowledge base that strategic technological projects require (Shrivastava and Souder, 1987).

A flavour of the strategic problems posed by these structural divisions of knowledge is conveyed by the following quote from our study. This is an IT manager's account of top management's role in the development of a customer database ('Client Management') in a life insurance company:

> They are all very capable and talented chaps, but they're heavy into politics. And they know which way the markets move but as to actually having information about something as boring as how Client Management would work . . . I think that might be kept away from the senior executives. . . I don't think they are likely to have enough information to be able to judge in absolute terms.

Although this kind of comment and the wider debates on strategic IT give great support to a focus on the management of expertise, the gulf between management and IS knowledges needs to be interpreted quite carefully. It is tempting, for instance, to take a mechanistic view of the means by which these different business and IT knowledges can be integrated. One corollary of the strategic IT debate, for instance, has been a call for the development of 'hybrid' business and IT skills through the shaping of internal career paths (British Computer Society, 1990; Earl and Skryme, 1990). A loose coalition of pundits and IS managers, centred on the British Computer Society, has urged the development of 'hybrid managers'. Unlike their narrowly specialised predecessors, these would be 'managers possessing business understanding, technical competence and organisational knowledge and skills' (British Computer Society, 1990, p. 3). These managers would be developed through a combination of IS experience, together with job rotation into business units and various forms of training and management development (Earl and Skryme, 1990).

This call for hybridity certainly expresses one strand in the evolution of IS expertise, namely the fusion of technical and organisational knowledges as reflected in the creation of systems analyst and business analyst roles (Friedman, 1989). However that evolutionary pattern also demonstrates the extent to which the formation of expertise is contingent on wider technological and occupational changes; in this case the advent of distributed IT and the operation of labour markets for IT skills. Given the role of these wider contingencies, the idea that hybrid expertise can be created as a matter of management policy is akin to a Frankenstein vision of creation in which living experts can be produced simply by assembling the requisite bits and pieces of knowledge. To underline the tendentious nature of this enterprise, this conceit unhappily echoes the, now discredited, assumptions of the designers of the earliest expert systems.

In contrast to these mechanical and functional treatments, the research described below took as its premise the socially constructed character of knowledge. Rather than seeing knowledge as free-floating ideas and cognitions, readily mustered in the appropriate places, social construction involves, in the first instance, a recognition of the social structural constraints on the production and distribution of knowledge. In this context the latter would encompass, for example, career patterns, occupational formation and the operation of labour and product markets. Again, to say that knowledge is socially constructed is not simply an assertion that social relations are integral to its development, but also points to the role of social action in actively constructing knowledge.

Applying these concerns to the debate around strategic IT amounts to both a critique and a challenge. Thus, on the critical side, the social constructionist approach cautions against both the rational and the political models of 'strategic IT'. Since it rejects assumptions of an objective environment (Smircich and Stubbart, 1985), it is bound to be sceptical about the ability of organisations rationally to identify and adapt to relevant contingencies in such an environment. Equally, though, it does not subscribe to the view that the internal political reality is the dominant one. Rather its focus is on the way in which social groups within and across organisations actually create the realities that seem to confront them through the painstaking construction of interpretive knowledge. This in turn creates the challenge that is addressed by the case-study material below. This is the challenge of explaining the process of strategy making in terms of the distribution of expertise and the empowering effects of particular bodies of knowledge.

Although the expertise perspective distanced our study from both the contingency and processual models of strategic IT, this did not mean that their concepts and empirical categories were entirely irrelevant, especially if interpreted in a non-deterministic way. For example, with evidence of the increasingly widespread diffusion of strategic IT concepts within organisations (Wilson, 1989), it would be crass to ignore their impact on managerial practice or to see it as a purely rhetorical exercise. Rather the rational model of strategy may provide a political resource for different groups within management (Knights and Morgan, 1991), and may also offer useful instruments for handling the uncertainties posed by the expanding roster of tasks addressed by IT applications. Exogenous forces are neither elevated to the status of imperatives nor reduced to the mental constructs of senior managers. Instead we see such contingencies being *enlisted* by interorganisational and occupational networks, suppliers and, of course, expert groups within the organisation to support the construction of their own particular interpretations of the sector. Strategic actions are shaped by the ability of such groups to achieve plausible and compelling interpretations of the wider environment.

A further element of the social constructionist view is the link between the work processes in which knowledge is created or applied and structurally embedded or widely diffused bodies of knowledge. Applying this view to technology, for instance, leads to a multilevel definition that ranges from the concrete artefacts of machines and software, through generic designs or infrastructures to occupational and disciplinary knowledge bases (Scarbrough and Corbett, 1992). Organisations also have a hand in this structuring of knowledge: distributing specialist knowledges across functional or divisional structures and embedding them in its politics, practices and routines.

In this perspective, strategic IT projects create a particularly acute knowledge problem for organisations. The knowledges needed to construct a strategic approach to IT are widely distributed and structurally embedded. They are unlikely to coalesce spontaneously because of business needs or external pressure. Nor is a top-down deployment of strategic IT likely to be effective since the unequal structural distribution of the relevant expertise precludes a mechanical or logical derivation from strategic plans. In short, as rational planning cannot conjure up a strategic approach to IT, nor top-down management impose one, we perforce have to look at the ways in which strategic knowledge can be *constructed* around IT.

As our case studies demonstrate, this is an uncertain and risky project. Strategies for IT have to be socially constructed by competing against the clamouring voices of senior managers from other functions and interests, all with equally strategic concerns. A strategic approach does not emerge spontaneously from this clamour. Particular groups, not least the IS function itself, have to labour carefully and painstakingly to make IT strategic. This involves making space within the existing routines of the organisation, cutting across organisational boundaries and acquiring knowledge from other groups. In doing so, such groups will be exploiting different aspects of their own expertise, including their functional competence in handling problems, their structural relationships with other groups and their connections with supplier or occupational groupings outside the organisation.

Thus the social constructionist perspective invites us to examine the resources used in constructing knowledge in organisations and in maintaining it against the competing aspirations of other groups. More than that though, it suggests that the expertise of such groups should be viewed not as a means of accessing an objective reality but rather as provisional knowledge claims that are always subject to social validation and review. In short, the critical question for strategic IT is not whether IS expertise can be mechanistically integrated with managerial expertise, but how particular groups can make claims to strategic knowledge around IT and how such claims are validated and advanced.

These questions are explored through case studies of strategic IT projects in the Scottish financial services sector. This sector offered an especially favourable context for the development of such projects and an ideal test-bed for the much touted claims of strategic IT. In the 1980s and 1990s, a combination of the deregulation of UK financial institutions together with the exponential growth of IT applications created a high level of interest and opportunity around 'strategic IT', in which Scottish institutions were well to the fore.

Sectoral context

Sectoral context is important in a study of expertise because the historical evolution of a sector shapes the technologies and knowledges through which products and services are produced. Although the role of IS expertise in our various cases was heavily influenced by the process of project development, these sectoral features were important structural elements in shaping the construction of IS knowledge in the organisational setting. Three key features are worthy of detailed focus: technological infrastructure, the occupational formation in the sector, and the operation of interorganisational networks.

On the first point, the evolution of financial services in the UK typically involved the elaboration of branch networks controlled from a central headquarters. This in turn established the classic infrastructural patterns for computing and IT, where large mainframes served a large number of branch systems. IS expertise developed through the emergence of central computing and, later, IT functions. Initial applications of computing technology focused not on products but on efficiency-oriented processes such as payments processing in banking and computerised policy records in insurance. Only later did product innovations such as home banking and on-line quotations emerge from the use of computing technology (Scarbrough, 1992). The second sectoral influence on the organisational role of IS expertise comes from the web of occupational and interorganisational networks that make up a sector. Management in each firm becomes 'part of a social network in which common perceptions, attitudes and behaviours are shaped and moulded' (Shearman and Burrell 1987, p. 328). Such networks help to transmit new sectoral 'recipes' to do with strategic and technological configurations (Child and Smith, 1987).

This is not to say, though, that organisations are simply passive receivers of the knowledge and information transmitted through sectoral networks. Senior manages proactively cultivate and develop network contacts as a means of generating knowledge about their sector. Moreover, they use their investment portfolio of new ventures and initiatives experimentally to extend further their sectoral knowledge. For example, in response to the question 'how do you go about keeping your finger on the pulse', the chief executive of the Bank of Scotland replied that discussions on commercial issues would be:

> internal or with suppliers. Like we would discuss them with IBM. We will discuss things with British Telecom. We will discuss things with the Halifax Building Society with which we have a joint credit card company or the AA for joint business. Or Standard Life whose insurance policies we sell or all sorts of different people. For example, we own 22 per cent of First Mortgage Securities Ltd. which is a competitor of the Mortgage Corporation of National Homeloans. Why did we go into that? Why do we own 22 per cent of it? Because it gives us another window in a different world.
>
> If you walk down Princes Street, you will see on shops 'VAT refunds for tourists'. We have an associated company, in which we own 50 per cent called the Foreign Exchange Company, which is the market leader in that business. Why did we go into that? . . . Because it gives us a different perspective . . . We try and have as many windows in as many different parts of the business as we possibly can. And we will try experiments here, there and everywhere.

In the financial sector particularly, an important feature of IS expertise is the development of intersectoral networks encompassing hardware and software suppliers (the historical influence of IBM is an obvious example here). At the occupational level, too, there are important flows of knowledge and information. One IS manager in a building society described how his staff;

> are always immensely quick and eager to go to other building societies and ask them about what we should buy and whether a package might be best or whatever. That's one thing about building societies – we're very good at communicating with one another, as compared to, say, insurance companies. They wouldn't tell you if they got a new pencil sharpener.

Another IS manager from the building society sector outlined some of the parameters for such knowledge-trading:

> We will meet at various times, at various conferences. In DP [sic], for example, there is a biannual meeting where we all exchange views on what we're doing in relation to technology. At that level, we may not exchange the various products we are working on. The details of those products. But certainly we don't mind saying 'We've purchased a number of PCs which are going to do this'. Or 'we've purchased a mainframe computer and a network which is going to do this'.

A third important consequence of sectoral evolution is the emergence of a variety of occupational groupings. This not only establishes the range of occupational groups employed in a sector, but also conditions the relationships between them. Thus in a sector with a 200-year history, the 30 years evolution of the IS occupation marked it out as an upstart group compared with the long-established financial intermediary roles occupied by specialist bankers, accountants and actuaries.

Occupational mobility and strategic knowledge

In relation to strategic IT, these sectoral factors are important in two major ways. First, they help to shape the technological and infrastructural context in which strategic IT is developed. Second, they have a generalised impact on the pecking order of different occupational groups within organisations. Occupational studies suggest that the strategic influence of particular groups broadly correlates with the wider 'mobility project' of their professional formation (Armstrong, 1987). In financial services specifically, the centrality of financial intermediary roles long guaranteed a place within senior management for bankers, actuaries and accountants. But one of the subtexts for strategic IT was the ability of sectoral and technological change to propel the IS occupation into challenging this dominant coalition or finding a place within it.

Again occupational studies suggest that the ability to mount such a challenge depends on the monopoly control of skills that are central to managerial functions. The importance of such monopoly control is outlined and elaborated in the work of Hickson *et al.* (1971), which describes the 'strategic contingencies' that afford political leverage to organisational subunits. These are, respectively: *centrality* (multiple linkages to other groups and the impact of the withdrawal of specialist services on the workflow of the organisation); *substitutability* (the availability of alternative suppliers); and the ability to *cope with uncertainty*. In these crude, structural terms the advent of IT certainly enhanced the power of IS functions. Where computing technology had previously been centred on back-office, labour-saving tasks, IT extended its scope to encompass product innovations such as ATMs and home banking. This not only reinforced the IS function's centrality but added a modicum of control over market uncertainty. Moreover the need to integrate new systems with 'core technology' meant that product development could not be split off from the mainstream IS organisation, as happens with specialist R&D departments in the manufacturing industry. Thus, in a sector whose products are effectively different ways of packaging information, the 1980s stimulus to new product development and the creation of new electronic delivery systems seemed to augur well for the future of IS functions.

However there were also important constraints on the pervasiveness and centrality of IT in financial services. These included the continuing importance of financial intermediary roles in profit generation, and more generally the weakness of IS professional groupings. Equally, it would be a mistake to see the role of IS functions as being wholly oriented towards product marketing and innovation. Much IT investment and IS expertise was still dedicated to the maintenance and development of infrastructural techologies for funds movement or shared ATM networks, which had little direct connection with product market competition. Even in the highly fragmented US banking industry, around 65 per cent of systems expenditure in banking went towards supporting 'invisible' functions such as funds transfer, with only 10 per cent going into potentially competitive product market areas. In short, it seemed that 'The vast bulk of systems investments support products or services that are commodities throughout the industry' (Steiner and Teixeira, 1990, p. 45)

Against these caveats about the sectoral importance of IS expertise, though, it is important to remember that key features of IS work were highly organisation-specific, reflecting the immediate contingencies of each firm's strategy as much as the wider sector. Our study found many instances of such organisational factors promoting the centrality of IS expertise, or at least imposing constraints on substitutability and deskilling. Organisations had to respond, for instance, to an IS labour market where a rapid growth in demand greatly limited deskilling by enhancing the mobility and marketability of IS specialists. Organisations adopting tight management controls or pursuing only routine IT projects might find it difficult to recruit and retain skilled IS personnel. In one of the banks in our sample, the organisation's inability to pursue major projects limited its attractions for IS staff who sought the CV-enhancing experience of such projects. As one IS manager noted, IS staff felt 'the need to be regarded as IT professionals rather than slightly irregular bank staff'. Similarly, while the management of IS expertise had moved on from the *laissez-faire* practices of previous decades (Friedman, 1989) and had been fully assimilated into the mainstream management structure, this was at least as much to do with accommodation as with control. With the management structure incorporating managers from an IT occupational background, hierarchy also meant the subtler blandishments of career ladders and an internal labour market.

Added to these factors, the nature of IS work itself continued to militate against detailed specialisation of jobs. For instance, both the proliferation and the nature of IT applications limited the incorporation of IS skills into hardware. Moreover the uncertainty generated by the spread of innovative applications effectively inhibited the routinisation of IS work. As Friedman notes: 'Technical progress . . . which arises from the cumulation of individually minor improvements is also important today. What distinguishes computer systems development is the extent to which technical change of this . . . type occurs. This is, in turn, dependent upon the inherent creativity which still characterises systems development' (Friedman, 1989, p. 360).

Just as product development could not be readily separated out from systems development at a departmental level, nor could innovative and routine elements be easily separated out from individual jobs. Many applications were dependent upon intensive user contacts into the final stages of implementation, thus encouraging the reintegration of analysis and programming into 'project teams' or individual job specifications as a means of pooling the knowledge and cooperation necessary to absorb technological uncertainty.

If IS expertise was sustained by constraints on management deskilling and rationalisation, its position was also underpinned by the inability of other organisational groups – specifically, users and accounting professionals – to exercise effective control over IS work. This is not to say that IS expertise was blissfully unaffected by these groups' expectations and pressures. The growth of distributed IT and the waning power of the mainframe, for instance, had greatly boosted the role and knowledge of user groups in shaping IT developments. Indeed the 1980s were dubbed the era of 'user relations' constraints by Friedman (1989). However, in our sample at least, the radical re-distribution of technological know-how that might have established effective user control over IS work was limited by a number of technical factors. A particular constraint here was the integrated and centralised character of IT systems in financial services – a product of the sectoral evolution noted earlier – which created a tension between the need for centralised control and development and the local demands of users. This tension expressed itself in the work organisation of IS staff and in the allocation of IS resources. For example, while IS personnel typically worked in teams that shadowed user departments, they were not devolved to those departments but were managed from the central IS function. Similarly, while IS work was largely driven by user demands, IS expertise was effectively rationed through systems of project prioritisation. Revealing asides from IS staff – 'priority four never gets done', or 'it's the greeting wean that gets fed' – demonstrated that prioritisation was as much a question of political expediency as of the rational allocation of resources. These tensions might have ultimately been resolved in favour of user control, but this decentralising tendency was countered in most of our sample firms by the continued need for a centralised IS resource to sponsor and develop organisation-wide IT projects.

Even in the era of distributed technology there seemed to be important recursive relationships between IS expertise and the control of computing technology. At the same time the above points also serve to demonstrate the crucial limits to the commodification of expertise created by the integral relationships between social groupings, knowledge and technologies. In particular, the systems of project prioritisation in our case studies show the organisation of IS expertise balancing on a knife-edge between the politics of the user–expert relationship and the economics of market control.

The problems and politics of commodifying expertise are given a further twist by the role of the accounting functions in our case-study organisations. The IS function poses a particular set of problems for the application of financial controls, and hence for the way in which it can be structured. These problems relate to what Steiner and Teixeira (1990) term the 'tyranny of shared costs': the difficulty of apportioning the central mainframe costs of development, maintenance and processing to user departments. Although such cost allocations were carried out in our sample, the precision attached to them was limited by the resulting costs of controlling and monitoring IS work and by the need for flexible relationships between IS and user departments. In addition, the tendency for many different financial service products to be distributed through a common delivery system – the bank branch being the classic example here – complicated the allocation of costs to products.

In this period our sample firms typically handled such accounting issues through cost-centre and budgetary controls for IS functions. The infrastructural and integrated nature of IS technology created significant constraints on the allocation of IS costs to users. At one bank, for instance, progress in linking IS projects to costs had only been made in the last three years: 'Three years ago . . . you didn't know if it would cost you £1/4 million or £10 million . . . we know the basics of the technology, but it didn't necessarily translate into the bottom line of cost'. Even accountants acknowledged the difficulty of achieving a precise breakdown of costs:

> You can look at an engineering factory and you can see the product being built and you can say 'well that should not have taken twice as long as that', except maybe there is a bit more stress or a bit more sophisticated welding in doing that. It's very difficult to do that with a development project when it is all done on a computer . . . If you can record your man-hours on the project, you have still got this problem with processing capacity. Its difficult to isolate completely.

This casts an interesting sidelight on the intractability of IS activities to accounting controls, compared with, say, their application to the discrete and visible products of an engineering function (Armstrong, 1987). But it would be wrong to see the development of financial controls over IS functions simply in terms of the relative strength of the accounting function. The group that most strongly favoured such controls was often IS management itself. In several of our case-study firms IS management were keen to develop more precise means of allocating IS costs to users. Such moves reflected a general trend (Price Waterhouse IT Review, 1990) towards the use of 'chargeback systems', which, by providing the IS function with a 'revenue stream' and its own measure of profitability, can help IS management to justify their operations in the face of increasing pressures towards cost efficiency: the Price Waterhouse surveys suggest that in 1985, 59 per cent of computer installations had no measures of efficiency compared with almost all installations having such measures in 1990.

Such controls clearly enhance IS management's knowledge of project costs. Nevertheless their adoption seems to have as much to do with the 'selling' of the IS function to the rest of the organisation. In a political context, centres of costs or overheads are seen as vulnerable to attack by profit centres – an attack that is likely to be intensified during periods of increasing competition.

The case studies

Research was carried out in the period 1989–91. It focused on IT projects in six Scottish-based financial institutions spanning the insurance and retail banking sectors. The latter have been organised so as to provide paired comparisons involving projects where the task, technology and product market context have some important commonality. The pairs of case studies described here are as follows:[2]

- Bank of Scotland VISA CENTRE and *Premier Financial Service (PFS) INDEX; customisation of card processing packages.
- Clydesdale Bank's TELEBANK and Royal Bank of Scotland's ROYLINE; remote banking systems.
- Bank of Scotland's CABINET and *Home & Auto Ltd's MIS; a branch information network and a corporate MIS (management information system) respectively.

Although a number of the projects were deemed 'strategic' by IS management, the focus in our research was not on a predefined conception of what constituted 'strategic IT', but on the social processes involved in constructing such concepts and categories. In that sense the local meanings attached to strategic IT were the end-point rather than the starting point of our study. Moreover we found that the processes of making IT strategic varied enormously from one company to another. In some firms the 'strategic' label was largely a symbolic matter, whereas in others it had important consequences for the direction, scale and evaluation of resources.

Bank of Scotland VISA CENTRE and Premier Financial Services' (PFS) INDEX card processing project

This first pairing of cases brings together two projects where the main IT developments involved the acquisition and maintenance of software packages for the processing of credit card accounts. Although there were important issues to do with customisation, the technology was well defined and the IT development process itself was reasonably routine. In short, in terms of its contingent features this IT development conformed to McFarlan and McKenney's (1983) 'Factory IT' model, where the key decision criteria are not strategic but rather operational goals of cost and efficiency.

To an extent this contingency model was reflected in the actual project development process. In the acquisition of the software package concerned, well-defined operational issues of cost, reliability and processing efficiency were paramount. However, in the PFS project in particular, the organisational context led to a routine technology acquisition taking on a much wider significance. The INDEX card-processing package was to be purchased for PFS, which was a credit-card firm and a recently acquired subsidiary of a larger clearing bank group – ScotBank Group. In the previous year the diversification of the group had prompted the establishment of a 'group services' function, which was dedicated to maximising the effective use of the bank's technical resources. As control of IT developments in the group had previously rested almost exclusively with the in-house IS function of the clearing bank part of the group, this aim brought group Services into direct conflict with the management of that function. It was at this politically sensitive juncture that the issues surrounding the acquisition of INDEX came to the fore and got caught in the cross fire, so to speak.

The members of group services saw IT developments at PFS as a unique opportunity to establish their influence over the allocation of IT resources. Exploiting their new mandate to the full, they were able to insist that both the customisation and the maintenance of the new package be turned over to the software supplier. Both these tasks would normally have been carried out as a matter of course by ScotBank's IS function, thus the effect was to establish an important precedent for the future organisation of IT resources. As a result the political symbolism of the project effectively overrode more immediate concerns of efficiency and practicality. Indeed the routine nature of the project actually made it a more powerful precedent in future decisions on the role of the in-house IS function. One member of the group management team hinted at the possible repercussions:

> I think what we're really talking about here is power. We're talking about a historical environment where nothing, but nothing, would happen in a computer development unless it was done either directly or under the control of IS Division. Now the implications of a user getting a system in and running without ever going anywhere near Management services . . . if you were in IS Division in a senior position, you would say, 'Wait a minute!'

The politicality of the PFS case is highlighted by the comparison with the Bank of Scotland Visa centre. The Bank of Scotland had not followed a diversification strategy of the kind pursued by Scotbank. Consequently there was no need for a group management function, nor the attendant conflicts. When the bank established its new Visa processing centre in 1988, it did so very largely under the auspices of the in-house management services division (MSD). Although labour market factors led to the centre being located a few miles away from the bank's computer centre, its senior management were in the main transferees from MSD and the Visa centre itself drew heavily on the division's technological resources. With no structural conflict to darken the mood, the decision-making processes around the Visa centre's systems were placid and uncontentious; the outline organisation chart, for example, was reputedly drawn up in a local hostelry over a quiet drink. The same untroubled calm pervaded the decisions on the processing systems that would form the technological core of the new centre. The selection, customisation and maintenance of the supplier package were all handled by MSD itself, with none of the obtrusive interventions that marked the Scotbank case.

Two points emerge from the comparison between the PFS and Visa centre cases. First, it shows that contingent factors such as the routineness of a technology are not exogenous determinants of the managerial discourses, criteria and practices that develop around a particular project. The significance which such factors possess for decision making is clearly related to the way in which they can be enlisted, symbolically or otherwise, in the rationales and interpretations promoted by particular groups within the organisation. On the other hand such interpretations are not so localised or malleable that they can sustain entirely divergent meanings for broadly similar technologies. Neither of these cases were seen as meriting the vocabulary or attention afforded to strategic technologies.

TELEBANK and ROYLINE

Our second paired comparison shows how the symbolic importance of a project may be parlayed into a full-blown strategic rationale if it is actuated by the advancing claims of a particular kind of expertise. The relevant comparison here is between the development of two remote banking systems. At Clydesdale Bank, the in-house IT staff both conceived and justified the TELEBANK remote banking system as a strategic project. They argued from the evidence of market and technological trends that remote delivery systems would play an increasingly important part in the bank's future product range. TELEBANK was conceived as one element in a range of remote banking products, and as an important competitive response in a rapidly changing marketplace:

> So we had made greater sense of home and office banking; we'd taken it a lot further than anyone else had. We'd moved from being second to Bank of Scotland, and

through the use of this telephone system which was innovative, we've moved ourselves to being market leaders in the UK.

In direct contrast, at the Royal Bank of Scotland no such strategic concerns developed around the design and implementation of ROYLINE, although in technological terms this was probably a more sophisticated remote banking system. The impetus for ROYLINE came from senior management, who were aware of similar developments in the USA and were concerned to extend the range of services available to business customers. Far from playing up the long-term or strategic aspects of the new technology, however, IS management took a decidedly downbeat view: 'There are business requirements for which we are finding technological solutions . . . You can't utilise technology for its own sake.'

Again, neither the technological characteristics of the projects nor the features of comparable market contexts can explain the variation in the way the projects were managed and developed. Although both projects clearly derived from a new sectoral recipe centred on remote delivery systems, the conceptual frameworks within which they were designed and justified were markedly different. In the Clydesdale Bank case we found an IT function that was increasingly unhappy with its role. Clydesdale was a relatively small subsidiary of a larger banking group – Midland Bank – and in recent years the same kind of managerial processes we noted at Scotbank had begun to impinge on the autonomy of the IS function at Clydesdale. In this context, TELEBANK not only represented a way of securing greater autonomy within the group structure, but also of securing a lead role in any future technological developments in that area. This was described by one of the system's major proponents: 'TELEBANK', he said;

> is not highly important in terms of our own systems; though, remember, it was extremely important at the time. Politically, it was immensely important politically. It was incredibly important that people here could see that we had something outwith the Midland Bank. Because beyond that point we were able to persuade Midland Bank that we should project manage the group developments in home and office banking.

This highlights the way in which the political interests of an IS function are not given by its structural position alone but also reflect the collective identity or self-image that its managers are seeking to cultivate. Clydesdale's IT specialists had been involved in a number of important innovations in the preceding decade, including the development of a unique branch network, and also of a prototype EFTPOS (electronic funds transfer at point of sale) system. To develop a crude typology here, the IT specialists at Clydesdale Bank seem to have seen themselves as *innovators*, with a responsibility for expanding the role of IT in the bank's services. They were therefore much more inclined towards exploiting the rhetorical and conceptual resources offered by strategic IT. Conversely, IS management at the Royal Bank of Scotland saw themselves as *professionals*, emphasising the need to serve specific needs of the bank and priding themselves upon achieving the closest possible relationships with user groups. Given this image, they eschewed the pursuit of 'strategic' projects, but interpreted developments in remote banking as involving a pragmatic and incremental response to customer needs.

Bank of Scotland CABINET and the Home & Auto MIS

In this pairing, we have a comparison of two important projects that were equally strategic in terms of the discursive moves and methodologies employed by IS management, but produced very unequal outcomes. In broad terms, one might say that CABINET was a successful project that validated the strategic knowledge claims of IS expertise, while the Home & Auto MIS (management information system) was a comparative failure that actually undermined the credibility and claims of the in-house IS function.

Here, the reasons for success and failure can tell us a lot about the social construction of strategic IT. In the first instance, these cases suggest that project success had little to do with the rhetorical use of a strategic vocabulary *per se*. This vocabulary was a feature of both cases – and if anything more explicitly so in the Home & Auto MIS case, which was termed the 'strategy project' by management itself. On the other hand the characteristics of the projects themselves do seem to have exerted a powerful influence. Even in its embryonic stages, the CABINET (customer and branch information network) project had all the hallmarks of a strategic initiative. As designed by the in-house management services division, this was to be the major infrastructural investment for the Bank's branches well into the 1990s. It would provide on-line, customer-based information to branches, replacing a current-account-based information flow that involved the daily updating and despatch of thousands of microfiches. Moreover it not only involved the development of a new information network connecting the bank's several hundred branches to its central mainframes, but also required the integration of existing account records into a central customer database. The significance of the latter move can be gauged from the fact that hitherto the bank, like most UK clearing banks, had only recorded information on its many millions of branch-based accounts. There was no centralised record of its customers – many of whom might have a number of different accounts and contacts with the bank.

For all these reasons, CABINET was widely hailed as a major part of the Bank's product strategy for the coming decades. As one senior manager said: 'CABINET itself is not a product. CABINET is a strategy. It's a strategy to attack the market place in the 90s'. The Bank's chief executive was equally convinced of its importance, even while recognising the risks: 'The danger with CABINET is that you go down a blind alleyway from which you cannot escape. The danger of not doing it is that you go out of business'.

With top management's backing, the massive capital expenditure required by CABINET managed to escape the normal criteria of return on investment. In their dealings with colleagues from the accounting function, IS management were able to argue quite successfully that the singular character of CABINET freed it from the need for detailed cost–benefit justification:

> We knew that if we tried to cost justify each application as it came up, we would never be able to do it . . . because the infrastructural costs would always be too high. We had to take on a longer-term marketing view and accept that we would have to implement one project that was actually not going to be cost justified . . . provided we were sure it was taking us in the right direction.

Even a management accountant was prepared to accept that CABINET was 'a strategic decision, and the cost of not doing it was more important than the cost of doing it'.

On the face of it this project seems an archetypal example of the strategic use of IT as identified by the McFarlan and McKenney matrix. However, attributing the strategic label to CABINET's intrinsic technical qualities alone would be neglecting the painstaking construction of strategic knowledge, which was an integral part of the project. In the first instance, the very fact that the bank selected this project from many other possible investment opportunities serves to highlight the role of MSD in making IT a strategic item in the deliberations of top management. In part, MSD's success here involved mobilising sectoral recipes that emphasised the quality of customer service. Such recipes dovetailed neatly with the operational facilities offered by new database technologies. However it also rested on the role that MSD had carved out for itself within the bank. The early 1980s had seen important structural changes in the IT area, with first a small strategic planning unit being established and then the merger of what had been separate (sometimes squabbling) divisions of management services and computer services. The new amalgamated management services division succeeded in establishing a unified mandate for interpretation and action in relation to the changing technological environment. That new mandate was simultaneously reflected in an outpouring of project proposals – CABINET being only one of a series of innovative projects – and the fostering of a self-consciously 'strategic' identity to define the division's role in the bank's affairs.

Given its mandate and self-image, the MSD function was keen to use the language of strategy to finesse the problems raised by new technological developments. Such problems came in two forms. Firstly, new technologies – such as customer database systems – tended to generate significant managerial and technical uncertainties. The latter, in fact, were less the result of intrinsic technical features than of the degree of fit between the new technology and the existing competences of the IS function. The greater the gap between the two, the more useful the discursive flexibility of strategic IT in patching over the resulting uncertainty. Secondly, one of the key problems raised by new technologies was the troubling effect they tended to have on the definition of task domains. Large-scale IT projects such as CABINET could not easily be accommodated within the established borders between the IS and accounting functions. Where previous 'back office' systems had been efficiency oriented and therefore amenable to the routine accounting criteria of payback or discounted cash flow, these new systems were predicated on less quantifiable gains in market share and customer loyalty. Hence the deployment of a strategic rationale not only helped to circumvent the standard accounting criteria, but also secured a new space for IS development that was freer of accounting controls.

These steps in the social and organisational construction of strategic IT can be usefully contrasted with parallel developments at Home & Auto Ltd. Although its development of a corporate management information system did not approach the levels of capital expenditure required by CABINET, it did offer important, if again relatively intangible, benefits. This was a system that promised to rationalise and improve what were hitherto rather patchy and sporadic information flows to product managers. The pay-off was to come through improving the quality and responsiveness of product managers' decisions on premium rates.

From the outset the MIS project was handled as a strategic initiative. This was reflected particularly in the development methodology employed. By adopting, in almost textbook fashion, the complete paraphernalia of a methodology termed 'business systems planning' (BSP), the director of the IS function sought to ensure that the project was responsive to the long-term needs of the organisation as a whole. This approach involved taking an holistic view of information needs, moving in logical sequence from corporate goals, as identified through interviews with senior managers, to the technical features of the operational system. The adoption of BSP was partly a reaction to an earlier abortive attempt by the rival 'statistical services' function to develop a workable system. This had ultimately foundered when it was belatedly discovered that supposedly up-to-the-minute MIS reports could take days of mainframe run-time to produce. BSP would avoid such oversights by beginning with a detailed assessment of information needs and then moving logically and carefully onto the possible IT solutions to those needs.

Like the CABINET project, one of the principal implications of the corporate MIS' strategic status was the relaxation of the standard financial criteria. The only financial justification ever devised for it claimed that it would lead to a 'decrease in claims ratio which in turn will be reflected as benefit on the Underwriting profit/loss in a year'. It noted the statistical services' estimate that a 1 per cent reduction in the ratio would lead to a £5 million benefit across all classes of business. However, while the report claimed that a 1 per cent reduction was a conservative estimate of the impact of a corporate MIS, it did not attempt to substantiate the relationship between the MIS and the quality of rate-setting within the company. One of the report's authors noted of the 1 per cent estimate: 'There was no grounding for that really. It was just a figure that everyone accepted would be the case'.

However, despite – or even because of – this rigorous attempt to drive the corporate MIS from strategic business needs, the project quickly encountered problems. This was partly because the MIS project depended from the outset on the local knowledge and cooperation of a wide range of user groups. Eliciting the information needs of the different groups involved proved to be no easy matter. Another major barrier was the complexity of the existing process and its dependence on the tacit knowledge of those setting premium rates. All these problems were further exacerbated because the IS function – located in the basement of the headquarters building – lacked the necessary status and credibility to gain the active commitment of the top management team, who were located on the top floor. One of the youthful team of systems developers noted: 'The topmost level was banned from us, perhaps because we were pretty scruffy'.

Not surpisingly, the IS developers were unable to squeeze these complex realities into their formal BSP model:

> We produced organisation charts but this was one of the more difficult tasks. In a complex business you may leave areas of responsibility slightly grey. Like the individual product managers formally had some responsibilities, but they varied in their approach to product pricing and left different decisions to their product managers . . . That was the first big hole we fell down.

The Home & Auto MIS project thus offers a stark contrast to the CABINET project. The latter attained strategic status through MSD's mandate and its infrastructural implications. Moroever, as it involved a product innovation, it did not have the same need to map existing norms and practices. Its early stages were therefore relatively independent of the local knowledge and cooperation of the user groups in the branches. In contrast the Home & Auto project rapidly fell into the 'big hole' of existing organisational practices. The complexity and time demands of the project were further compounded by political pressures from impatient user departments. There was a feeling that the IS function had 'analysed it to death'. Ultimately this combination of political pressures and technical failure prompted a change in both the personnel and the policy of the IS function. This involved a switch to a more 'realistic' and pragmatic approach: 'evolution not revolution', as the new IS manager put it. The holistic, strategic approach was abandoned and the MIS design was simply tailored to the specific needs of the largest (and most vociferous) user department.

The contrast between the CABINET and Home & Auto Ltd cases is revealing. It suggests, for example, that mapping a 'strategic' methodology onto a development process is not in itself enough to construct strategic knowledge. Instead, factors to do with the internal distribution of expertise and the scope of the project at hand seem to play a crucial role. These include the credibility of the IS function itself, especially in the top management arena; the function's basic competences in making the technology work; and the characteristics of the project, most notably dependence on user groups.

Discussion

Each of these case pairings tells us something about the social construction of strategic IT. Even the first pairing (of non-strategic projects) has some counterfactual relevance, and usefully underscores the importance of the IT project to the management process. At the same time though, the PFS case challenges the contingency model of IT management by demonstrating that expert groups are not passive in the face of the tasks they are set, but actively seek to exploit them in ways that enhance their own stature. But if this leads in turn to the political aspirations of expert groups, the pairing of TELEBANK and ROYLINE also reminds us that such aspirations are malleable and closely related to the collective identity that such groups construct for themselves.

Our final pairing of cases shows that strategic IT is a more complex construction than narrowly political models would suggest. Although the structural power bases of the IS functions involved were certainly relevant, broader questions of expertise were revealed by the unfolding of project development. For example the distribution and range of knowledges enlisted by each project was a uniformly important factor. Thus to cite just one example, CABINET's strategic standing was more easily secured because the bank's MSD function controlled so much more of the relevant knowledge.

Apart from highlighting the distribution of expertise between specialists and users, the CABINET case also has more far-reaching implications for our understanding of the character of such expertise. It suggests that two distinct elements of expertise are involved in constructing strategic knowledge around IT. As well as individual competences such as programming and systems analysis, what can be termed the 'interpretive capacity' of different groups seemed to be crucial. Whereas competences involve individual or group performance of predefined tasks, the capacity to interpret market and technological contingencies is ultimately crucial to defining the range of tasks an organisation sets itself (Smircich and Stubbart, 1985). Of our case sample, the Bank of Scotland is the clearest example of an IS function developing such a capacity. In other cases, IS functions signally failed to project a compelling world-view for the organisation as a whole, even where, as in the Royal Bank case, they possessed a high level of competence and professionalism.

This emphasis on the interpretive role of IS practitioners is not to say that their narrowly technical competences are entirely irrelevant to the construction of strategic knowledge. By ensuring control of the work flow within organisations, they undoubtedly help to secure task domains and perceived power amidst the rough and tumble of organisational politics (Lucas, 1984; Stevens, 1993). Indeed, following Miles and Snow (1978), it is possible to discern important recursive relationships between organisational contingencies, competences and interpretive capacities. For example a firm may make an initial move into new product market niches by exploiting the underlying competences of its IT function. As success in this niche comes to depend on technical innovation, the firm becomes more dependent on its technical experts' competence. At the same time the expert group's ability to interpret the market context is greatly enhanced. As a result, firm strategy places even greater emphasis on technical innovation and the circularity is reinforced.

On the other hand such recursiveness can equally operate in the reverse direction. It is by no means certain that the control of technical competences will necessarily entail interpretive responsibilities for the organisation at large. In the history of manual occupations, for instance, the crucial Taylorist intervention involved the separation of thinking from doing. It may be that for knowledge workers the separation of competence from interpretation will prove to be equally fateful. In that sense the experience of our sample of IS practitioners may have something to tell us about the prospects for downward as well as upward occupational mobility.

More generally, there is more to achieving interpretive roles, thereby securing strategic claims, than achieving knowledge of either the technological or the market context. Studies have shown that the performance of interpretive functions is not only a matter of mobilising wider knowledge of the task context, but also of controlling the symbolic means of representing the organisation's activities within that context (Armstrong, 1989). This last point suggests that even the strategic successes in our sample, such as the MSD's role at the Bank of the Scotland, be treated with a degree of caution. Significantly, MSD's strategic mandate was based on the development of CABINET and a stream of other projects. This project-based character of IS expertise seems to be a much more fragile platform for strategic knowledge than the continuous monitoring power of accounting (Armstrong, 1991). In short, IS expertise only becomes critical to strategy making during those occasional episodes when large-scale IT-based projects are being designed and implemented. The rest of the time IS expertise is primarily engaged in a support role, and is subject to the direction of general managers and the operation of accounting controls.

Conclusions

This study suggests that the strategic nature of a particular IT project is not something that can be determined at the outset. Persuading top management to invest major resources into a project, or to slacken the usual investment criteria, is as much a matter of the internal management structure and culture of the business as it is the 'objective' merits of a particular proposal. In suggesting that such persuasion reflects the social construction of technology, I have sought to show how the expertise of the IS function, combined perhaps with the degree of IS ignorance amongst top management, can sometimes project a compelling world-view in which the strategic possibilities of IT are central. Although it obviously helps if such a world-view is supported by wider sectoral features, the contingencies of the immediate environment are probably secondary to the way in which they are interpreted. In this process, the IS function's history, status and self-image are important factors.

The practical implications of this study are manifold. It suggests that the rational model of strategy is relevant, but only as a resource that is generally available to competing functions and which reflects both the latter groups' aspirations and the problems they experience in handling particular projects. Similarly, the competence of the IS function and of users is also relevant, but again not in a straightforwardly functional way. Perceived competence both influences and reflects credibility and political influence. Moreover, competence is embedded in a specific philosophy or approach that may not be readily integrated into the kind of overarching interfunctional framework needed to create the bridging knowledge between business and IT issues.

The social construction perspective cautions against simplistic prescriptions; however rational the model or methodology, it will normally come unstuck if it conflicts with what people really 'know' in organisations. Instead of imposing strategic plans and frameworks from the top down, this study suggests that managers would do better to construct organisational capabilities and strategies from the bottom up; shaping and regulating the development and interaction of different forms of expertise.

Notes

1. This chapter reports on a research project – 'Stategic Innovations in Financial Services' – supported by the Joint Committee of the ESRC/SERC. Robin Fincham, James Fleck, Rob Procter, Margaret Tierney and Robin Williams were the other members of the research team. A fuller version of the research findings is reported

in Fincham *et al.*, *Expertise and Innovation: Information technology strategies in financial services* (Oxford University Press, 1994).

2.   Wherever possible the actual names of firms and projects have been used. In some cases, however, which are asterisked, confidentiality is preserved by the use of pseudonyms.

References

Armstrong, P. (1987) 'Engineers, management and trust', *Work, Employment and Society*, vol. 1, no. 4, pp. 421–40.

Armstrong, P. (1989) 'Management, labour process and agency', *Work, Employment and Society*, vol. 3, no. 3, pp. 307–22.

Armstrong, P. (1991) 'Contradiction and social dynamics in the capitalist agency relationship', *Accounting, Organisations and Society*, vol. 16, no. 1, pp. 1–25.

British Computer Society (1990) *From Potential to Reality: A Report by the British Computer Society Task Group on Hybrids* (London: British Computer Society Publications).

Child, J. and Smith, C. (1987) 'The context and process of organisational transformations – Cadbury Limited in its sector', *Journal of Management Studies*, vol. 24, no. 6, pp. 565–593.

Currie, W. (1994) 'The strategic management of a large scale IT project in the financial services sector', *New Technology, Work and Employment*, vol. 9, no. 1, pp. 19–29.

Dey, S., Metzer, R. O. and Banks, J. D. (1988) 'Making Management–DP conflict a thing of the past', *National Productivity Review*, vol. 8, no. 1, pp. 59–64.

Earl, M. J. and Skryme, D. J. (1990) 'Hybrid Managers: What do we know about them?', *Working Paper RDP90/6* (Oxford: Oxford Institute of Information Management).

Earl, M. (1989) *Management Strategies for Information Technology* (London: Prentice-Hall).

Firdman, H. E. (1991) *Strategic Information Systems: Forging the business and technology alliance* (New York: McGraw-Hill).

Friedman, A. L. with Cornford, S. D. (1989) *Computer Systems Development: History, organisation and implementation* (Chichester: Wiley and Sons).

Gunton, T. (1990) *Inside Information Technology* (Hemel Hempstead: Prentice-Hall).

Hickson, D. J., Hinings, C. R., Lee, C. A., Schneck, R. E. and Pennings, J. M. (1971) 'A strategic contingencies theory of intra-organisational power', *Administrative Science Quarterly*, vol. 16, no. 2, pp. 216–229.

Knights, D. and Morgan, G. (1991) 'Corporate strategy, organisations and the subject', *Organization Studies*, vol. 12, no. 2, pp. 251–73.

Lucas, H.C. (1984) 'Organisational power and the Information Services Department', *Communications of the ACM*, vol. 27, no. 1, pp. 58–65.

McFarlan, F. W. and McKenney, J. L. (1983) *Corporate Information Systems Management: The issues facing senior executives* (New York: Dow Jones Irwin).

Miles, R.E. and Snow, C.C.(1978) *Organisational Strategy, Structure and Process* (New York: McGraw-Hill).

Mumford, E. and Ward, T.B. (1968) *Computers: Planning for people* (London: Batsford).

Murray, F. (1989) 'The organisational politics of information technology: studies from the UK financial services industry', *Technology Analysis and Strategic Management*, vol. 1, no. 3, pp. 285–98.

Scarbrough, H. (ed.) (1992) *The IT Challenge: Strategy and IT in financial services* (Hemel Hempstead: Prentice-Hall).

Scarbrough, H. and Corbett, J.M. (1992) *Technology and Organisation: Power, meaning and design* (London: Routledge).

Shearman, C. and Burrell, G. (1987) 'The structures of industrial development', *Journal of Management Studies*, vol. 24, no. 4, pp. 325–45.

Shrivastava, P. and Souder, W.E. (1987) 'The strategic management of technological innovations: A review and a model', *Journal of Management Studies*, vol. 24, no. 1, pp. 25–41.

Smircich, L. and Stubbart, C. (1985) 'Strategic management in an enacted environment', *Academy of Management Review*, vol. 10, no. 4, pp. 724–36.

Steiner, T.D. and Teixeira, D.B. (1990) *Technology in Banking: Creating value and destroying profits* (Homewood, Illinois: Irwin).

Stevens, G. (1993) 'Power and EDP departments: A case study', *New Technology, Work and Employment*, vol. 8, no. 2, pp. 111–21.

Willcocks, L.P. and Mark, A.L. (1989) 'IT systems implementation: research findings from the public sector', *Journal of Information Technology*, vol. 2, no. 2, pp. 92–103.

Wilson, T.D. (1989) 'The implementation of information systems strategies in UK companies: Aims and barriers to success', *International Journal of Information Management*, vol. 9, pp. 245–58.

PART 3

INSTITUTIONAL CHANGE AND THE MANAGEMENT OF EXPERTISE

CHAPTER 7

Information systems for knowledge management

Harry Scarbrough

This chapter deals with management concepts and technologies that are explicitly focused on the management of expertise. It reports on attempts by five UK-based multinationals systematically to identify and represent their 'knowledge assets'. Their efforts and achievements are a powerful illustration of a number of the wider themes highlighted in the introductory chapter. These include (1) the shift from 'Mode 1' to 'Mode 2' knowledge production and the importance of identifying and configuring knowledge assets for competitive advantage; (2) new-found managerial responsibilities for cultivating and deploying such knowledge-assets given the demise of traditional professional and functional structures; and (3) the application of IT to the codification and representation of expertise.

The management of knowledge-assets

The notion that competitive performance is dependent on what can broadly be termed 'knowledge assets' has emerged as a powerful unifying theme in recent years. Studies in the fields of industrial economics (Nelson and Winter, 1982), human resource management (Schultz, 1971) and latterly business policy (Klein *et al.*, 1991) have coalesced in a remarkable consensus around the critical role played by knowledge assets in industrial competitiveness. But this growing interest in knowledge assets is not only a theoretical progression. It also reflects important changes in the market and technological environments. One of the key features of recent industrial change, for instance, is the progressive reduction in the length of product cycles – new products are being designed, produced and replaced at an ever faster rate. Pralahad and Hamel, in one of the most influential accounts of knowledge assets, argue that as product cycles shorten, competitive advantage increasingly depends on the underlying competences that generate a stream of product innovations:

> In the short run, a company's competitiveness derives from the price/performance attributes of current products . . . In the long run . . . the real sources of advantage are to be found in management's ability to consolidate corporatewide technologies and production skill into competencies that empower individual businesses to adapt quickly to changing opportunities (Pralahad and Hamel, 1990, p. 81)

Moreover the global spread of IT and rationalised management systems may have reduced the size and labour-intensity of business organisations, but they have also increased *pro rata* the performative impact of the skills and knowledge of those who remain. Hall (1992), in an analysis of the contribution of intangible resources to the success of businesses, found that UK chief executives rated employee know-how above aspects such as specialist physical resources, contracts and intellectual property rights.

In themselves these changes represent a powerful injunction to lavish greater management attention on the technological infrastructures, human resources and collective skills from which competitive advantages are being sought. But what gives the resulting interest in knowledge assets an extra piquancy is the coincidence of these new strategic calculations with wider institutional changes that actually threaten the existing knowledge bases of business firms. Deregulation, global competition and the spread of market controls have delivered a powerful challenge to conventional ways of sourcing and organising knowledge and expertise. Thus the development of interfirm networks and alliances has encouraged collaborative development and transfer of knowledge, but it has also forced companies to identify their key corporate skills so that they can be protected and strengthened. Similarly the decentralisation of business activities into market-facing units has also entailed the erosion or extinction of specialist forms of expertise that had previously thrived in the habitats furnished by central R&D functions and functional management structures.

In sum, these factors create an overarching tension between, on the one hand, the increasing competitive importance of knowledge assets, and, on the other hand, the devolution of responsibility for and control of such assets. This tension is felt at many different levels of the organisation and provides the backcloth for a variety of management responses. Strategic concerns for 'core competences' and the like are certainly an important component of such responses, but they can also take more mundane or operational forms too, as middle managers grapple with the problems thrown up by more decentralised and market-responsive forms.

The empirical study outlined here[1] explores these managerial responses at both strategic and functional levels. In broad terms, it examines attempts to implement new managerial models for understanding and identifying knowledge assets. Implementation seems to hinge upon the translation of such models, through various classificatory methodologies, into detailed sources of management information. A particular concern of the study, therefore, is the design and impact of information systems, notably knowledge databases, in representing knowledge assets and influencing management practices. In short, the overall focus is upon the interplay between managers' conceptual models of knowledge assets, the resulting methodologies and classifications, and the information systems created to identify such assets.

Before reporting the case-study findings, with their patchwork pattern of success and failure, it is worth noting some of the methodological and practical constraints that the literature would lead us to expect in these cases. For a start, there are important epistemological questions here to do with limits on the reflexivity of organisations; their ability to know what they know. First, much of the competitively important knowledge in an organisation is tacit knowledge. Polanyi (1967) defined this as 'knowing more than we can say.' It means, for instance, that even highly proficient experts find it difficult to describe their own knowledge and practices (Stubbart and Ramaprasad, 1990). Second, knowledge in organisations is not simply the aggregate cognitive capacity of individual experts. To a large extent it is a collective phenomenon rooted in the structure and social relations of the concern (Kogut and Zander, 1992). Although studies of such knowledge often describe it in tactile terms – exhibiting fluidity, adhesion and porosity, for instance (Badaracco, 1991; Cohen and Levinthal, 1990) – this robust impression overstates the impacted and involuted quality of certain forms of knowledge. Moreover, while these studies seek to define *logical* relationships between knowledge assets and competitive performance, this is not the same as defining the *mechanical* relationships between the two at a level of specificity amenable to managerial action. The distinction is highlighted, for instance, in Pralahad and Hamel's (1990) citing of the whole domain of 'microelectronics' as an organisational 'core competence'.

While these factors highlight the problems of building conceptual models of knowledge assets, there are also important practical constraints to do with the organisational processes capable of translating such models into detailed and descriptive databases. All information systems, whether IT or paper-based, involve the possibility of political influences on their design and use. One group of writers, for example, has highlighted the political and contested nature of technological change. In this *political design* perspective, as it can be termed, different groups within management operate as self-consciously political actors, attempting to secure their functional goals and interests by shaping systems design and implementation (Wilkinson, 1983; Willcocks and Mason, 1987). In contrast an alternative perspective, which has emerged more recently, focuses on the *informational effects* of IT systems rather than their technology or design (Bloomfield, 1991; Bloomfield and Coombs, 1992; Poster, 1992). Instead of viewing information systems as the crystallisation of political interests, this perspective emphasises their more insidious effect on the perceptions and world-views of organisation members. Management practices are seen as the medium through which power is exercised, as managerial world-views reproduce themselves in technical and representational forms. Thus the informational content of the system, and in particular its way of representing reality, exercises a powerful influence on user behaviour. Bloomfield, for example, notes the 'dual capacity' of information systems in this context: 'both to facilitate surveillance and (self-)control – that is, individuals may monitor their own performance, or that of others, through the visibilities made available by IT – and to represent and redefine what organisations are' (Bloomfield, 1991, p.702)

Case-study findings

The case studies outlined below show management in five major UK-based firms attempting to identify and represent their knowledge assets. Of course, this sample was partly constrained by the relatively small number of firms that have made specific attempts to link corporate strategy with the skills and abilities of the workforce. Within that constraint, however, the sample encompasses firms from a diverse range of industrial and product contexts. Also, the case material relates not only to IT-based databases but also, counterfactually, to cases of paper-based rather than IT-based systems, and also cases where skills databases had failed to emerge at all, despite apparently similar concerns to make corporate skills visible and manipulable. Moreover tensions in the management of knowledge assets are currently associated with the strategic concerns signalled by the 'core competences' debate. But our case studies demonstrate that such tensions can equally arise, sometimes in an even more acute form, in middle management and functional areas of the business.

We begin with two strategic cases. The first, *TechCo*, was a medium-sized firm that had grown rapidly in the 1980s by exploiting a technological lead in the provision of network services and bespoke and standard software products. By the early 1990s top management were starting to take a serious strategic interest in identifying the company's knowledge assets. This interest partly reflected a perceived need to establish a platform for future strategic decisions. At the time of the research study, this refrain had been taken up at the level below top management by strategic planners and senior managers in the recently established technology planning group. The issue had also been brought into sharper focus by the company's acquisition in 1989 by a US-based multinational grouping.

In this context, management's concern to identify 'core competences' was officially presented as a matter of generating relevant information for key product-market and acquisition decisions. It would also assist in decisions on the 'roll out' and implementation of two important innovations in software development. However, to an extent these arguments were really a gloss on more sensitive concerns about the privileging of short-term market success over long-term skills formation. The mid-1980s adoption of a market-facing structure of six strategic business units (SBUs) encompassing sectors such as health, manufacturing and finance, had led to a fragmentation of the IS and networking expertise upon which the company's success was founded. Alarm bells began to ring for corporate management, as one of the members of the technology planning group commented: 'We were starting to find customers weren't coming to us and asking us to quote because they thought we were technically backward. We were unable in some cases to address customer queries because we didn't have the competence internally'. Moreover the SBUs concern with their own short-term profit targets effectively discouraged line management from sharing knowledge and expertise with other groups:

> Knowledge is not shared across these units. Some units are willing to invest in a lot of training and application of their people in skills which are available somewhere else. There's no exchange of people. Rather than send one person of one group to another group, people would actually get contractors in.

Although important in their own right, these strategic concerns did not emerge in a vacuum but were driven by important political interests. In particular, the market-facing structure had created significant ambiguity around the respective roles of business unit management and corporate functions. These led corporate management to see the core competence framework as having an important dual function. Firstly, it was a means of legitimating their concerns about the impoverishment of technical skills. As a senior manager in technology planning put it:

> What we've got is a technical community . . . what they've lacked is an externally validated framework to legitimise the concern they've had . . . There has been a surge of support for the core competence debate because it allows a technical community to articulate something they think is very important.

But, secondly, the core competence debate would also serve to define their role and *raison d'etre* against the powerful centrifugal tendencies created by the new structure. As the same manager admitted: 'The search for core competences is also the search for a role for central management'.

While such factors help to explain corporate management's immediate interest in the core competences issue, it proved more difficult to sustain the continuing use of competences as a feature of the top management vocabulary. As the company's strategic problems multiplied with the recession of the early 1990s, the debate on competences was absorbed into and then marginalised by a more critical debate on future strategy. Moreover the technology planning group found it difficult to move from the rhetorical position afforded by the core competence model to the practical plane of information and planning. Attempts to do so rapidly collapsed into more routine data-gathering exercises that simply aggregated occupational categories and skill levels across the company's different operations.

The second firm with a strategic interest in knowledge assets was CommCo, a large-scale supplier of telecommunications and software products. In recent years it had shifted away from the production of electro-mechanical telecommunications systems towards 'value-added' software products. Interest in core competencies at CommCo exhibited many of the features observed at TechCo. Again there was a level of uncertainty attributable to acquisition and merger activity – in this case, takeover by a large UK firm followed by merger with a large Continental telecommunications supplier. This kind of activity prompted senior management to apply the core competence framework to their strategic practices. But here the aim was not so much to define the company's existing core skills as a base for strategic development as to determine the corporate skills needed for future competitiveness. A list of competences – for example 'project management', 'gaining market share' and 'customer focus' – was defined by top management and the different divisions of the firm were reviewed against this list.

Both TechCo and CommCo, then, drew on the same conceptual framework in their attempts to strategise the knowledge base of the organisation. However at CommCo talk of core competences was not restricted to an internal dialogue between different levels of senior management. Having defined their list of core competences, senior management sought to apply it as a template to development and training across the business. The personnel function was enlisted to define and bridge the resulting 'skills gap' between existing and desired competences within each of the business units. This involvement had a double-edged quality, however. While personnel were able to give greater attention to the translation of core competences into individual skills and learning than had happened at TechCo, this functional delegation was gained at the expense of diminishing support from top and line management. A related consequence of this approach was a conflict between the generic competences defined for the company as a whole and the design of development programmes for individual managers and experts. Although a competence such as 'project management', for example, could be tentatively operationalised by using repertory grid techniques with existing project managers, others, such as 'gaining market share', had no obvious application to the level of individual development.

The TechCo and CommCo cases echo many of the concerns that underpin the literature on knowledge assets. Both firms were in high-tech sectors, employing large numbers of 'knowledge-workers'. Moreover both firms were afflicted by some of the strategic ills that the knowledge assets prospectus claimed to address. At TechCo, for instance, the cannibalising of the corporate skills base by market-facing SBUs was an almost classic illustration of the Pralahad and Hamel thesis – as were the challenges posed by collaboration and strategic reorientation at TechCo. However there were other features of these cases that highlighted important organisational constraints on identifying knowledge assets, even when the strategic impulse to do so was strong. Some of these constraints were political, others arguably methodological. Thus, the strategic concerns at TechCo were driven by the corporate planning group within corporate management. This group saw its own salvation in the application of the core competences approach. At the same time they ultimately found it difficult to use the model as anything more than a debating weapon because it could not be translated into categories and measures capable of meaningful application.

These two cases shed much light on the processes involved in translating the persuasive rationale of knowledge assets to the plane of managerial action. There were certainly overtones of the political design perspective, for example in the way in which the knowledge assets approach was both driven and constrained by intramanagement conflicts and interests. Meanwhile the failure to translate that approach into meaningful categories and representations is suggestive of some of the informational factors at work here. Beyond that, though, there are also intimations of other important constraints. Thus the different groups involved were not only working from within a given structural location and political interests, but also from bounded knowledge bases that heavily conditioned the way in which they applied the knowledge assets framework. In other words, the implementation of this framework necessarily had to take place *through* the expertise of particular groups, and consequently reflected such groups' knowledges and partisan concerns. CommCo personnel function's radical distillation of collective core competences into what was for them the more manageable form of individual skills and development plans is a perfect instance of the mediating impact of specialist expertise.

These points are further reinforced by two cases in which there is an even clearer link between the content and representations of information systems and the expertise of the management groups responsible for designing them.

MetalCo had a corporate strategy that focused on quality through technical improvements in production methods within tight financial controls. An interest in the identification of skills and knowledge assets came from a desire to demonstrate clear, cost-effective links between the extensive training carried out by MetalCo and the corporate strategy. The approach therefore focused entirely on individual employees and the development of a standards-based analysis of all the competencies required for particular jobs as well as possible routes for acquiring such skills. The informational element of the system, which was paper-based, involved measuring employee performance against the required standard, thus giving a graphical representation of the job holder's abilities relative to the job requirements in each specific competence identified for the job. For those individuals who had areas of weakness the system defined possible training courses and other routes such as secondment or distance learning. Although control of the system lay with the line managers who defined job profiles and assessed their staff in relation to them, the definition of standards, ways of measuring them and routes to acquiring them were carried out with strong personnel involvement and centralised monitoring. This produced clear and robust classifications – for example competences were defined at four levels: strategic, advanced, implementation and practice, and fundamental. However the paper-based system did not allow for the aggregation of data very far beyond the individual level. Even summary data on a plant or department's competence changes over time involved time-consuming clerical exercises.

The other company, VehCo, was a volume vehicle producer whose competitive strategy focused on reducing cost and improving quality. VehCo had made a commitment to continuity of service for its employees and to being a 'people orientated' company. Again the attempt to identify knowledge assets reflected a mixed bag of policy and operational objectives. The personnel function, which played the major role in this attempt, saw its wider mission as ensuring that employee skills matched the demands of the job. At the same time the company's commitment to job security meant that centralised allocation of staff was increasingly necessary to cope with the effects of technical change. These policy issues were allied to more specific concerns. The system to identify knowledge assets was piloted in the various engineering functions of the firm, where there was concern about the unfocused and costly training resulting from an existing system of individual development. More importantly, engineering activities were increasingly being organised through project teams rather than functional structures.This created a need to collate centralised information on individual engineers' skills so that project teams could draw on the best available expertise.

To meet these objectives, and with the assistance of an information systems manager, Personnel developed a prototype computerised 'skills database', which formed a module within a broader management information system. Details of the individual skills and job profiles of 600 engineers were fed into this system. The categories used to define such details provided, in effect, a common language to mediate between personal experience and job requirements. They were developed, however, from the bottom up; that is to say within existing divisional and functional boundaries. Thus the skills on the database were defined hierarchically in relation to specific engineering systems: from 'family' (for example chassis engineering), through 'group' (for example brakes) to 'skill' elements (for example brake pads). Each job was defined in terms of a particular skills profile. Manager–subordinate discussions produced an agreed report on the job-holder's skills in relation to that profile. Individual skills were ranked from 'NA' ('new area') through 'basic', 'developing' and 'comprehensive' against the job profile.

Once collated through the skills database, this information provided visual representations (a string of pluses, minuses or equals) of 'skills gaps' at both the individual and the departmental level. This was indeed the primary objective, as the system's major personnel champion noted: 'The basic thing is to identify skills gaps and allow us to close them in the most cost-effective manner'. A secondary benefit, though, would be facilitating the assembly of project teams where particular skills were needed. However, neither the implementation of the system nor its use were free from unanticipated problems and consequences. Defining a list of skills that was detailed enough to be meaningful and acceptable, yet generic enough to allow comparison proved an immensely tortuous task. The 'objective' evaluation of skills also threatened personal sensitivities, as the personnel champion noted:

> If you say to an individual you have a low level of skill. Of course we're not bothered – we can manage with a low level of skill. Then the guy's going to go out thinking, 'I'm pretty low and the department's not very good either because they can manage with a low level of skills'.

Nor did the local champions of the skills database find it easy to persuade their colleagues that its benefits would outweigh the emotional and intellectual agonising involved in relating individual competences to job profiles. Managers simply did not think of their subordinates as bundles of specific skills, and what would not come naturally had to be coached and learned.

While these factors limited the adoption of the system, its methodology and design also placed important limits on its use. Most importantly, the corollary of focusing on 'skills gaps' was to define the employee's skills narrowly in terms of the skills profile required for the job. This limited the pursuit of flexibility to the movement of individuals across existing job specifications. Added to this, the interpretation and application of the system lay in the hands of the personnel function. Having little control over the way job profile skills were defined by line management or the negotiations that defined personal skill attainments, Personnel tended to fall into the role of policing the system. This they did by ensuring standardisation in the inputting of the data, using their tacit knowledge of the organisation to 'correct' abnormal entries and control staff movements based on system data. For example, one personnel manager commented that transfers to and from the 'non-metallic materials' area (in effect, trim and upholstery, where the workforce was almost 100 per cent female) would have to be carefully vetted.

Discussion

Comparison of our case-study firms suggests a number of conclusions as to the way the knowledge assets issue emerges and is handled in different organisational contexts. The first point to make here is the importance of the strategic context behind the identification of knowledge assets. This was not only reflected in the strategic concerns that stimulated the pursuit of core competences, but in the broader impact of differing product-market strategies. Thus both MetalCo and VehCo saw the primary purpose of their skills databases in terms of the delivery of an already predefined strategy. This flowed from a strategic focus on incremental improvements in existing processes rather than new markets and new products. Human resource specialists played a primary role in systems development and this was reflected in the way the systems were tied in to appraisal systems, training, and internal labour markets. At the same time the personnel function was very concerned not to jeopardise the line management 'ownership', which provided legitimacy for the initiative. For both organisations this created problems of 'consistency' and 'objectivity' in skill definition and measurement – precisely the aspects the system claimed to deliver. In contrast the high-tech organisations took a much more strategic view of the knowledge assets issue, and their attempts to define such assets were driven from a more senior level. Their concern with corporate skills was played out in the context of decisions on the future development of the business. The aim of making 'core competences' more visible was to provide a framework for such decisions.

Different strategic orientations were not the only factor at work here, though. Crucial to the eventual outcomes of these initiatives was the way in which the competitive environment was internalised and assimilated via the specialist expertise of groups within the management structure. This distribution of knowledge within and about the organisation, together with its representation in existing information systems was crucial in shaping the emergence, content and impact of knowledge databases. Thus, in the bureaucratic context of Metalco and VehCo, knowledge of the relationship between individual skills and wider corporate capabilities was already embedded in the existing structural 'grid' of jobs and skills. As management saw no strategic need to challenge the distribution of skills embodied in that grid, their databases could focus on the relatively narrow issue of bridging the skills gap between the requirements of the job and the competences of the individual. In the high tech context, however, the interest in knowledge assets was largely a reflection of needs for innovation and change. This effectively ruled out the use of existing job descriptions as a template for the development of competences. As a result the problem of translating strategic models of knowledge assets into operational terms was much greater, and in CommCo at least, was only partially resolved by the personnel function intervening to reinterpret it as a manageable 'skills gap' problem. The problems of the high-tech firms were further aggravated by the distribution of managerial expertise. It appeared that the senior managers who deployed the strategic language of competences lacked the technologies needed to make it effective. Conversely, personnel functions possessed some of those tools, but their expertise involved a redefinition of knowledge assets into highly individualised terms. Thus, while Personnel were equipped with the tools and existing information systems to do the job they lacked the necessary organisational stature and strategic knowledge.

Conclusions

Applying these findings to the two above-noted models of information system design and use produces some interesting revisions. The study found both intramanagement politics and informational issues shaping the design and use of databases. The role of corporate planning at TechCo and the sometimes perverse effects of the skills categories at VehCo stand out as examples here. Significantly, however, these influences did not operate unilaterally but seemed to be heavily mediated by the concerns and conceptual dispositions of the different groups involved. Not to put too fine a point on it, the expertise of the various management groups involved had an important effect on the way in which knowledge assets were modelled, interpreted and methodologically translated into information systems. The application of Personnel expertise, in particular, led to knowledge assets being defined in a highly individualistic, developmental fashion. This provided a more quantifiable calibration of knowledge assets, and hence a more viable methodology for the development of skills databases. However this was at the expense of neglecting the collective aspects of knowledge assets, and also, given personnel's marginal role relative to line management, at the cost of some loss of credibility and political impact for the systems thus designed.

Although these findings suggest a fairly pessimistic outlook for the development of skills and knowledge databases, this has to be set against the escalating incentives to seek greater information and central control over knowledge assets. Moreover, many of the informational problems posed by such systems may well submit to the sheer information-processing power of

IT. However a more enduring constraint revealed by our study is the established division of expertise within management. Bloomfield (1991) claims that the implementation of IT systems serves to promote new perspectives and managerial practices and thus 'empowers' particular forms of expertise. The present study, however, suggests a more cautious view of the extent to which information systems alone can reshape meanings and practices that are already inscribed by the preceding distribution of expertise. In other words, while information systems may systematise and extend what organisations already know, they cannot change the conditions of knowing.

Note

1. This study was carried out jointly with Sonia Liff of the Warwick Business School and was supported by pilot funding from the school.

References

Badaracco, J. (1991) *The Knowledge Link: How firms compete through strategic alliances* (Boston: Harvard Business School Press).

Bloomfield, B. P.(1991) 'The role of information systems in the UK National Health Service: Action at a distance and the fetish of calculation', *Social Studies of Science*, vol. 21, no. 4, pp. 701–34.

Bloomfield, B. P. and Coombs, R. (1992) 'Information technology, control and power: The centralisation and decentalisation debate revisited', *Journal of Management Studies*, vol. 29, no. 4, 459–84.

Cohen, W. M. and Levinthal, D. A. (1990) 'Absorptive capacity: A new perspective on learning and innovation', *Administrative Science Quarterly*, vol. 35, pp. 128–52.

Hall, R. (1992) 'The strategic analysis of intangible resources', *Strategic Management Journal*, vol. 13, pp. 135–44.

Klein, J. A., Edge, G. M. and Kass, T. (1991) 'Skill-based competition', *Journal of General Management*, vol. 16, no. 4, pp. 1–15.

Kogut, B. and Zander, U. (1992) 'Knowledge of the firm, combinative capabilities and the replication of technology', *Organization Science*, vol. 3, no. 3, pp. 383–97.

Nelson, R. and Winter, S. (1982) *An Evolutionary Theory of Organisational Change* (Cambridge, Mass.: Harvard University Press).

Polanyi, M. (1967) *The Tacit Dimension* (New York: Doubleday Anchor).

Poster, M. (1992) 'Databases as discourse', Conference on 'Knowledge-workers in contemporary society', Lancaster, September.

Pralahad, C. K. and Hamel, G. (1990) 'The core competence of the corporation', *Harvard Business Review*, May–June, pp. 79–91.

Schultz, T. W. (1971) *Investment in Human Capital* (New York: Free Press).

Stubbart, C. and Ramaprasad, A. (1990) 'Comments on empirical articles and recommendations for future research', in A. Huff, (ed.) *Mapping Strategic Thought* (Chichester: Wiley).

Wilkinson, B. (1983) *The Shopfloor Politics of New Technology* (London: Heinemann).

Willcocks, L. and Mason, D. (1987) *Computerising Work: People, systems design and workplace relations* (London: Paradigm Press).

CHAPTER 8

Beleaguered professionals: clinicians and institutional change in the NHS

Lynn Ashburner and Louise Fitzgerald

This chapter addresses the impact of institutional changes in the UK National Health Service on the expertise and professionalism of doctors. It not only surveys the scope and content of change, but also explores the implications for present understandings of the role of doctors in society. Medical practitioners are well worth studying in this context because they can be seen as the extreme end of the spectrum of professional and expert formation, the archetypal model of professional power and disciplinary knowledge. It follows, however, that while this group has much to tell us about the management of expertise in general, it is also one the most difficult groups to locate in a comparative study of expertise. Indeed there is a good case for arguing that their massively ramified professional formation is a unique historical phenomenon that defies ready comparison or generalisation.

But without denying the unique features of the medical profession's history, there are equally powerful arguments for a re-evaluation of their knowledge claims and powers in the context of wider institutional and technological change. First, any professional grouping needs to be located within a 'system of professions' (Abbott, 1988) where interprofessional competition helps shape its control of certain 'jurisdictions' of work and knowledge. Secondly, and more importantly in the current context, the evolution of professional jurisdictions themselves needs to be related to rapidly changing institutional contexts. The pincer effect of market forces, technological change and managerial control tends to break down the tightly defined jurisdictions formed by *interprofessional* competition into more contingent combinations of knowledge, work and status defined by *interorganisational* competition. The effects of this paradigm shift in institutional form are too complex to be squeezed into the one-dimensional plane of 'deprofessionalisation'. They raise important questions about the interpenetration of management tasks and medical expertise, and the distribution of medical knowledge between different occupational groups. There are political issues at stake here, but these are being worked through indirectly by the construction of quasi-market disciplines that create autonomous organisations and a consequent blurring of managerial and medical practices. The emerging parallels with the management of other expert groups, R&D scientists for example, are clear. So too are similar constraints on management action, including the professional stigma attached to dilution or 'hybridisation' of the knowledge-base, the wider managerial problem of the interdependency of practical knowledge and social relations, and the uneasy interface between hierarchical controls and membership of a cohesive knowledge community.

Introduction

The concept of professionalism has been the traditional means of under-standing the role of certain workers, distinguished by their monopoly of knowledge or expertise, in their relationship with other occupational groups. With the expansion of specialised knowledge and the increasing variety of technological developments, there has been an equally diverse development of relationships within organisations, between 'experts', professionals, other workers and managers.

Given the privileges traditionally afforded professional status, its attain-ment has been the objective of many occupational groups. Now the concept is in danger of losing its usefulness as its defining features are constantly being broadened or redefined. This usefulness was always limited, since much of the research on professions focused somewhat narrowly and tended to examine the differences between professions and other occupations, rather than the similarities. Some facets of the professional model could be seen as almost tautological; for example, professionalism embraces a need for autonomy, and autonomy reflects the fact that this is professional work. This leads us to the view that in trying to understand the ever-changing relationships and boundaries between the medical profession and manage-ment, the concept of profession may not be adequate. One might question whether it remains useful to talk narrowly of professionals or more broadly of experts? Has the concept of the professional been superseded or do unique features still remain that distinguish professionals from experts? Crompton

(1990) presents a useful discussion of the conflicts and contradictions inherent in previous research on professions. She puts forward the argument that the concept of a profession does not describe a generic occupational type, but rather a mode of regulation of the exchange of expert labour. With this point in mind, we shall argue that it is more useful to examine key characteristics of 'professions', such as their monopoly of expertise and autonomy and their impact within a given context, than to seek to justify a profession as a distinct and different occupational group.

Another reason for questioning the utility of the concept of 'profession' lies in the fact that a profession is said to be based on a common and definable body of specialist knowledge. Indeed in the UK and the USA great stress is placed on the rational/scientific nature of medical decisions and judgements. In reality, medical 'knowledge' and the practice of medicine can be seen as highly culturally influenced. Payer (1988) draws attention to the wide variations in medical thinking in the USA, the UK, France and Germany. She raises the question: how can medicine, which is supposed to be a science, be so different in four countries whose people are genetically similar? In a thought provoking (and highly amusing) text, she documents the wide differences in medical thought and treatments, for example low blood pressure treated with 85 drugs and hydrotherapy in Germany would entitle the sufferer to lower life insurance rates in the USA. For widely different reasons, it is interesting to compare the position of Soviet doctors with that of their counterparts in Europe and the USA. Field (1988) indicates that the status of Soviet doctors is lower and their degree of autonomy negligible. Nevertheless, in the Soviet scheme, a doctor maintains a very dominant position over the patient. These comparative examples serve to demonstrate that some of the criteria for assessing 'a profession' are not as absolute and clear-cut as one might assume, and indeed are contextually and culturally framed.

The focus in this chapter is on the impact of the changes in the UK health care system on doctors and on the interfaces between medical professionals and managers. In the UK, doctors have historically been widely recognised as having 'professional' status. As such, this profession in the UK has a long and unique history, with very different foundations from those of the newer and more technologically based areas of expertise, for example IT specialists and engineers. Medicine as an area of specialist knowledge still remains largely inaccessible to the layman, unlike 'newer' areas of expertise, which are relatively more accessible or transparent. Whilst the practice of medicine has become increasingly reliant on high-tech equipment, the basic foundations of medical and scientific knowledge that form the undergraduate programme of learning in the UK have remained relatively static (Stevens, 1966). One indicator of the stable body of knowledge is that the five year duration and the content of the undergraduate programme, established before the inception of the NHS, remains in place. As a result this occupational group, in this context, has been able to identify and define the body of knowledge over which it has monopoly. Furthermore it has achieved state support for this monopoly and its accreditation procedures. Finally, despite the assumption in 1961 by the then Ministry of Health of formal control over the national supply of medical manpower, it has maintained control over the supply of skilled experts through setting targets for the number and standards of the intake to medical schools. In summary, it is this combination of historical, cultural and relational factors that has allowed this occupational group to acquire the 'professional' label.

This is not to suggest that technological advances have not led to pressures for change. The main pressure has been towards increasing the volume of curriculum content rather than dramatic shifts in the programme. Thus current undergraduates have a limited introduction to the uses of information technology. Similarly, considerable emphasis is placed on formal knowledge and much less on the acquisition of skills, such as interpersonal skills in dealing with patients. This approach lies at the heart of the doctor–patient relationship, which tends to be conceptualised as a relationship of dependency rather than the meeting of two 'experts' from different domains. Whilst the public image of medicine tends to focus on its technological advances – nuclear magnetic resonance machines – changing medical technology has impacted differentially on medical specialities. Thus techno-logical and scientific advances have radically altered the capabilities and modes of service delivery in radiology and surgery in the last 15 years, but have had little impact on the field of mental illness.

This chapter examines evidence from two studies of the medical profession in the UK, which in the past has been relatively successful in maintaining its traditional powers of control and autonomy. The studies focused on how this form of 'expertise' has reacted to continual attempts to manage it. How is the medical profession reacting to the introduction of the quasi-market and the increase in managerialism and the consequent attempts to change the balance of power between doctors and managers?

We begin by examining briefly the historical, political and economic context of the development of medicine as a profession and its relationships with management and other professions. Next we explore the various theoretical traditions that have attempted to account for the evolution of the professions and consider some of the wider societal and organisational influences that are in operation. Trends in the UK are compared with those in the USA where several writers suggest that a process of 'deprofessionalisation' (Haug, 1973) or 'proletarianisation' (McKinlay and Arches, 1985) is occurring. We assess the extent to which these ideas are useful in understanding current developments that are a consequence of recent government reforms. The third section will introduce the empirical data from the two studies and examine the implications of this for the development of theory. The main focus of the studies is on clinicians in provider units, but the data also show that the relationship between clinicians and management varies between different sectors of the NHS and within different sections of acute and primary care.

Thus a wide range of changes are beginning to emerge. Finally, the issue of the relative value of the concept of professionalism will be assessed in relation to medicine.

The complexity of the changes currently facing the NHS – and within it, the medical profession – have led us to identify three main themes to be explored through the examination of the empirical data:

- Changes that have occurred within the profession, in terms of losses and gains by medical professionals in different parts of the service.
- The evolving relationships between management and the medical profession.
- The impact of the quasi-market on the medical profession.

The historical and political context

The history of the changing relationship between medical professionals, managers and government shows the continuing growth in the influence of management. At the time of the formation of the NHS in 1948, what determined its structure and hierarchy was the relative power positions of the medical profession and the government. In the process of negotiation to draw an independent profession into a universal health system where practitioners' remuneration to a certain extent would be controlled by the state, many other aspects of their independence and autonomy were in fact strengthened and even protected by statute. For example, as Harrison and Schultz (1989) show, the government guaranteed the medical profession clinical freedom in order to ensure their participation in the NHS.

Organisationally, the NHS was best understood not as a public sector bureaucracy but as Burns (1981) described it, a collaborative system comprising a complex set of relationships between administrators and various professional groups that produced a loosely structured order. Thus the medical profession was effectively free of direct control from either government or management. A further facet of 'management' was the role of health authorities, with their tripartite membership of elected local government representatives, professionals and lay people. One might argue that differences could be played out in this forum so that the directives passed to the officers and administrators responsible for the day-to-day running of the service, reflected a balance of interests. The alternative view, which emerged from several empirical studies such as that by Day and Klein (1987), was that such bodies had limited effectiveness due to role ambiguity and lack of corporate identity.

With no conventional hierarchies or lines of managerial responsibility, the medical profession had an indirect but key influence over the management of their own parts of the service. This level of clinical freedom was enhanced by the continuation of medical dominance over other health service professionals. As Larkin (1988) shows, the government was instrumental in protecting the autonomy of the medical profession in relation to particular medical practices in the face of competition from other professions. The British medical profession has consistently managed to resist inroads into its autonomy. Halpern (1992) shows how the use of political and institutional processes have enabled the medical profession to remain dominant throughout all its interprofessional struggles.

In a period of economic growth, the efficiency and effectiveness of this organisational form was not questioned, but from the 1970s it was increasingly recognised that some change was necessary to create a more responsive form of organisation. The relentless upward trend in the costs of health care, with the gradually ageing population and the desire to eradicate inequities in the level and distribution of health service provision, has led to increasing pressure for greater 'management' control. In the face of such a well-established medical power base, the transformation of administrators into managers and their empowerment has been a gradual process.

In the name of efficiency and economy, in the 1980s the government challenged the power of the growing bureaucracies – and the professional groups within them – across the whole of the public sector. In Britain, as in most Western economies there was the growing pressure of a reducing GDP and what McKinlay (1988, p. 2) calls the 'modest contribution of medicine to the health status of populations'. What was perceived to be a lack of a conventional management hierarchy within the NHS meant that there were inadequate mechanisms for controlling expenditure in any precise way. In professionally dominated organisations such as the NHS, change could only be achieved by increased control over the activities of professionals.

Studies of the structural changes introduced in 1974 (Elcock, 1978), which aimed to introduce a team approach to decision making via consensus, found a very high degree of cultural and organisational resilience and minimal actual change. Its domination by professionals, loose structure and strong internal culture had apparently enabled the NHS to withstand attempts at fundamental change. Governments were not deterred and new reforms aimed at restructuring continued. The Griffiths Report (1983) was a continuation of this effort and is generally credited with the introduction of general management into the NHS.

Besides introducing personnel and structures from the private sector, Griffiths stated that a crucial target for the health service was to encourage more doctors into general management. The aim was for a single accountable individual to head each unit as a general manager with a clear corporate remit. This represented the introduction of hierarchy into the NHS, but there was no sustained flow of clinicians into general management posts. The obvious pay and status differentials deterred most doctors from making what might have been an irrevocable move to what could be seen as a less desirable career and an alien value system. General management was still not the complete answer. Consultants were still responsible for the majority of decisions involving large resource implications in the course of providing individual care. Nevertheless the introduction of general management did result in considerable changes in management processes. Power shifted more towards managers as a result of budgetary control and resource constraints, or more indirectly through the introduction of new information technology. Even before the Griffiths reforms had been fully established, plans were being laid for further changes.

The 1990 NHS reforms

Since the Griffiths restructuring had not achieved all that was expected, the government made moves to build on what progress had been made, and in 1989 a White Paper called *Working for Patients* (Cmnd 555), was published. This became the NHS and Community Care Act (1990), and unlike its predecessors it introduced a wide range of reforms that were more ideological than structural in nature. The central idea was that the roles of purchaser and provider should be separated and that the mechanisms of health care provision should be governed by an internal quasi market, rather than by local and central planning.The introduction of a 'market' in health care was a radical change, and can be seen as part of the 'free market' ideology of the Conservative government. But more particularly it represented a shift in the locus of control, with the 'market' and competition now driving economic efficiency. Another main strand of this policy was the opportunity for hospitals and other provider units to cease being managed directly by district health authorities (DHAs) and to go for trust status. As increasing numbers of units have achieved trust status, this has removed the whole gamut of managerial functions from DHAs and left them primarily as purchasers of health care on behalf of their local populations. Their purchasing strategy was to be based upon priorities set at both a central and a local level.

The autonomy given to trusts, although limited, can be seen as part of a process of management decentralisation, but it is also an important component of the move away from an essentially planned approach to service provision to one governed by market forces.

The role of the general practitioner in the purchasing of health care was another central aspect of the reforms. The introduction of fundholding was directly acknowledged in the White Paper as a means to make hospitals – that is, hospital clinicians – more responsive to GPs' needs. By the third wave, it was estimated that over £40 million of purchasing power would lie with GPs, involving a significant movement of resources away from health authorities (Ashburner, 1993), and further reducing the capacity of DHAs to control the purchasing and thus the planning of the provision of health care in their locality. An important result of this change has been that it has fundamentally altered the relationship between GPs and hospital clinicians.

The third major strand of the reforms was the change in the composition of health authorities. Underpinning the purchaser–provider split was another central 'idea'; that the structures, culture and models of the private sector were somehow more efficient and effective in the management of any organisation. The new health authorities and the newly formed trust boards were modelled on the pattern of private sector boards. Health authorities had formerly comprised three main groups: health service professionals, elected local authority representatives and 'lay' members. The new composition specifically excluded any form of representation, removing both the professional and local authority representatives (Ashburner and Cairncross, 1993). Now, in addition to the five non-executive members and the non-executive chair, there are five executive members. This has removed the reporting role of officers and brought managers directly into the higher, strategic level of management. This change was intended to make the new bodies 'more businesslike', but one consequence has been the loss of representation for paramedic and nursing professionals. Although there is a statutory place for a clinician on trust boards, this is not the case for district health authorities, where the main purchasing decisions are made. However, immediately following the reforms almost 80 per cent of DHAs did appoint a medical practitioner to the board. This again has the potential to change the balance of power between managers and clinicians.

Structurally, the position of clinicians may appear to have weakened and that of managers considerably strengthened. In reality the relationship between the two groups is more complex. Our data explores the role of clinicians in management with the development of clinical directors and clinical management teams in provider units. Alongside these changes, the development of a public health role in purchasing and the new breed of GP fundholder have the potential to increase the power of certain groups of clinicians, in specific circumstances. From this it is clear that the wide range of changes that are now impacting on the medical profession cannot be understood by any single concept. We need to examine the theoretical baggage of the study of the medical professions, and establish whether it can provide a sufficiently explanatory capacity.

The theoretical context

There are many approaches to the study of the professions. The three key ones are the functionalist perspective, the interactionist perspective and the theory of closure. The earliest analyses focused on the internal dynamics of what constituted a profession and how the profession developed, while later ones have considered the wider political, economic, historic and social contexts of professions, their relationship to organisations and inter- and intraprofessional boundary disputes. In this section it will be argued that the concept of a profession is an ambiguous one, and therefore what needs to be explored are the constituent key concepts that have been used in defining a profession, such as that of professional autonomy. Similarly, since in common with some other writers we are interested in the impact of change processes on doctors, we would argue that the social and political context must be incorporated into the analysis. The debate around the professional model tends to imply a linear process of change, focusing on unidimensional, quantum changes, for example deprofessionalisation and proletarianisation, irrespective of context. It is our intention, in a later section, to use our empirical data to challenge some of these explanations.

The earliest theoretical approach to the medical professions came from the functionalist tradition (Parsons, 1951), which analysed the defining features of professions as credentialism, universalism, neutrality, homogeneity, control of entry and autonomy. This approach is highly selective in focusing on particular features of work. Atkinson and Delamont (1990) have described it as merely uncritically reproducing the professionals' own claims, overemphasising the degree of homogeneity and not accounting for the differential distribution of power, control and rewards within a profession. As Murray, Dingwall and Eekelar (1983) emphasise, a distinction needs to be made between the 'outward' and 'inward' face of a profession. The functionalist approach only considers the 'outward' perspective. This narrows the focus to a collective view of the professions as neutral, knowledge-based and working for the 'general good'. Turning the analysis 'inward' requires a very different set of dynamics.

A distinction thus needs to be drawn between the collective position of a profession and that of the individuals within it. From the interactionist tradition has emerged a perception of the professions as merely a specialised form of division of labour, and any differences just those of degree. An emphasis on the internal characteristics has led to the questioning of the level of homogeneity within professions and a highlighting of the exchange relationships and negotiating that exist both within a profession and between related professions and which result in differential distribution of power, control and rewards.

Closure theory focuses on the strategy adopted by groups to achieve closure and control and in its examination of process has similarities with the interactionist approach. Its focus on the meaning of exclusivity, by which groups ensure occupational closure, however, has similarities with the functionalist approach. The attempts of occupational groups to seek professional status depend on labour-market strategies aimed at achieving occupational monopoly over the provision of certain skills and competencies.

Such a perspective is rooted in the neo-Weberian tradition and expounded by writers such as Parkin (1979), who described the tactical means of obtaining exclusionary closure as being based on the seeking of legal monopoly – through licensure by the state – and credentialism, which is used as the means to monitor and restrict entry to the profession. Whilst this process may have been successful in the past, it is arguably more difficult to achieve today, with the proliferation of newer and less stable fields of knowledge and the fuzziness of boundaries between fields of knowledge.

Across these various perspectives there are some commonly agreed characteristics of a profession. Firstly, there is a body of expert knowledge over which the profession exerts a degree of control and, in the purest form, a monopoly of practice. Then there are issues around credentialism. Within the profession, individuals as the holders of specialist expertise expect to exercise a degree of autonomy over their work and work processes. This control may even extend to control over the work of others and related professions. From this emerges two central concepts, those of professional dominance and professional autonomy, both of which reflect the collective and individual aspects of the 'outward' and 'inward' faces of the profession.

With regard to the medical profession, the concept of professional dominance is most closely related to the work of Freidson (1970). He discusses it primarily in terms of the dominance of the medical profession over other health care professionals and managers, whilst others would extend this to include dominance over patients. Navarro (1988) suggests that the extent of the dominance can only be understood in relation to the profession's interrelationships with other professions and occupations in a societal context.

Professional autonomy, of which clinical freedom is a part, can be conceptualised at the individual and collective level and refers to the various forms of autonomy exercised over the content and condition of practice. This potentially ambiguous concept can be used emotively to defend the position of doctors and so it is especially important that it is critically evaluated. Professional or clinical autonomy cannot be seen as an absolute, since total freedom for any individual or group is bound to impinge on the freedom of others. Thus any definition will have limitations. What must be assessed when considering the relative positions of two groups, such as clinicians and managers, is the scope and boundaries of autonomy and how these are changing.

The relative importance ascribed to autonomy by different writers depends on which aspect of autonomy they see as critical. Wolinsky (1988) sees it as a red herring since there have always been constraints on clinical freedom, especially limited resources. On the other hand Harrison and Schultz (1989) place the concept at the heart of the professions debate. In these terms, for management to be able to secure greater control over the provision of health services they would need to curtail clinical autonomy.

Here it is necessary to distinguish between collective and individual autonomy. Increased managerial control may threaten individual autonomy and has given rise in the USA to arguments about 'deprofessionalisation' (Haug, 1973) and 'proletarianisation' (McKinlay and Arches, 1985). Freidson (1983) would argue however, that from the American experience, at a collective level the medical profession is as powerful as ever. The key difference between the concept of autonomy as used in the USA and Britain, is that in the USA it includes the assumption of economic freedom. In Britain, economic freedom was surrendered in exchange for greater state safeguards for other aspects of autonomy, primarily that of clinical freedom. Elston (1991) reviews several classifications of autonomy (Freidson, 1970; Ovreteit, 1985; Harrison and Schultz, 1989) and also stresses the importance of state support.

Setting the changes the medical profession is undergoing into their theoretical context requires the use of a much broader analytical base. Most writers would acknowledge the importance of social context, whilst others stress specific aspects such as historical context, politics, economics, gender and race. Less common are analyses of how professions impact on organisational forms (Scott, 1985) and how they are linked into the class and labour-market systems (Hall, 1988). McKinlay (1988) warns against a too narrow focus on the managerial changes that are now happening because without a political and economic analysis there will be little contribution to understanding.

There is now a partial meeting of theorists from different perspectives. Abbott (1988) for example, is an interactionist who has broadened his perspective to include historical and social context. He describes professions and occupations as interdependent systems each with their own jurisdiction, with different levels of control and with boundaries that are in perpetual dispute. This dynamic model of the professions is useful in that it focuses attention on the constantly changing boundaries between a profession and other occupational groups and underlines the role of power in renegotiating these boundaries. This model stresses the interrelationship between the inner and outer contexts of professional systems. It also helps to explain why general forces such as bureaucratisation or knowledge changes do not have a uniform effect but are highly idiosyncratic in their outcomes. Crompton's (1990) work also presents a broader frame of reference, seeing the differences and similarities between professions and other occupations more in terms of differing modes of control.

Scott (1985) comments on the effects of constantly changing professional, organisational and environmental developments on the structure and performance of medical organisations. He does this at two levels of analysis: the changes in relationship between managers and professionals; and the changes in relations between health care organisations and their environments. His conceptual framework has relevance for the current changes in the UK. He disputes early theorists' ideas that professionalisation and bureaucratisation are opposing forces and even that they are alternatives. He sees them as companion processes. This is similar to Hafferty (1988), who shows that bureaucracies can and do make accommodations to professionals, and Davies (1983), who maintains that bureaucracies and professionals can work well together.

Scott suggests that there are three main trends. He shows how the growth of management influence is partly the result of the needs of the medical profession's increasing complexity and need for coordination and management. As organisational environments become more complex and as medical specialities subdivide, there is the consequent need to manage the boundaries with the environment and to coordinate the increasing range of different and often conflicting interests. Secondly, he highlights the increasing intraprofessional divisions, for example between public health physicians, who relate to patients as collectives, and GPs or hospital consultants, who relate to patients in one-to-one care; where the former are increasingly trying to control the work of the latter. The third trend he identifies is the huge growth in allied health professionals. All three represent incursions into the domain of medical professionals and present the potential for increased conflict.

Thus there are many trends that might be seen as a threat to the autonomy of the medical profession, of which an increase in management power is only one. In order to begin to understand the transformation that the medical profession is undergoing, we need to consider the data that has emerged from two recent studies.

The evidence from recent research

This section discusses the results of two different research projects, both of which took place during the critical period of changes in health care in the UK: 1990–93.

The first project tracked a cohort of clinicians as they assumed management responsibilities and followed their progress as they undertook management training. The methodology adopted for this research was a staged, processual one. This enabled the clinician's situation prior to training to be examined, and data to be gathered at a number of key stages, during and after the training period. In order to understand the professional position of the clinician, one must analyse the context in which he/she works. This approach of contextualising the doctors' position is a key feature of this analysis. Previous research has been criticised for failing to take account of the sociopolitical context in which a profession is currently operating (Davies, 1983). Adopting a methodology that embeds the role and activity within its context and traces that context longitudinally is a route to understanding the nature of professions and of professional power. The second advantage of the methodology is that it produces an account of development and progression through time, in a context that is changing rapidly. Whilst the data are insufficient to track trends, they do offer indications of the inhibitors and supports to progress.

The characteristics of the cohort are also pertinent. The cohort was small and consisted of 31 clinicians who were assuming or had already assumed management roles, mainly as clinical directors or medical directors within a health-care provider unit. All the roles assumed carried and still carry major management responsibilities, but the position of medical director is usually the most senior and carries automatic membership of the unit's board. As an example of the level of management responsibility involved, by the latter phases of the study virtually all clinical managers were budget holders, with budgetary responsibility ranging from £1.9 million to £4.5 million. Medical directors had corporate budgets ranging from £36 million to £42 million. A wide range of specialisms were included in the group, from acute medicine – anaesthetics, surgery, obstetrics and gynaecology – to community health and psychiatry. Within the group there were 26 males and five females, aged between 35 and 56.

The second project had a broader focus and studied the operation of the 'new' boards of the DHAs, family health service authorities (FHSAs) and trusts. Again, a longitudinal methodology was adopted, and nested hierarchies of boards were studied for periods of between six and 18 months. Data were collected by direct observation of board meetings, interviews with board members and through archival data. Within the research, professionals are observed as members of boards, advisors to the boards, those in specialist professional positions, such as director of public health, and as professional members of senior management teams.

The introduction to this chapter detailed a number of themes to be explored through the data. These were: the changes that have occurred in the profession in terms of losses and gains by medical professionals in different parts of the service; the evolving relationships between management and the medical profession; and the impact of the quasi-market on the medical profession.

Hafferty's (1988) work sets out some of the threats to the dominance of the medical profession within the current context. This list provides a useful starting point for examining specific issues in the light of the changes under examination. He suggests five areas of threat, including the threat that a marketplace in health care will increase competition between professionals and cause divisions; that rifts may develop within the profession between the clinical managers and the clinicians who are being managed; and that greater managerialism will reduce the power of the profession. This chapter will discuss these threats in the light of the research results.

As illustrated in the introduction, some authors have debated the relative importance of the issue of professional autonomy at both the individual and the collective level (Wolinsky, 1988; Harrison and Schultz, 1989), whilst others (Goode, 1960; Hetherington, 1982) have debated the conflicts between professionalism, professional autonomy and management. As much of the literature is premised on the conflicts between professional and bureaucratic approaches, it tends to adopt the view that any professional moving into management is effectively moving out of the profession. This perspective is clearly open to dispute, as the evidence from this research will demonstrate. However the research data will illustrate that the language of confrontation, using terms such as 'betrayal' and 'desertion', is still employed to exert social pressure on clinical managers.

The key changes affecting professional roles

At the core of the process of contracting for health-care delivery is the split between purchasers and providers. On the provider side, it is essential to be able to specify a level of service from a group of clinicians and other paramedics, to a specified cost and quality. This is a major impetus for involving clinicians actively in management decisions. It is virtually impossible to imagine how managers, in isolation, could carry out the tasks required to specify the type, form, quality standards and volumes of a specific medical service without the active involvement of the clinical specialists. Following the White Paper 'Working for Patients' in 1989, there was a dramatic shift in the organisation of many acute units, with the majority adopting a clinical directorate structure. In many regions, in a period of eighteen months units moved from having no clinical directors to having them in about 80 per cent of acute units. As a result, role definitions were rushed and suboptimal solutions produced. The majority of these clinical director roles were taken by clinicians.

As stated in the second section, the subsequent legislation – the NHS and Community Care Act (1990) – specifies the inclusion of clinicians in the management process in a more particular way. A place is reserved for a medical specialist in the boards of trusts and on FHSAs, though there is no guaranteed place for a clinician on purchasing authorities. This gives clinicians access to the most senior and strategic decision-making forums.

Fundamental shifts have also been generated by the establishment of GP fundholder practices. Not only are fundholders purchasers of services, but their purchasing power has caused a shift in the behaviour of specialists towards taking greater account of the GP's perspective. There has therefore been a major, top-down, transformational change in the UK health-care sector. The change is described here as transformational because the introduction of the quasi-market has been complemented by a vast service change at the unit level, and certain areas of service change represent substantial shifts in the way care is provided, for example the policy of moving the majority of mentally ill patients from institutional settings into the community. The range of these changes and the processes of implementation are well-documented and analysed elsewhere (for example, Pettigrew *et al.*, 1992; Harrison, 1988) and will not be dealt with here.

The impact of the changes on professional roles

The first and most notable impact of the recent changes on professional roles is that many more doctors have now accepted medical management roles, either at the clinical director level or the medical director level. Hitherto there had been a series of unsuccessful attempts to coax doctors into management (for example, in 1983 following the Griffiths Report) so this change was a substantial achievement. In the past the members of the medical profession were not persuaded of the benefits of moving into management, and having adopted this viewpoint they were very successful in resisting pressures to do so. The motivations behind their recent change of heart are complex and, as one might anticipate, varied. There is evidence (Fitzgerald, 1994), however, of three interlocking dimensions, which in combination represent an important change from the past and explain the doctors' revised views. First, the roles currently on offer are part-time and allow clinicians to continue in clinical practice. This is of prime importance to the majority of clinicians. The following view of a clinical director is typical: 'I didn't spend that length of time becoming an expert in a teaching hospital to chuck it all away, and as I said, the symbiosis has got to be there. I've got to continue to practice, so that's my first priority'.

In addition, clinicians appear to have made the judgement that the current changes in the health-care system are fundamental and will not disappear. And finally, many clinicians are excited by the challenge of a new role. The adoption of management responsibilities is not without its critics and there are also many clinicians who have accepted their new medical management role with some reluctance (Dopson, 1993).

The second major impact of the changes on professionals is that they have real influence and decision-making power. Professionals are now budget holders and are responsible for major spending decisions. They play a key role in contract setting and service development. It is clear that these clinical management roles offer members of the medical profession the opportunity to take and participate in major decisions, affecting the delivery of health-care. One clinical director described the approach he is adopting to strategic planning as follows:

> The directorate executive, that is, the consultants and nurse managers, have had two 'time-outs' and worked out what we are good at and then built a strategic plan for the next five years. Our key objective is to be one of the top ten units (in their

speciality) in the UK. We have defined the criteria for a 'top' unit by benchmarking against other such units in the UK, Europe and the USA. We have developed a scoring system based on cost, quality and effectiveness of treatment outcomes. This afternoon, I am going to Holland for a meeting with doctors who are trying to set up a similar management system.

This quote exemplifies a clinical manager who has already, in a relatively short period of time, learnt to develop a competitive approach to service development based on the distinctive competencies of the group and founded on data on 'competitors'.

Moreover the clinical directors, and especially the medical directors, have new spheres of influence as members of the trust board or trust executive. As such they have access to the highest-level management discussions and are involved from the outset in the process of planning changes.

This positive interpretation of the impact of the changes has to be balanced against the more negative recognition that this is largely a part-time role. To work effectively, the role needs careful specification and appropriate support. From the actual descriptions of their work and from the examples cited in the research, one can conclude that the clinical management role involves a considerable degree of change management and strategic management. For example one clinical director described his current priorities as follows: 'Over the next six months, I am developing the integration of the services of two hospitals and planning the transfer from one which is closing to the other, in a year's time. I am also working on the routine development of my service and the strategic planning of future services'.

Giving doctors other operational tasks could waste a valuable resource. Also, one might argue that confining the role to one of conventional management means failing to utilise the unique skills already developed by clinicians. Their prior medical training enables them to contribute in a critical way to the service strategy, to the appropriate allocation of resources, both staff and equipment, and to improving the quality of patient care.

A third impact of these changes is to establish the key, pivotal role of the medical director in a provider unit and the potentially key role of director of public health in the purchaser organisation. The evidence (Ferlie *et al.*, 1992; Ferlie *et al.*, 1993; Fitzgerald *et al.*, 1993) suggests that medical directors (and their colleagues representing teaching hospitals) in trusts and public health directors in health authorities are exercising considerable influence on boards. Whilst the newly constituted boards have provided evidence of an improved level of debate and questioning from the non-executive directors in particular, the independent viewpoint adopted by professionals on boards is remarkable. In several examples, the challenges to consensus in the group have come from a professional. Indeed in a minority of the boards they have been allowed to take on the role of 'licensed' dissenter. Such dissenters have a more secure base from within the system, more self-confidence and a more subtle approach to the raising of issues than other directors. 'I sometimes think that we do need the radically different view, the challenging position that says "well, hang on, you are going to completely disadvantage this geographical area", not necessarily going along with the position guided by the chairman. It is often my role to do that' (director of public health).

Again however a note of caution must be struck, particularly in relation to public health professionals. It is undoubtedly the case that the medical director's role is central to the success of the organisation and the managerial nature of the position is clearly recognised. Whilst the public health roles have great potential for influence, the historical context of the speciality is more chequered and the responses of professionals more uncertain. Lewis (1987) illustrates the struggle of public health as a speciality to establish a niche. Even now, Dawson *et al.* (1993) show that public health professionals still feel uncertain about their role and some feel considerable concern about embracing a 'management' role with, as they see it, a loss of their independence as the representative of community interests.

Nevertheless, in the three case studies of purchaser authorities, the public health director was an executive member of the board, the public health function was represented on all the purchasing teams and took a key role in the development of contracting. In two of the case-study sites, the annual report of the director of public health was gradually evolving into a vehicle for the dissemination of purchasing intentions and new thinking and acting as a conduit of ideas to the public.

With the advent of general management in the post-Griffiths era, power could be seen to have shifted towards management, and these new senior roles for professionals redress the balance in favour of the medical profession. They offer an opportunity to develop genuinely collaborative decision-making processes and structures, so long as managers and clinicians can be found with the willingness and managerial capacity to engage in health-care management. (The issue of doctors' management capability will be touched on in a later section.)

A fourth area in which the current changes impact on professionals is shown in the evidence of altered relationships within the professional group, between colleagues. The evidence suggests that clinical managers are grasping some thorny problems and dealing with long-standing issues that have been allowed to fester up to now. These issues relate to differential levels of performance among colleagues, which may be revealed through a medical audit. Another set of issues focus on the inequitable distribution of workload. These latter problems are currently highlighted by the need to reduce the hours worked by junior doctors'. Hitherto, clinical freedom meant that few general managers dared to deal with these issues. Significantly, it appears that there are some indicators here that issues of professional performance and professional standards are being addressed and handled by clinical managers.

A number of important issues are raised when the management role moves from the hands of a general manager, drawn from outside the professional group, into the hands of an individual who is a member of the profession. Firstly, there is the broad question of the distinctive management needs of experts and professionals. Secondly, there is the impact of such managerial actions on the concept of collegiality among professionals. In theory, one of the distinguishing features of professions as collective groups is that, whilst high standards of entry are set, once attained, all members of the profession have 'equal' status. Though developments that ensure the quality of care may be good for the health service and for the patient, will they cause dissent among clinicians?

A fifth and final impact of these changes on professionals also focuses on the relationships within the profession itself. The establishment of GP fundholders, with the buying power to purchase specified items of care for the patients on their lists, has led to an overhauling of relationships between GPs in primary care and clinicians in secondary care. Hospital clinicians now need to attract the custom of GP fundholders and a process of communicating and marketing to GPs has been quickly established. Consultants in secondary level care are now asking for the views of GPs, and indeed are shaping the service to meet their needs. This marks a considerable shift in behaviour, illustrating the shift in power. Calnan and Gabe (1991) illustrate how GPs have been traditionally viewed within the profession as being of lower status and how this has been shaped by the professional development of hospital medicine. The reversal of this trend is likely to continue with the downward pressure on costs, encouraging the use of more day surgery, with aftercare provided by the GP and the extension of the GP's role to include minor surgery performed on the GP's premises.

The changing relationships within the profession and with management

In the previous sections we have sought to establish the complexity of the changes and their impact on relationships within the medical profession and between professionals and managers. The simplistic notion of a shift of power from professionals to managers, which has been hypothesised for the USA, is not substantiated by the evidence in the UK. We would argue that the picture is richer and more complex. In a number of key ways, medical professionals have adapted to their changed circumstances and whilst their power base has altered, it has not been lost or eroded. One of the most profound impacts of the introduction of the quasi-market has been to disturb long-established power bases of particular specialities. As a result, some of the most substantial shifts of power have been intraprofessional, with different specialities losing and gaining. Overall the professionals have gained some important new roles, and with them new spheres of influence.

Budget holding at the clinical directorate level requires a shared collaborative approach to resource allocation, with discussion of priorities. The clinical director role is a part-time one in the vast majority of cases and the incumbent must therefore work as part of a management team in order to be effective. A clinical director needs to establish a core team with balanced and complementary skills to work alongside him/her. Another recent research project (Harwood and Boufford, 1993) reinforces this theme of team management. The authors describe team management as an essential prerequisite to the successful management of a clinical directorate. Thus at the directorate level one sees the evolution for the first time of a composite management team consisting of professional managers and medical professionals working together. This raises a number of issues concerning the processes of sharing expertise and learning from each other in order to capitalise on the complementary assets, and the interesting problem of developing and blending a management team of colleagues, which overcomes the 'baggage' of historical differences of status. This represents a great challenge to many medical professionals.

At the level of the whole organisation, be this an acute hospital or a community or mental health unit, the establishment of an executive team with at least one medical professional as medical director also creates a new mixed forum of general managers and professionals. One important difference from the past is that professionals are included in the executive team as equal, corporate contributors to the management team and not as more 'advisors'. General managers do still hold key positions and generally have the advantages of greater management expertise and of being in full-time management. But now professionals are actively involved in the management process.

The role of the medical director, in particular, is critical. It is important to establish the role as a strategic one, with a key contribution to strategy formulation. Thus the profession could influence strategy and not just have the negative power to block decisions. All clinical managers see themselves playing a critical boundary role between management and clinical professionals. They describe part of their role as 'translating' ideas from one forum to the other. The medical director acts as an important bridge between management and the medical profession. Particularly in the early period of transition, following the implementation of the quasi-market, this role is highly vulnerable. On the one hand relatively few clinicians have had the management training that would enable them to feel competent and confident when operating at the strategic board level. On the other hand a considerable number of clinicians, especially older ones, remain hostile to the idea of medical management roles and resent 'interference' in or management of their activities by anyone. Whilst many clinical managers experience support from colleagues and managers, there are some who see themselves as separated and on occasion, isolated from clinical colleagues. The extent of this isolation varies considerably from one location to another. In some instances, it is merely a question of occasionally employing management terms that are not understood by medical colleagues. In other examples clinical managers are subjected to a degree of downright hostility from some colleagues, which causes stress.

In the medium term the willingness of consultants to take on clinical management roles may be influenced by these events and pressures. To quote one medical director: 'If I decide to leave this role, it will be because of the isolation and the sense of distance from colleagues' (and this was in a setting where both professional colleagues and managers were on the whole supportive). If high-quality, experienced clinical managers are to be recruited and retained, then these are issues of concern.

Management training for professionals

It is clear that many professionals in health-care are being asked not only to adapt to major changes in the national systems of health-care, but also to take on new and unique medical management roles. Yet in the past few clinicians had any training in management, so there is a comprehensive development task in equipping professionals for these roles. This section will briefly present data on the clinicians' perceptions of management and the ways in which these have been influenced by training.

Clinicians are an extreme example of specialists moving into a corporate or generalist role. As a profession, they are academically orientated. Whilst some at least are keen to learn management subjects, their perceptions of what management entails are coloured by their contact with managers in health-care and by the frequently held view that managers are not well qualified and management is easy to learn (Stewart, n.d.).

The cohort of clinicians in the first project were unusual in that they had all had prior management training, even if this was only a course lasting a few days. Similarly they all had experience of management. Nevertheless their perceptions of 'management' were still relatively unsophisticated. At the start of the study the majority of the cohort described management in terms of a set of skills that frequently focused on 'people' skills, such as appraising, selecting and performance management.

Few clinicians in the cohort showed an awareness of the full range of areas of functional management, such as might be covered on an MBA course. Similarly, few consultants described management as operating at a strategic as well as an operational level in an organisation. Perhaps as a result, even the skills of management that were discussed were skills that are relevant to the management of individuals or units, such as those quoted, rather than analytical or creative skills, that might be used to formulate plans and proactive strategies. Only a couple of individuals quoted change management as a management topic of relevance. This is important because most of the clinicians described the context in which they operated and the tasks facing them as involving high strategic and change-management content.

In this cohort, clinicians went to programmes of management training based in high-quality business schools and undertook intensive courses for middle or senior managers alongside participants from all sectors of business. It is notable that following the period of study there was a shift in the clinicians' perceptions of management, and more particularly, the areas of management learning that might prove most useful to them in the future. For some, there was the discovery a functional area of management that had been largely unknown to them and proved to be relevant to their own management problems: 'Operations management was very relevant and interesting and I'm working on how to apply it. I found the finance absolutely fascinating', and 'I think it was the emphasis on quality as the concern of everyone; that is, that we are all a customer of each other, interdepartmentally. That struck me most. And the positive emphasis on welcoming complaints and dealing with them. All of these things are quite radical and different concerns from those we are used to in the NHS'.

For others it was the discovery of areas of management that are outward looking and deal with the interfaces between the whole organisation and its competitors, customers and suppliers. These would normally be described in terms of strategic management, marketing and business policy. After training, consultants frequently mentioned these areas as offering particular relevance to their roles. Clinicians stressed the conceptual development of thinking about the NHS as a business, albeit a 'not-for-profit' business. The overwhelming reaction of the cohort members to their training was positive. Unanimously, consultants saw the programmes as beneficial, and were particularly supportive of the opportunity to mix with and learn alongside managers from other sectors. A majority of the cohort stated that they had gained confidence as a consequence of their training.

Conclusions

The concepts of deprofessionalisation and proletarianisation are not adequate to explain or help us to understand what is happening within the medical profession in the UK. The problem lies with theories of the professions and their tightly defining features, which, for example, emphasise broad concepts such as autonomy without discussion of the processes by which autonomy is achieved. The research shows that medical autonomy in terms of total clinical freedom has never been possible in any real sense. In relation to the characterisitics of a 'professional', there is the suggestion, certainly in the USA, that doctors are being deprofessionalised. The UK research data show that the process of change that is certainly enveloping the medical profession cannot justifiably be interpreted in this way, unless only the negative effects on the profession are acknowledged. The reality is far more complex. Given their position of power in terms of their ownership of specialist expertise, doctors are generally able to negotiate either the level or the extent of change, to influence changes directly and indirectly and to adapt and find new ways of continuing to exert power and influence. This process cannot reasonably be termed deprofessionalisation.

The evidence also suggests that some clinicians have made assessments of the overall, long-term impact of the current changes. The clinicians' response to these changed circumstances is to adapt. The response is at once opportunistic and proactive. The clinicians in the research were motivated by a desire to influence the form of care provided, and in some cases to improve on the way decisions have been taken in the past. They are also motivated by career ambition, against the background of a changed organisational setting where many believe that management skills will become more, rather than less important.

In this context, the clinicians in the cohort were assuming new and powerful managerial roles as clinical directors and as medical directors. These roles will provide the chance to influence decisions about the service or business plan of each directorate and to participate in decisions about the allocation of resources. The role of medical director gives guaranteed access to senior management discussions and the role of public health director has considerable potential, which, as our research cases show, can sometimes give powerful leverage. These changes, it may be argued, potentially strengthen the sphere of influence of the medical profession. They offer access to decision-making fora that were not guaranteed prior to the Act. In this respect, the evidence in the UK seems to support the thesis put forward by Friedson (1987) in the USA, that the medical profession collectively has not lost its position of dominance, but has adapted to suit changing circumstances.

The study suggests a number of dangers in the current scenario. One is that, as rapid change occurs, clinicians assume roles that are ill-defined and do not use them effectively. Two negative outcomes are likely from such a process. On the one hand clinical management will not improve, indeed it may deteriorate and the service will not gain. On the other hand competent and motivated clinicians will become discouraged when trying to perform a range of management duties on a part-time basis. Such clinicians are likely to withdraw from management. It is evident that, for clinicians, all the time spent on management activity is constantly assessed against what could have been achieved by using that time for clinical practice. Another danger is that without training, in this period of transition, the part-time management roles will not attract clinicians who are committed and have credibility among their colleagues, and the potential of the roles will not be fulfilled.

Another potential threat lies in the difficult relationships and isolation that a number of clinical managers have to face. This may inhibit the development of collaborative and productive 'hybrid' roles. The data suggest that where clinical managers are addressing long-standing issues of quality audit and performance standards, there is a danger that rifts between the managers and the managed will increase, as Hafferty (1988) predicted. Much will depend on the views of the majority of the profession and whether they support the need for such developments. It may be judged that a more unpalatable alternative would be the imposition of centrally driven standards, or greater managerial intervention. In sum, the changes of perception following management training do serve to further distance clinical managers from some of their colleagues. At least initially, this is likely to generate some dissent within the ranks of the profession.

If one shifts the level of analysis, it can be seen that at the interorganisational level, contracting for services and the quasi-market may have a further impact on professionals. Whilst at the unit level it can be demonstrated that individual clinicians may have gained positions of influence, it can also be argued that competition between hospital trusts is growing and that this constitutes competition within the profession itself. As the specification of contracts develops and the information systems supporting contracting improve, the distinctive 'competencies' of a particular service will emerge. This may help the purchasers to discriminate between services, but it is also a fundamental challenge to the collegiality of the profession, which is premised on the equality of professionals. It is this aspect of the changes that many in the profession dislike most. Thus there are early indicators that the 'threat' expounded by Hafferty (1988) of an internal market inducing intraprofessional competition may have some foundation.

The jury is still out on whether the introduction of the quasi- market will reduce the central control of the state in the NHS. The policy of introducing market-like mechanisms could be seen as an attempt to curb professional powers by introducing mediating devices and delegating rationing decisions. It is difficult at this stage to assess how the final balance sheet will look. This complex picture includes multiple changes to the system of health-care, changing patterns of relationships, new roles and shifts in the balance of power, both inside the medical 'profession' and between doctors and other groups. The current context requires either a reassessment of the concept of profession, or the employment of a broader concept, such as that of 'expertise', which acknowledges the increase in other categories of specialist and expert workers. This would enable the more complex sets of relationships that are developing and the issues of expertise and its management to be more usefully analysed.

Out of the current studies and in the light of earlier research on professions, it can be argued that some enduring elements or characteristics are worthy of further attention. These need comparative investigation across a wider spectrum of expert roles. The first of these elements is the level of individual autonomy that can be and needs to be exercised by the individual expert in order to perform effectively. An expert whose judgements are completely contained and constrained by regulation or bureaucracy cannot usefully function as an expert. In pinpointing this element, we emphasise the need to examine the processes by which autonomy is exercised. The second factor relates to the collective autonomy of a group of experts and the extent to which they control not just entry standards, but the real quality standards of members' work. A research focus on this factor would yield data on the interrelationships between the 'professional' group and management, as well as the impact of these arrangements on consumers of the professional service. The third factor relates to the values held by group members and the ways in which these are maintained and monitored. Investigation of this factor is critical to developing an understanding of the processes by which different modes of control operate and their relative efficacy. Comparative research on these elements would yield greater understanding of the management of expertise in the current context.

References

Abbott, A. (1988) *The System of Professions: An essay on the division of expert labour* (Chicago and London: University of Chicago Press).

Ashburner, L. (1993) 'FHSAs: authorities in transition', Research for Action Paper 8 (Bristol: NHSTD).

Ashburner, L. and Cairncross, L. (1993) 'Membership of the "newstyle" health authorities: continuity or change?', *Public Administration*, vol. 71, no. 3, pp. 357–75.

Atkinson, P. and Delamont, S. (1990) 'Professions and powerlessness: female marginality in the learned occupations', *Sociological Review*, vol. 38 (Feb.), pp. 90–110.

Burns, T. (1981) 'A Comparative Study of Administrative Structure and Organisational processes in Selected Areas of the NHS', Research Report (London: Social Science Research Council).

Calnan, M. and Gabe, J. (1991) 'Recent developments in General Practice', in J. Gabe *et al.*, *The Sociology of the Health Service* (London: Routledge).

Crompton, R. (1990) 'Professions in the Current Context', *Work, Employment and Society*, special issue, pp. 147–66.

Davies, C. (1983) 'Professionals in Bureaucracies: The Conflict Thesis Revisited', in R. Dingwall and P. Lewis (eds), *The Sociology of the Professions* (London: Macmillan).

Dawson, S. *et al.* (1993) 'In or Out of Management? Dilemmas and Developments in public health medicine', paper presented to the Professions in Management in Britain Conference, Stirling University.

Day, P. and Klein, R. (1987) *Accountabilities: Five public services* (London: Tavistock).

Dopson, S. (1993) 'Management: the one disease consultants did not think existed', paper presented to the Professions and Management in Britain Conference, Stirling University.

Elcock, H. (1978) 'Regional government in action: the member of two RHAs', *Public Administration*, vol. 56, pp. 379–97.

Elston, M. A. (1991) 'The politics of professional power: medicine in a changing health service', in J. Gabe, M. Calnan and M. Bury *The Sociology of the Health Service* (London & New York: Routledge).

Ferlie, E., Ashburner, L. and Fitzgerald, L. (1993) 'Board Teams: Roles and Relationships', Research for Action Paper 10 (Bristol: NHSTD).

Ferlie, E., Fitzgerald, L. and Ashburner, L. (1992) 'The Challenge of Purchasing', Research for Action Paper 7 (Bristol: NHSTD).

Field, M. G. (1988) 'The Position of the Soviet physician: The Bureaucratic Professional', *The Millbank Quarterly*, vol. 66, Suppl. 2, pp. 182–201.

Fitzgerald, L. (1993) 'Management Development for Consultants: Formative Evaluation of the Doctors in Business Schools Programme. Final Report', unpublished report, Trent RHA/Department of Health.

Fitzgerald, L. (1994) 'Moving Clinicians into Management: A Professional Challenge or Threat?', *Journal of Management in Medicine*, vol. 8, no. 6.

Fitzgerald, L., Ferlie, E. and Ashburner, L.(1993) 'Leadership by Boards in Health-care', Research for Action Paper 12 (Bristol: NHSTD).

Freidson, E. (1970) *Professional Dominance: The social structure of medical care* (New York: Atherton Press).

Freidson, E. (1983) 'The Theory of Professions: state of the art', in R. Dingwall and P. Lewis (eds), *The Sociology of the Professions: Lawyers, doctors and others* (Basingstoke: Macmillan).

Friedson, E. (1987) 'The Future of the Professions', *Journal of Dental Education*, vol. 53, pp. 140–144.

Goode, W. J. (1960) 'Community within a community: the professions', *American Sociological Review*, vol. 22, no. 194.

Griffiths Report (1983) *Report of the NHS Management Inquiry*, (D83) 38 (London: HMSO).

Hafferty, Frederic (1988) 'Theories at the crossroads: a discussion of evolving views on medicine as a profession', *The Millbank Quarterly*, vol. 66, no. 2, pp. 202–225.

Hall, R. H. (1988) 'Comment on the sociology of the professions', *Work and Occupations*, vol. 15, (Aug.), pp. 273–5.

Halpern, S. A. (1992) 'Dynamics of professional control: internal coalitions and cross-professional boundaries', *American Journal of Sociology*, vol. 97, pp. 994–1021.

Harrison, Stephen (1988) *Managing the National Health Service: Shifting the frontier?* (London: Chapman and Hall).

Harrison, S. and Schultz, R. I. (1989) 'Clinical Autonomy in the UK and the USA: contrasts and convergence', in G. Freddi and J. W. Bjorkman (eds), *Controlling Medical Professionals* (London: Sage).

Harwood, A. and Boufford, I. J. (1993) *Managing Clinical Services. A consensus statement of principles for effective clinical management*, BAMM, BMA, IHSM, RCN (London: Institute of Health Services Management).

Haug, M. R. (1973) 'Deprofessionalisation: an alternative hypothesis for the future', *Sociological Review Monograph*, vol. 20, pp. 195–211.

Hetherington, R. H. (1982) 'Quality assurance and organisational effectiveness in hospitals', *Health Services Management Research*, vol. 17, no. 2.

Larkin, G. (1988) 'Medical dominance in Britain: image and historical reality, *Millbank Quarterly*, vol. 6, suppl. 2, pp.117–31.

Lewis, J. (1987) 'From public health to community medicine: the wider context'. in L. Willcocks and J. Harrow (eds), *Rediscovering Public Service Management* (London: McGraw-Hill).

McKinlay, J. B (1988) 'Introduction', *The Millbank Quarterly*, vol. 66, no. 2.

McKinlay, J. B. and Arches, J. (1985) 'Toward the proletarianisation of physicians', *International Journal of Health Services*, vol. 15, no. 2, pp. 161–95.

Murray, T. R., Dingwall, R. and Eekelar, J. (1983) 'Professionals in bureaucracies', in R. Dingwall and P. Lewis (eds), *The Sociology of the Professions: Lawyers, Doctors and others* (Basingstoke: Macmillan).

Navarro, V. (1988) 'Professional dominance or proletarianisation? Neither', *The Millbank Quarterly*, vol. 66, no. 2, pp. 57–75.

NHS and Community Care Act (1991) (London: HMSO).

Ovreteit, J. (1985) 'Medical Dominance and the Development of Professional Autonomy in Physiotherapy', *Sociology of Health and Illness*, vol. 7, pp. 76–93.

Parkin, F. (1979) *Marxism and Class Theory* (New York: Columbia University Press).

Parsons, T. (1951) *The Social System* (London: Tavistock).

Payer, L. (1988) *Medicine and Culture: Varieties of treatment in the USA, England, West Germany and France* (New York: Henry Holt).

Pettigrew, A., Ferlie, E. and McKee, L. (1992) *Shaping Strategic Change: The case of the NHS* (London: Sage).

Reuschemeyer, D. (1986) *Power and the Division of Labour* (New York: Polity Press).

Scott, W. R. (1985) 'Conflicting levels of rationality: regulators, managers and professionals in the medical care sector', *Journal of Health Administration Education*, vol. 3, no. 2, pt II, pp. 113–31.

Stevens, R. (1966) *Medical Practice in Modern England: The impact of specialisation and state medicine* (New Haven and London: Yale University Press).

Stewart, Rosemary (n.d.) 'Involving Doctors in General Management', Templeton Series, Paper 5 (Bristol: NHSTA).

Wolinsky, F. D. (1988) 'The professional dominance perspective re-visited', *The Millbank Quarterly*, vol. 66, no. 2, pp. 33–47.

CHAPTER 9

Commodifying professional expertise: IT in financial services

Harry Scarbrough

This chapter addresses a number of key issues in the management of expertise. Its principal focus is on the use of different institutional mechanisms to organise expertise in the context of innovation projects. In particular, it examines the differing effects of market and hierarchical forms through a study of the roles played by in-house IT functions and external suppliers in the development of IT-based innovations. These roles have often been understood as the product of 'make–buy' decisions, but the empirical study outlined here suggests that this is too crude a dichotomy to describe the complex knowledge flows and inter-organisational relationships involved in innovation projects. Trends towards marketisation make it increasingly important to understand the respective advantages of market and hierarchy as means of managing expertise. At the same time, too much emphasis on institutional forms risks neglecting the tacit significance of micro-level social organising processes. In the development of innovations, only the latter can achieve the social closure needed for the effective communication and acquisition of knowledge and expertise.

Introduction

Recent years have seen the remarkably uniform advance of market forces into domains once controlled by professional groups. Both classical professionals such as doctors and organisational professionals such as R&D scientists have experienced the increasing use of market mechanisms to regulate their work. But of all the major occupational groups touched by advancing marketisation, perhaps the most far-reaching effects have been amongst IT specialists, whose particular fate is addressed in the empirical study reported here.

IT staff have never been immune from market change, of course. Their professional formation is relatively weak, and over the last thirty years their survival as an occupational group has been constantly under threat from the expanding power of computers to objectify human programming skills in the form of hardware and software. Until recently, however, the recurrent waves of major technological change had somehow only succeeded in creating an enormous cumulative increase in the labour-market demand for IS skills. Now, this pattern of steady occupational expansion is under severe threat due to a widespread shift away from the use of in-house IS functions towards the outsourcing of IS services. In the UK, in particular, the market for the outsourcing of IT services has been growing at a rate of 20 per cent per annum throughout the 1990s (Willcocks and Fitzgerald, 1993). Many major organisations have outsourced some or all of their IT activities, with 'facilities management' being an especially attractive candidate. For the purposes of this chapter then, IS work serves as an outstanding example of the contemporary impact of marketisation on professional work.

The widespread advance of market relations obviously owes a good deal to specific technological and institutional changes. However the cumulative pattern of market penetration seems too uniform across sectors to be simply a product of localised causes. It suggests that the advance of market forces is not simply a matter of managerial fads or political ideology, but is part of a deeper epochal shift in the societal appropriation of knowledge. As a corollary, it raises important questions about the intellectual frameworks that are applied to the analysis of professional practices. If such practices are increasingly shaped and commodified by the penetration of market forces, does the professional model of work organisation retain a viable prospectus? Or is professionalism in the grip of secular trends that lead inexorably to increasingly normalised forms of managerial and market discipline?

Re-framing the professional model

The study outlined below[1] of so-called 'make–buy' decisions in financial services cannot claim to offer a complete answer these questions. However it does allow us to explore them through a particularly apposite sample of IT-based innovation projects. The latter were a relatively typical group of IT projects in that they were distinguished by extreme pressures of commodification, and by the fluidity of the boundaries between professionalism, hierarchy and market relations. Without preempting later discussion of this study's findings, the initial impressions of the wider questions noted above are briefly summarised below.

Firstly, the study highlighted the increasing need to locate the professional model of work within the wider repertoire of societal means of appropriating knowledge, including both hierarchical control and the commodification of knowledge into artefacts or services. Contextualising the professional model against these alternatives is not to suggest that professionalism will be simply swept away by marketing and management. Indeed one of the points highlighted by detailed examination of the case studies is the innate resistance of certain forms of knowledge to hierarchical control or commodification. Rather, this is a recognition that where professional controls are weak – or have been weakened by the state – the effect is to place professional practices in a more nakedly competitive relationship with alternative organisational forms. Thus even surviving professional regimes are likely to experience the indirect effects of market criteria. Professionals increasingly have to justify their practices not just to their peers, but also to wider constituencies. Likewise the outcomes of professional work are evaluated against market goods rather than conformity to professional norms. The competition for knowledge acquisition is fiercest, though, where market forces and institutional restructuring are furthest advanced. In these contexts, professionalism is likely to represent but one, declining, variant of the embodiment of knowledge in human expertise – such expertise itself being under threat from technology and commodification. Professional services are subjected to market testing, for instance, while at a generic level human forms of expertise compete with software packages and expert systems. In short, even where the competitive interaction between different modes of appropriating knowledge does not eliminate professional functions, it is likely to transform the character of professional work towards more distributed and diffusely organised forms of expertise.

Although the above passage highlights the competition between professionalism, hierarchy and commodification, this should not detract from the coevolutionary development of these different means of appropriating expertise. As I noted of IS expertise earlier, particular groups of professionals may actually benefit from the wider diffusion of knowledge through commodification if it serves to enhance the overall demand for their services. Similarly, increasing hierarchical control of expertise tends to enhance its status as a corporate currency of significant if variable value, even as it ceases to be the calling card of professional elites.

Secondly, locating professionalism in the competitive flux around the appropriation of knowledge is also a statement about the increasingly *contingent* and fragile character of human expertise. Such contingency means that expertise is not so much asserted by autonomous professional authorities as actively constructed out of particular conjunctions of knowledge, tasks and social relations. The aggregate effect is to reinforce the tendency towards diffusely distributed and professionally attenuated forms of expertise. Canonical bodies of knowledge and powerful professional associations are displaced by transitory knowledge networks that exploit the liberal connectivity of the market.

Knowledge and organisational forms

The above points have sought to reframe the debate about the post-professional organisation of knowledge work towards a focus on the contingent deployment of expertise. The latter brings with it several important changes in perspective. The first, which will be explored in detail through our case studies, is a shift in the level of analysis from wider institutional influences to the micro-level strategies of groups and individuals in responding to the contingent circumstances of their work.

The second, which is signalled here by an inclusive concern with expertise rather than professionalism alone, is the need to question the elective affinities between particular forms of social relations and particular bodies of knowledge. For example the expertise and the institutions of professionalism have usually been seen as one and the same, shaped by the same unidimensional trajectory of professionalisation. Under the strain posed by recent lesions of knowledge and status, however, this assumption is beginning to give way to an increasing awareness of the decoupling of expertise and professionalism. Moreover this is only one symptom of the pressing need to address the *modal* interactions between social forms and knowledge bases; to explain, for instance, why knowledge should be vouchsafed to professional groupings rather than to bureaucracies or markets, and vice versa.

Of course the ability to encompass all of the modalities of knowledge and institutional forms poses a stringent test for any theory of organisation. Not only would such a theory need to address the social processes of *organising* that operate in the interstitial spaces and times of existing institutional forms to determine the boundaries between professional, hierarchical and market forms of *organisation*, but it would also have to recognises the organisational implications of different forms of knowledge, including, for example, the social distribution of knowledge between formal and tacit varieties and across different social groups.

One existing body of theory that claims to answer these questions is 'transaction cost analysis', which has been pioneered by Williamson (1975, 1985). This views societal institutions in terms of their differential ability to regulate economic transactions. Williamson makes the point that accounts of organisational growth based solely on political factors are unable to explain with any precision the boundaries to organisational growth. In his account institutional forms, including markets, hierarchies and professional group-ings, emerge to achieve efficiency in the regulation of different kinds of transaction. Assuming the adjudication of long-run market pressures, the boundaries of different organisational forms can be explained precisely and entirely with reference to their relative efficiencies in regulating different kinds of transaction.

As far as knowledge is concerned, Williamson's account suggests that the relative appropriative success of different institutional forms will depend on their fit with the specific transactions in which knowledge is exchanged. In other words, the key organisational feature of knowledge is its tradeability. As markets are seen as the most efficient transactional mechanism in absolute terms, only forms of knowledge that cannot be handled through the market would be appropriated through professional or hierarchical structures. This would encompass, for instance, knowledges that are highly firm-specific ('asset specificity') or which are opaque to a potential purchaser ('information impactedness').

Williamson's treatment of the appropriation of knowledge is based on a theoretical strategy that explains institutional forms in terms of the efficiency characteristics of transactional fit. As the market is assumed to be the most efficient institutional form, hierarchies and other forms of social control are effectively relativised to the transaction. Hierarchies are seen as the result of 'market failure', and social control – the paradigmatic focus of much conventional organisation theory – is daringly transmogrified into a dependent variable.

This theoretical strategy pays dividends in terms of the institutional compass of Williamson's work. However it can equally be turned against the transaction cost approach. Thus a number of organisational theorists have sought to repay the compliment by relativising markets in relation to the exercise of social control. Zucker (1991) argues, for instance, that markets can equally well be seen as the product of 'hierarchy failure'; in other words, as merely alternative means of enhancing control over particular social groups. Indeed a number of writers on professional groups (for example Whalley, 1986) have argued that market disciplines are a powerful means of reinforcing hierarchical controls over professional groups. Moreover, to turn Williamson's argument completely on its head, social control may actually be transferred from one organisational context to another through processes of commodi-fication. Such commodified control is exemplified in the IT field, for example, by proprietary methodologies that seek to impose a tight discipline on the work of systems developers.

Defining control, rather than transactional efficiency, as the axial principle of social organising places a radically different complexion on the appropria-tion of knowledge. In this perspective, knowledge is appropriated by certain social groups in the pursuit of power and control over others; a formulation that is reflected in some aspects of the professions literature where the acquisition of knowledge is viewed in terms of an interprofessional struggle to control jurisdictions and exercise power over client groups (Johnson, 1972). More generally, privileging social control over economic exchange produces a concern with the problematic coexistence of different forms of social order, not with the competition between them.

Clearly the oppositional discourses of control and exchange pose different vectors of explanation. However, both theoretically and empirically the wider validity of their dichotomised treatment of social and economic life-worlds is being increasingly brought into question. In particular, empirical studies of what has been called the 'swollen middle' of transactions (Hennart, 1993), encompassing interorganisational relations, make–buy decisions and the like, consistently report hybrid patterns of socio-economic activity. Thus Macauley's (1963) study of salesmen highlights the functional role of social norms and trust in reducing the need for monitoring and surveillance in market structures. And Butler and Carney (1983) suggest that in complex make–buy situations, so-called 'managed markets' are developed, 'augmenting' market structures through the deployment of mechanisms normally associated with hierarchies, notably 'trust', 'routines' and 'mutual adjustment'. Even in relatively pure market situations we find the operation of market mechanisms resting upon the lubricating effects of social norms and shared meanings (Martin, 1993).

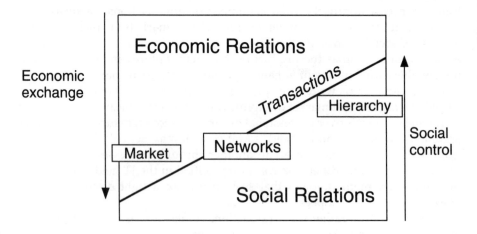

FIGURE 9.1 Continuum of transactions between market and hierarchy

The interpretation of such hybrid activities can take many different forms. We could simply note, with Commons (1970), that all exchanges involve a transfer of control. Or we could note the way in which studies of social networks help to challenge monolithic conceptions of institutional forms. More importantly though, these studies of hybrid activities make the point that exchange and control relations are not bounded by institutional forms. They challenge the assumption that social control is confined to (over-socialised) hierarchies and exchange relations to (undersocialised) markets. Rather control and exchange relations involve a mutual dependency which, as Figure 9.1 denotes, can be seen applying even in an attenuated way across a continuum of socioeconomic interactions. Even the most clannish hierarchies are influenced by market forces by way of the employment relationship, while diffuse forms of social control operate even in inter-organisational or market contexts through occupational networks and cultural norms.

More specifically in relation to the commodification of knowledge, these points tend to refute Williamson's claim that the 'fit' between transactions and organisational forms alone suffices for complete institutional closure. In other words there are many situations where both markets and hierarchies fail and keep failing. This particularly applies to chains of transactions where one transaction is contingent on another. Williamson suggests that these chains are only sustained by 'technological inseparability' – for instance through long-linked technologies or technological infrastructures – or learning effects that produce human asset specificity. In all other cases he sees transactional chains being decomposed by efficiency pressures such that transactions are redistributed to market or quasi-market forms. Such chains are thus transformed into a front end that delivers products into a wider marketplace and a back end where technological or other factors demand hierarchical control of production processes (or a front-stage and a back-stage, to put this in Goffman's, 1971, terms)

However Williamson's account rests on the assumption that efficiency pressures are all-powerful – an assumption that is already highly qualified by the pervasive role of social controls. A more plausible explanation for such institutional changes takes us back to the role of strategic social action. Given the absence of institutional closure the stalemate of control and exchange relations can only be resolved by social actors strategically deploying the rules of market relations and social control as 'organising methods' (Hennart, 1993). Of course the motives of such actors are likely to be mixed, being coloured by economic or political factors alike. For example there is a wealth of recent examples of strategic interventions designed to shift the locus of control away from producer groups to managers and customers (Willman, 1983). By enhancing the impact of exchange relationships, for instance, the pressures of commodification effectively confer power on those who occupy strategic positions in such relationships. Although the most egregious instances of such intervention have been seen in the public sector, the privileging of customer relations has been an explicit aim of practically all the most recent fads and techniques in management, including TQM, JIT, BPR and other acronyms (Scarbrough and Burrell, 1994).

The communication of knowledge

The transactional continuum outlined in Figure 9.1 defines the appropriability of knowledge in terms of its amenability to exchange or control. However the wider literature on technological change suggests an additional organisational characteristic; that of communicability. The significance of communicability is greatest in the context of innovation, but even more generally it is easy to conceive of situations in which significant economic pressures are thwarted by problems of communication. Nor is communication simply a cypher of social control, although social relations obviously provide important channels of communication. Rather the communication of knowledge seems to involve the sharing of cognitive frameworks and shared meanings. Thus the acquisition of knowledge depends upon the possession of certain kinds of prior knowledge (Cohen and Levinthal, 1990). And the production of knowledge typically involves 'bootstrapping' (Hofstadter, 1980); that is, using existing knowledge as a platform for innovation. In other words, such transactions seem as dependent on social and cultural processes of communication as they are on economic exchange (Boisot, 1986).

The role of communication processes is widely evidenced in the literature on technological change. The diffusion of innovations, for instance, is often interpreted through analogies with broadcasting. Similarly, more recent studies of technological change have drawn on the notion of 'actor networks' and 'translation' (Callon, 1980; Latour, 1987) where innovations simultaneously exploit and rework existing patterns of social relations. Drawing on this literature suggests three basic forms of knowledge communication:

- *Professionalism,* that is, the communication of knowledge through its embodiment in the learning and experience of individuals and groups.
- *Objectification.* Here the communication process revolves around the pursuit of portability (Cooper, 1992), and universal applicability through standardisation. The knowledge needed to use the technology is kept to a bare minimum.
- *Organisational sedimentation,* where knowledge is communicated via rules, standards, routines and structures (Argyris and Schon, 1978; Lyles and Schwenk, 1992; Whipp and Clark, 1986).

These forms of communication not only operate through mainstream social institutions, but also through specialised institutions of education and training. Their implications for the mechanisms of appropriating knowledge can be usefully gauged by mapping the parameters of communicability on to the continuum outlined earlier (Figure 9.2).

The distinctive importance of communication applies with particular effect to innovation projects. The latter involve a complex simultaneous equation in which social actors develop effective means of communicating their respective knowledges, define and order their different interests and relationships, and do so, moreover, in such a way as to incentivise both through the prospect of shared economic gains. Thus the expert groups involved in these projects gradually delimit the rules, relationships and rewards of the innovation process at the same time as communicating and sharing the relevant knowledges.

The need for such organising processes, as well as their fraught and uncertain character, are a result of the contradictory clash between different bases of action. As widely noted in organisation studies, the dynamics of control, exchange and communication imply conflicting objectives – communicability implies extensive networks and organic informality, for instance, while the crystallising of rules and relationships demands tightly bounded social interaction and well-defined outcomes.

Strategies of social closure

In our case studies of IT projects reported below, the organising processes of the various in-house and external groups involved were central to resolving

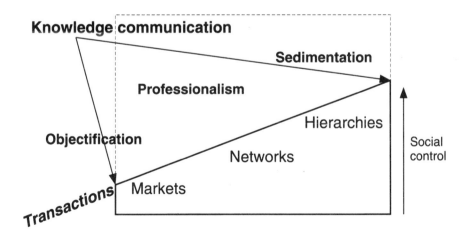

FIGURE 9.2 Knowledge communication and tradeability

the tensions between these conflicting tendencies in knowledge acquisition. In this context, background institutional effects were less important than what can broadly be termed the 'strategies of social closure' developed by the groups and managers involved. The notion of social closure is normally identified with wider occupational groups and the pursuit of exclusionary strategies based on monopolies of specialist knowledge (Parkin, 1974). However the micro-level strategies described below also involved a degree of interpretive closure of the kind normally associated with technological development; the meaning of particular technologies becoming progressively stabilised as users, inventors and producers come to share common frameworks as to the meaning, critical features and purpose of the technology (Pinch and Bijker, 1987). In the emergent context of innovation, closure was by definition a more localised affair, but the sharing of common frameworks was no less crucial to the effective communication of technical knowledge.

Although our case studies could not produce an exhaustive taxonomy of such closure strategies, three major types could be discerned, varying roughly according to the distribution of knowledge, economic interests and social relations involved in each innovation. These have been termed 'blackboxing', 'hostage' and 'prisoner' strategies. Their location in relation to the communication and trading of knowledge in highlighted in Figure 9.3. Rather than presenting an exhaustive account of each of our case studies, in the rest of this chapter I will use the case-study material to illustrate the way such strategies were worked out in particular contexts.

The blackboxing strategy

The blackboxing strategy was developed in a number of our cases as a way of coping with the dilemmas posed by commodified forms of technical knowledge such as software packages. It involves organising transactions for the economic exchange of objectified artefacts, with minimal dependence on social relations. This seems to be a widely used strategy in the IT area, in large part because the technology itself pushes the possibilities of objectification to the extreme. Information processing power makes it easier to objectify knowledge, and this is reinforced by the powerful economic incentives to recoup the costs of labour-intensive software development by exploiting its relatively low cost of reproduction and distribution (Friedman, 1989; Pelaez, 1990).

Although this strategy seeks to exploit economies of scale in knowledge production (Swann, 1990; Brady *et al.*, 1991), it also depends on social processes for communicating that knowledge. It requires that technical knowledge be separated from its original social and technical locale by being progressively stabilised, segmented and made portable (Latour, 1987; Cooper,

1992). Stabilisation involves the establishment of a 'dominant design' for the technology, such that computer hardware, for instance, has become more standardised and more robust (and in the process significantly cheaper). Segmentation, meanwhile, involves separating systems development into different phases, or dividing software into categories such as systems/utilities and applications. Hence, portability involves minimising the knowledge needed to use a technology by careful design of the user interface, thus allowing elements of a technological system to be removed from one context and applied in another.

In the financial services context especially, blackboxing is a long-established strategy for handling technical knowledge. Computing technology was applied originally to 'back office' functions such as accounting and transaction processing. Over time the hardware component became increasingly black-boxed, reflecting both competition between suppliers to provide complete solutions, and user needs for reliable systems. This allowed the separation of routine 'operations' tasks from systems development and eventually their complete automation through the use of supplier diagnostic systems. Indeed by the late 1980s blackboxing had become almost a literal reality for mainframe hardware, with one of our sample of cases, the Royal Bank of Scotland, making great strides towards the 'dark room' concept for managing mainframe operations. This involved excluding human workers from the machine room, locking the doors and 'throwing away the key'. Supplier

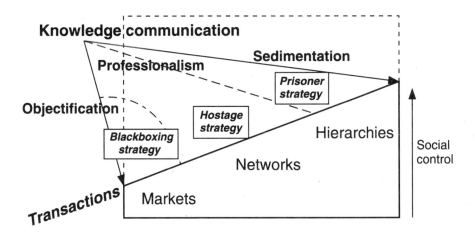

FIGURE 9.3   Strategies of social closure in organising technical knowledge

maintenance and back-up systems would ensure the continuous smooth running of the machines.

While organisational routines colluded in blackboxing mainframe hardware and processing tasks, the product-market developments of the 1980s spawned important new opportunities for blackboxed applications. Deregulation of the UK financial services sector encouraged a flurry of product diversification moves, with the vast majority of providers seeking to develop and extend their existing product range. These product-market pressures encouraged providers to look for two types of IT applications; product innovations such as remote banking systems that could augment their existing product range; and customer database applications that would improve the quality of service to customers and at the same time allow a greater degree of cross-selling through the integration of customer information.

As these applications generally involved 'front office' systems – that is, they affected the interface with the customer rather than the internal operation of existing accounting and processing systems – they were relatively amenable to the discrete functionality of the blackboxing approach. A number of our case-study firms embraced this possibility with enthusiasm. For example one building society purchased a customer database package ('Baron'), which the IS manager described in glowing terms:

> It is an all-singing all-dancing package which will control all our lending portfolios, various products which we hope to put out such as a checking account, insurance services and so on. 'Baron' is very much a customer-based system, as opposed to an account-based system. We're looking to have a customer-based system for the cross-selling opportunities that may exist. For example, if a guy comes in and gets a mortgage, he may need a loan for a car or need insurance or a personal equity plan (user services manager, Buildsoc).

Here the advantage of the blackboxing approach derived not only from its economic advantages (principally cost and time) over in-house systems development, but also from the building society's willingness to change its organisational routines in the face of changing product-market conditions. The software package, in fact, was seen as an important element in shifting to customer- versus account-based procedures for handling records.

The same favourable context existed in one of our other case studies: the development of a card processing system for the Bank of Scotland VISA Centre. The establishment of a credit card operation represented a significant diversification move for the bank into a market and a technology with which it was relatively unfamiliar. With no preexisting organisational routines to grapple with, the economic advantages of a software package were overwhelming. There was little or no debate on the make–buy issue itself, as management quickly focused on the choice of a particular package. Once the new package had been selected, management designed the new centre's organisation around it. Much of the basic organisational design was developed by two of the most senior managers, who drew up a rough blueprint over a drink in a local hostelry.

These cases clearly demonstrate the advantages of the blackboxing strategy in economic terms. However such advantages need to be set in context. First, questions of exchange only predominated because communication and social control issues were secondary in these particular cases. The organisational infrastructure within which the technologies were to operate was relatively malleable, either for reasons of strategic choice or because management were designing the organisation from scratch. Even so, communication and control issues were not entirely absent from these cases. In particular, while blackboxing seeks to instantiate all social relationships and all relevant knowledge in the form of a one-off purchase, it often encounters problems in a complex and dynamic context. Such problems may arise through constraints on the surfacing of all relevant knowledge, especially where it is organisationally or professionally embedded. Thus managers at Buildsoc, for instance, were later to acknowledge that the decision to install the system as a complete blackboxed package, without any preparatory customising to link it into the company's systems and organisational practices, had created serious problems: 'Unfortunately, we have had some problems with it. It's an American-based system. There's some Anglicisation required to be done and that's led to problems. We've had problems of sizing and unfortunately the whole thing has been beset with problems' (user services manager).

Of course some managers may be happy to accept marginal misalignment between commodified technology and organisational practices. They may see it as a small price to pay for the cheapness and functionality of standardised packages. A longer-term constraint arises, however, where the blackboxed technology has the potential to act as a platform for future technological innovation. The selection of software packages in our sample, for instance, often revolved around the possibilities and prospects of future supplier 'updates' to enhance the functionality of the package. Such updates involve highly specific knowledge of the technology. As this cannot be crystallised out as a one-off exchange, it raises issues of long-term relationships and possible dependency on the supplier.

The hostage strategy

The more that blackboxing raises the spectre of supplier dependency or, alternatively, relies on the buttressing of in-house systems development, the less powerful its attractions for the user firm. This points the way towards an alternative strategy for organising technical knowledge. For if dependency on the supplier's knowledge base cannot be avoided, it can be made safer by pursuing a strategy based on mutual dependency and mutual benefits. In broad terms, the 'hostage strategy' involves the use of occupational networks to communicate knowledge, and a mixture of occupational norms and economic incentives to organise transactions. This strategy is uniquely distinguished, however, by its incentive basis, described by Nooteboom as follows:

> A special measure that carries less risk of expropriation is that which takes the logical form of a hostage; something is given in custody which is of value to the giver (who will therefore comply with agreements lest he lose it) but not to the receiver (who will therefore not be tempted to expropriate) (Nooteboom, 1992, p. 342).

We can see this strategy clearly in the case study of the Clydesdale Bank's 'TELEBANK' remote banking system. Here there was a collaborative product development involving a bank seeking to develop its product range and a supplier (SoftHouse) wishing to develop a marketable remote banking product. The development of TELEBANK did not involve the one-sided 'lock in' threatened by package acquisition. Rather the relationship between Clydesdale Bank and SoftHouse was based on a kind of mutual hostage-taking, in which each side controlled assets that were more valuable to the other than to itself. Where dependency is usually inimical to the market appropriability of knowledge, in this case mutual dependency seemed to work effectively for both sides.

However it would be wrong to present the TELEBANK project as simply the rational calculation of interests around a particular transaction. Many of the reasons for successful knowledge trading here are to do with social relations rather than economic factors alone. Thus Clydesdale management had initially identified SoftHouse as a likely partner through occupational networks, and the subsequent development relied heavily on the degree of trust that a shared occupational identity helped to engender. Also, the shared knowledge made communications easier and meant that each group had the expertise to evaluate the other's contribution to a complex and uncertain process. Such social relations not only served to lubricate the coordination of work, but also extended the sanctions against opportunism: Clydesdale's position within the sectoral networks of the UK banking sector gave it reputational leverage over SoftHouse, with a 'high profile' project such as TELEBANK carrying 'enormous embarrassment potential' if it failed.

Factors such as these help to explain the relatively informal organisational arrangements that were applied to this project. Despite its importance to the Bank, there was little attempt to monitor SoftHouse's work, for example. Clydesdale management only needed informal discussions and general information about the development process to feel 'happy' with SoftHouse's programming standards. We can relate this informality to the 'organic' relationships involved in innovation, and to the tacit implications of the social controls noted above. In addition, however, a decisive influence seems to have been the potential economic gains arising out of the project. The benefits of a successful outcome would be both significant and complementary for each side. Once completed, SoftHouse aimed to market TELEBANK as a generic, blackboxed product to other UK banks. In return for providing this development opportunity, Clydesdale stood to benefit in a threefold fashion: by a reduction in development costs; the acquisition of an important new product, and royalties from the sale of that product to other banks.

It is a distinctive feature of interorganisational innovations that the joint pursuit of economic gains depends not only on the innovation process itself, but also on defining a division of labour that is compatible with the sharing of said gains. The degree of 'technological separability', to use Williamson's term, was important here in that it allowed the communication, application and proportionate reward of different kinds of knowledge within the same innovation process. To elaborate: TELEBANK could be implemented as a segmented appendage to existing processing systems, without requiring radical changes in them. Moreover the front end of TELEBANK could be designed and built by the supplier as virtually a buffer system between various end-user devices and the bank's secure databases. These architectural features of TELEBANK facilitated a broadly segmented division of labour between SoftHouse and Clydesdale's in-house systems development function, with the latter maintaining control over sensitive internal banking systems and data. Equally importantly, it allowed the supplier firm to concentrate upon the development of the stable blackboxed functional architecture as a potentially portable and marketable product.

The advantage of separability, however, lay not simply in allowing subcontracting of work, as Williamson would have it, but also that it permitted more effective communication of different kinds of technical knowledge. The TELEBANK innovation demanded a combination of banking expertise with specific technical skills and a more generalised understanding of the market. As the director of the software house reflected later:

> Unavoidably we've picked up a lot of expertise and knowledge about what really matters to a bank. I would not for a moment suggest that we are the kind of organisation that understands banking as a business to the same level of the people who are responsible in those areas. But what we do understand is what is important. We can make sensible judgements when we assess or incorporate technology. We can tell what really counts and what doesn't. And I think it's the 'what doesn't' which is the most important. So that puts us in a position that is very much apart from the standard provider of a package which is not necessarily providing banking functions. We know in any package, including our own, what it is that's attractive to the bank, and what is irrelevant.

Equally, Clydesdale recognised that, through using this supplier, it could gain access to information about what was happening in the *sector* in relation to out-of-branch banking and thereby obtain a more 'competitive' solution than would have been developed in-house. As one of the Clydesdale managers put it: 'There can be a danger sometimes in doing it in-house. You miss the proper understanding of the market . . . of the options and the technology because you tend then to tailor your cloth to suit your purse too much perhaps'.

Prisoner strategy

In the TELEBANK case the involvement of Clydesdale's in-house IS function primarily reflected the need for organisation-specific knowledge – the bank had no concerns about the exclusivity of the innovation process. In some of our other cases, though, we found organisations who were concerned to achieve competitive advantage by securing exclusive control of innovation outputs. In these cases, firms were much more likely to deploy a 'prisoner' strategy to achieve social closure around the relevant skills and people. This involved knowledge communication through professionalism and an intensively cultivated employment relationship that sought to bind individuals tightly to the organisation.

The prisoner strategy was especially evident in the CABINET case. This was the project whose outcomes were most unique to the innovating organisation and involved the greatest dependency upon in-house expertise. CABINET involved the development of a customer information network linking all of the several hundred branches to the bank's databases in Edinburgh. This network was designed to replace existing manual records and thereby both speed up responses to customer queries and assist the introduction of new financial services. This project was both large scale and long term. The actual design stage of the project began in 1984 and even at that stage it was understood that implementation through various phases of development (each one adding some new element of functionality to the basic network) was likely to extend well into the 1990s. Significantly, as a strategic infrastructural project, the financial controls applied to the project were less stringent than would have applied to more routine projects.

But the strategic commitment to the CABINET system as a whole did not imply that it was all carried out in-house. Some elements of the system, notably the office automation hardware and routine software elements, were blackboxed. Others, including the development of the network management software, were subcontracted to an external supplier. However the use of outsourcing was heavily constrained by the organisation-specific forms of expertise needed in the systems development process. The need to restructure existing databases, and the importance of banking knowledge in developing the user presentation software, meant that the greater part of that process had to be performed by the in-house IS function.

As CABINET demanded the long-term deployment of people with a combination of banking and IT knowledges, a fairly elaborate strategy was developed to retain this skilled resource. In line with findings from other studies (Tierney and Wickham, 1989; Storey, 1985), the elements of this strategy were fairly heterogeneous; some were concerned, for instance, with employee commitment, others with effort control. Thus IS employees were recruited to a strong internal labour market, with nine grades from trainee to senior manager and high levels of job security for IS employees. Career patterns showed a steady pattern of development, with staff joining the organisation in junior technical roles and gradually working their way up through the grades. This approach allowed the (selective) invocation of professionalism – both rhetorically and in expectations of personal initiative and teamwork. For instance one manager within the function defined a 'good' systems analyst as someone who 'defines the thing [system] properly and gets the specification correct the first time and does not have to make lots of changes. Someone who actually thinks ahead of anything that is going to impact on it'.

Ironically, however, normative commitment through elaborate career ladders ran alongside (indeed was facilitated by) the more mechanistic forms of social control built into a detailed division of labour. Strict programming standards were enforced and management insisted that programmers 'sign' their work – that is, indicate their responsibility. Work schedules and management monitoring were sometimes uncomfortably tight, as one employee noted: 'every program you get you are told initially what the completion date is, and then monitoring every week or two, how you are progressing, and how much work you can do, whether you are going past schedule dates and all this sort of stuff'.

Conclusions

This chapter has argued that a seismic shift in knowledge production towards distributed social networks and market mechanisms demands a reorientation in our theorising of professional work. In this reorientation, the contingent incidence of expertise displaces the more measured advance of professionalisation. One implication of this is a change in the relationship between professionals and managers. As professional groups become more thoroughly assimilated into market-hierarchy structures, conflict between professional and managerial goals is no longer based on differing value systems but derives from functional trade-offs between efficiency and expertise. A further, broader implication of these institutional and technological changes is the need to relate the human embodiment of knowledge in expertise to wider societal repertoires for the appropriation of knowledge.

In the latter context, the incursion of market forces into professional domains was seen as enhancing the prospects both for direct commodification and for indirect reshaping of the character of professional work. At the same time though, the ability of market forces entirely to sublimate human expertise was seen as limited by the cross-cutting dynamics of control, exchange and communication in the appropriation of knowledge. Market forces could not be seen as operating autonomously in shaping the deployment of expertise. This depended on strategic interventions by social actors that often had as much to do with shifting the locus of control over professional groups as with the efficiency pressures of market regimes. Thus the promotion of market relations could effectively naturalise certain forms of control by relocating them outside the organisation itself.

Finally, the role of social actors in organising knowledge flows was outlined through three prototypical 'strategies of social closure': blackboxing, hostage and prisoner strategies. Interestingly, the notion that the appropriation of knowledge cannot be achieved through the free play of market forces finds support from the new wisdom in, for instance, studies of R&D networks, firm–supplier relationships and corporate strategy. For example one study of informal networks encompassing academic scientists and R&D specialists found a three-stage process of network development: discovering opportunities, exploring possibilities and finally crystallising collaborative relations (Kreiner and Schultz, 1993). Such findings seem to be closer in spirit to the notion of 'social closure' than to the ruthless pursuit of transactional efficiences. Likewise the manifesto of 'lean production' (Womack *et al.*, 1990), for example, rejects the tyranny of cost as the basis for firm–supplier relations. Instead it highlights the advantages of close relationships with suppliers as a means of sharing knowledge and developing mutually beneficial innovations.

Note

1. This study was supported by a grant from the Joint Committee of the SERC/ ESRC. It was carried out by an interdisciplinary group drawn from the Universities of Edinburgh, Stirling and Warwick. A complete account of its findings are reported in *Expertise and Innovation: information technology strategies in the financial services sector* (Oxford University Press, 1994).

References

Argyris, C. and Schon, D. (1978) *Organizational Learning: A theory of action perspective* (Reading, Mass: Addison-Wesley).

Boisot, M. H. (1986) 'Markets and hierarchies in a cultural perspective', *Organisation Studies*, vol. 7, pp. 135–58.

Brady, T., Jagger, N., Tierney, M., and Williams, R. (1991) 'The Objectification of IT Software', paper presented to the PICT National Network Conference, Wakefield, Yorkshire, March.

Butler, R. and Carney, M. G. (1983) 'Managing markets: implications for the make–buy decision', *Journal of Management Studies*, vol. 20, no. 12, pp. 213–31.

Callon, M. (1980) 'The state and technical innovation: A case study of the electrical vehicle in France', *Research Policy*, vol. 9, pp. 358–76.

Child, J. (1987) 'Information technology, organisation and the response to strategic challenges', *California Management Review*, vol. 30, pp. 33–49.

Cohen, W. M. and Levinthal, D. A. (1990) 'Absorptive capacity: A new perspective on learning and innovation', *Administrative Science Quarterly*, vol. 35, pp. 128–52.

Cooper, R. (1992) 'Formal Organisation as Representation: Remote Control, Displacement and Abbreviation', in M. Reed and M. Hughes (eds), *Rethinking Organisation: New directions in organisation theory and analysis* (London: Sage).

Crompton, R. (1992) 'Professions in the current context', *Work, Employment and Society*, Special Issue, 'A decade of change', pp. 147–66.

Friedman, A. (with Cornford, D.) (1989) *Computer Systems Development: History, organisation and implementation* (Chichester: John Wiley & Sons).

Gibbons, M., Limoges, C., Nowotny, H., Schwartzman, S., Scott, P. and M. Trow, (1994) *The New Production of Knowledge: The dynamics of science and research in contemporary societies* (London: Sage).

Goffman, E. (1971) *The Presentation of Self in Everyday Life* (Harmondsworth: Pelican).

Hennart, J-F. (1993) 'Explaining the swollen middle: Why most transactions are a mix of "market" and "hierarchy"', *Organisation Science*, vol. 4, no. 4, pp. 529–47.

Hofstadter, D. R. (1980) *Godel, Escher, Bach: An eternal golden braid* (Harmondsworth: Penguin).

Johnson, T. (1972) *Professions and Power* (Basingstoke: Macmillan).

Kreiner, K. and Schultz, M. (1993) 'Informal collaboration in R&D. The formation of Networks across Organisations', *Organisation Studies*, vol. 14, no. 2, pp. 189–209.

Latour, B. (1987) *Science in Action* (Milton Keynes: Open University Press).

Lyles, M. A. and Schwenk, C. R. (1992) 'Top management, strategy and organisational knowledge structures', *Journal of Management Studies*, vol. 29, no. 2, pp. 155–74.

Macauley, S. (1963) 'Non contractual relations in business: a preliminary study', *American Sociological Review*, vol. 28, pp. 55–67.

Martin, R. (1993) 'The new behaviourism: A critique of economics and organization', *Human Relations*, vol. 46, no. 9, pp. 1011–1085.

Nooteboom, B. (1992) 'Information Technology, Transaction Costs and the Decision to "Make or Buy"', *Technology Analysis and Strategic Management*, vol. 4, no. 4, pp. 339–50.

Parkin, F. (1974) 'Strategies of social closure in class formation' in F. Parkin (ed.), *The Social Analysis of Class Structure* (London: Tavistock).

Pelaez, E. (1990). 'Software', paper presented to PICT Workshop on Social Perspectives on Software, Oxford, 13–14 January.

Pinch, T. and Bijker, W. (1987) 'The social construction of facts and artifacts: or how the sociology of science and the sociology of technology might benefit each other', in W. E. Bijker, T. Hughes and T. J. Pinch, T.J. (eds), *The Social Construction of Technological Systems* (London: MIT Press), pp. 10–17.

Pisano, G. P. (1990) 'The R&D Boundaries of the firm: An empirical analysis, *Administrative Science Quarterly*, vol. 35, pp. 153–76.

Powell, W. W. (1991) 'Neither market nor hierarchy: network forms of organisation', in G. Thompson, J. Frances, R. Levacic and J. Mitchell, *Markets, Hierarchies and Networks: The coordination of social life* (London: Sage), pp. 265–77.

Pralahad, C. K. and Hamel, G. (1990) 'The core competence of the corporation', *Harvard Business Review*, May-June, pp. 79–91.

Saviotti, P. (1992) 'Economics of Expertise', Edinburgh PICT Workshop, Edinburgh.

Scarbrough, H. and Burrell, G. (1994) 'From down-sising to de-managing? Knowledge work and the prospects for radical change in managerial roles', British Academy of Management, Annual Conference, Lancaster University.

Storey, J. (1985) 'The means of management control', *Sociology*, vol. 19, pp. 193–211.

Swann, P. (1990) 'Standards and the Growth of a Software Network', in J. L. Berg and H. Schumny (eds), *An Analysis of the Information Technology Standardisation Process* (Amsterdam: Elsevier Science/North-Holland).

Teece, D. J. (1988) 'Technological change and the nature of the firm', in G. Dosi (ed.) *Technical Change and Economic Theory* (London: Frances Pinter).

Tierney, M. and Wickham, J. (1989) 'Controlling software labour: Professional ideologies and the problem of control', ESRC/PICT Workshop on Critical Perspectives on Software, Manchester, July.

Whally, P. (1986) *The Social Production of Technical Work* (Basingstoke: Macmillan).

Whipp, R. and Clark, P. (1986) *Innovation and the Auto Industry: Production, process and work organization* (London: Frances Pinter).

Whittington, R. (1991) 'Changing control strategies in industrial R&D', *R&D Management*, vol. 21, pp. 43–53.

Willcocks, L. and Fitzgerald, G. (1993) 'Market as opportunity? Case studies in outsourcing information technology and services', *Journal of Strategic Information Systems*, vol. 2, no. 3, pp. 223–42.

Williamson, O. E. (1975) *Markets and Hierarchies: Analysis and antitrust implications* (New York: Free Press).

Williamson, O. E. (1985) *The Economic Institutions of Capitalism* (New York: Free Press).

Willman, P. (1983) Chapter 6 in A. Francis, J.Turk and P. Willman (eds), *Power, Efficiency and Institutions: A critical appraisal of the 'markets and hierarchies' paradigm* (London: Heinemann).

Womack, J. P., Jones, D. T. and Roos, D.(1990) *The Machine that Changed the World* (Oxford: Maxwell Macmillan International).

Zucker, L. G. (1991) 'Markets for bureaucratic authority and control: information quality in professions and services', *Research in the Sociology of Organizations*, vol. 8, pp. 157–90.

Index